# THE BLACKCOATED WORKER

STUDIES IN SOCIETY

CHILDREN UNDER FIVE
by J. W. B. Douglas and J. M. Blomfield

TECHNICAL EDUCATION AND
SOCIAL CHANGE
by Stephen F. Cotgrove

STUDIES IN SOCIETY

*Edited by Ruth and David Glass*

# THE BLACKCOATED WORKER

*A Study in Class Consciousness*

BY

DAVID LOCKWOOD

*Ruskin House*

GEORGE ALLEN & UNWIN LTD

MUSEUM STREET LONDON

FIRST PUBLISHED IN 1958

PRINTED IN GREAT BRITAIN
*in 10-point Times Roman type*
BY HAZELL WATSON AND VINEY LTD
AYLESBURY AND SLOUGH

*To*
*My Mother*

———————————————

# PREFACE

THIS book forms part of the long-term research into social stratification which is being carried out at the London School of Economics in conjunction with similar studies in other countries under the auspices of the International Sociological Association. The framework of the British programme of investigation was indicated in a symposium published four years ago—*Social Mobility in Britain*, edited by D. V. Glass—which focused on the general problems of social differentiation and mobility. Since then there has been a series of studies whose aim has been to examine in greater detail the process of educational selection and also the position of particular occupational groups in the class structure. Falling into the latter category, and most closely related to the present work, are R. K. Kelsall's *Higher Civil Servants in Britain*, 1955, and A. Tropp's *The School Teachers*, 1957. Both these books were the outcome of the original research intention to concentrate on the problems of recruitment, social status and professional organization in middle-class occupations that play an important part in the national power structure or in the process of social mobility. It is in this sense also that clerical workers constitute a rewarding subject of study, though one which has been curiously neglected since the publication of F. D. Klingender's *The Condition of Clerical Labour in Britain* in 1935. Clerical work has always been the major channel of upward social mobility from the working to the middle class. And, because of their highly marginal position and sheer numerical strength, the class identification of clerical workers raises important issues for the study of industrial and political behaviour. In this book, I have traced the reaction of clerks to the working-class movement, and tried to show how changes in their economic position, working relationships and social status have affected their class consciousness and the nature and intensity of their trade-union activities.

My work has benefited from the comments of Professor Asa Briggs, Mrs J. E. Floud and Professor D. V. Glass. On the general problems of social stratification I have had the stimulus of many discussions with Dr R. Dahrendorf and Dr A. Tropp. Among the persons who have patiently answered my questions or provided facilities for research, I should like to thank the following: Mr Alec Spoor, Public Relations Officer of the National and Local Government Officers Association; Mr T. G. Edwards, General Secretary of the National Union of Bank Employees; Mr L. A. Wines, Deputy General Secretary of the Civil Service Clerical Association; Mr G. Thomas of the Government Social Survey; and Dr H. Durant of the British Institute of Public Opinion. My greatest debt, however, is to my wife, to whom this book must now be an old acquaintance.

The present work incorporates the substance of a thesis which was approved by the University of London for the award of the degree of Doctor of Philosophy.

*London School of Economics*, April 1958.          D. L.

# CONTENTS

PREFACE                                                    *page* 7

INTRODUCTION                                                      11

I The Counting House                                              17

*The Modern Office: Introduction*                                36

II The Modern Office: Market Situation                           39

III The Modern Office: Work Situation                            69

IV The Modern Office: Status Situation                           97

V Trade Unionism                                                135

VI Conclusion                                                   199

APPENDIX A: Proportionate Increases of Clerical Salaries
        and Manual Earnings between 1905–6 and 1955             217

APPENDIX B: The Dwelling Areas of Clerks in Greater
        London                                                  218

INDEX                                                           221

# INTRODUCTION

'A body of men with strong distinctive traits, yet uncounted, uncared-for, misunderstood, or not understood at all, even by those who mix most closely with them—indeed, not even by themselves.'

B. G. ORCHARD,
*The Clerks of Liverpool*, 1871

'A docile being, chiefly noticeable as the first hope of suburbia at any time, and the last hope of the master class during strikes. If he has given the world any other impression than that of a professional Judas for Capitalism it is the vague idea that he has created the demand for five-a-penny cigarettes, the half-penny press, and guinea macintoshes.'

President of the National Union
of Clerks, *Annual Report*, 1915

'Those chaps who sit on their you-know-whats in offices and push pens.'

*The Bradford News*, 1951

# INTRODUCTION

EVERY social investigation must in some measure abstract from the mass of material which might be gathered on a particular subject. It is as well, therefore, to begin by trying to clarify some of the principal ideas that have guided the selection of data in this study. Its subject—the clerk, the typical blackcoated worker—would seem simple enough.[1] But the same subject can be approached from a variety of viewpoints and, depending on the particular viewpoint, different aspects of the problem will be emphasized or ignored. We have chosen to focus on the 'class consciousness' of the blackcoated worker, and, far from being simple, the notion of 'class consciousness' has a tortuous history of its own in which sociological and metaphysical themes are freely intermingled. It is not our intention here to flood the reader with the arguments and counter-arguments that spring from the controversy about the Marxian view of class and class consciousness. Yet just because of the emotive overtones of these concepts it is necessary to avoid any misunderstanding at the outset by reducing the idea of 'class consciousness' to a manageable category of research.[2]

To study the class consciousness of the clerk is to study the factors affecting his sense of identification with, or alienation from, the working class. More precisely, such a study should aim at an understanding of the relationship of the blackcoated worker to the trade-union movement, the main vehicle of working-class consciousness. In the course of the last seventy years the number of clerks has increased more rapidly than that of any other comparable occupational grouping, and today one out of every ten workers is a clerk. The Labour Movement could not remain indifferent to this occupational change, and by the early decades of the present century the problem of the class loyalty of the clerk was an urgent one in the minds of those concerned with unionization and working-class solidarity. For, almost without exception, the clerk was regarded as belonging to the working class and sharing the same interests as the

---

[1] The terms 'blackcoated worker' and 'clerical worker' are used interchangeably throughout the study. Clerks make up the greater part of the group of blackcoated workers, and common usage, throughout the greater part of the period under discussion, has preferred 'blackcoated' to 'white collar' worker.

[2] For a fuller discussion see T. Geiger, *Die Klassengesellschaft im Schmelztiegel*, 1949, Chapter VI, esp. pp. 123–7.

manual wage-earner. The vital question was whether the clerk himself was conscious of this community of interest, and whether he would align himself with the working-class movement.

In the face of these expectations the behaviour of the clerk was a disappointment. There can be little doubt that, throughout the greater part of the period stretching from the Trade Union Act of 1871 to the outbreak of the Second World War, the reaction of the blackcoated worker to trade unionism was, to say the least, lukewarm. There were, inevitably, some notable exceptions to this rule, but they were nevertheless atypical of the general tendency. Disappointment led easily to disparagement, and the view that the clerk was 'of different clay' from the manual worker, and that therefore little could be expected of him, was frequently expressed. Indeed, if there is one consistent and recurring theme which can be taken as the *leitmotif* of the present study it is that of the 'snobbishness', the 'self-deception' or the 'false consciousness' of the clerk. The contemptuous term, 'white-collar proletariat', was coined specifically in the inter-war years to emphasize the pathetic self-deception of the blackcoated worker who was seen as indulging in middle-class pretensions on a working-class level of living. Clerical workers were time and again singled out as the target for abuse by left-wing critics who regarded them as the saboteurs of the Labour Movement. Canute-like they were standing out against the irresistible tide of 'proletarianization'.

The charge that the blackcoated worker had a 'false' class consciousness of his real class position and real class interests is a particular expression of the general proposition that there is no necessary correspondence between what an individual believes his class position to be and what his class position actually is. Tawney, for example, warns us against confusing, 'the fact of class with the consciousness of class, which is a different phenomenon. The fact creates the consciousness, not the consciousness the fact. The former may exist without the latter, and a group may be marked by common characteristics, and occupy a distinctive position *vis-à-vis* other groups, without, except at moments of exceptional tension, being aware that it does so.'[1] In the case of the clerk, the common characteristics in terms of which he may be said to share the same class position as the manual wage earner are two-fold. First, that he is divorced from the ownership and control of the means of production. Secondly, as a consequence, he is obliged to sell his labour-power in order to make a livelihood. He is, like the manual worker, propertyless, contractual labour; in Marxian terminology, 'proletarian'.

[1] R. H. Tawney, *Equality*, 1952, pp. 50–1.

While this definition of class position presents us with the interesting problem that individuals who fall into the same economic category may develop differing ideas about their class identity, it tells us singularly little about the reasons why there should be a divergence in the class awareness of clerks and manual workers. In fact, such a broad definition of class has the disadvantage of obscuring actual variations in the situation and experience of those who share the common position of 'propertyless' labour. It is quite obvious that Marx himself clearly realized that the mere fact of 'propertylessness' provided no explanation of the actual presence or absence of class consciousness in a group. What he regarded as decisive for the development of class consciousness were the actual experiences to which the members of a class were subjected by reason of their common economic position. And by this he understood not only the material deprivations or indulgences which they shared, but also the sense of alienation from other classes and the sense of identification with one another which they experienced in the social relationships of production.[1] If then we are to make an empirical investigation of the class consciousness of the blackcoated worker it is best to postpone judgement on the question of 'false' class consciousness and to look in detail at his actual position in the administrative division of labour. In particular, it is advisable to jettison the blanket term 'proletarian' and to ask how far, in fact, the common fact of 'propertylessness' has resulted in identical economic consequences and identical social experiences for clerk and manual worker. In this way the ground is cleared for an examination of the variations in actual class position which may account for variations in actual class consciousness.

Under 'class position' will be included the following factors. First, 'market situation', that is to say the economic position narrowly conceived, consisting of source and size of income, degree of job-security, and opportunity for upward occupational mobility. Secondly, 'work situation', the set of social relationships in which the individual is involved at work by virtue of his position in the division of labour. And finally, 'status situation', or the position of the individual in the hierarchy of prestige in the society at large. The experiences originating in these three spheres may be seen as the principal determinants of class consciousness. 'Market situation' and 'work situation' comprise what Marx essentially understood as 'class

[1] See R. Bendix and S. M. Lipset, 'Karl Marx' Theory of Social Classes', *Class, Status and Power: A Reader in Social Stratification*, edited by R. Bendix and S. M. Lipset, 1953, pp. 26–34.

position'; 'status situation' derives from another branch of social stratification theory.[1]

The aim of the following chapters will be to determine how far clerks and manual workers may be said actually to have shared the same class position at different stages of industrial development. The main contrast in time will be between the 'counting-house' of the mid-nineteenth century, and the 'modern office' of the twentieth. Following this, we shall try to see how the class position of the black-coated worker is related to his class consciousness, marking especially those factors associated with the varying extent and character of clerical trade unionism. Only in this way can a closer understanding of the problem of 'false' class consciousness be arrived at.

[1] It is hoped that the meaning of these terms will become clear in the course of the discussion. The distinction between 'class' ('market-' and 'work-situation') and 'status' ('status situation') is made by Max Weber, *Essays in Sociology*, translated and edited by H. H. Gerth and C. W. Mills, 1948, Chapter VII.

# CHAPTER ONE

## THE COUNTING HOUSE

'The "average, undifferentiated human labour power" upon which Karl Marx bases his gigantic fallacy does not exist anywhere on this planet, but least of all, I think, is it to be found among clerks.'

CHARLES BOOTH, *Life and Labour of the People in London*, Vol. VII, 1896.

'The filial relationship in which they stood to their masters gave the latter a double power—on the one hand because of their influence on the whole life of the journeyman, and on the other because, for the journeyman who worked with the same master, it was a real bond, which held them together against the journeymen of other masters and separated them from these. And finally, the journeymen were bound to the existing order by their simple interest in becoming masters themselves.'

KARL MARX, *The German Ideology*

# THE COUNTING HOUSE

THE type of office that existed prior to the changes which ushered in the modern office of the twentieth century evades accurate description. The evidence bearing upon the condition of clerical labour between the eighteen-fifties and eighteen-eighties is meagre. The organizations of clerical workers whose journals later throw an indirect light on their mentality and problems are, if existent, inarticulate. Only in the novels of the time, in an occasional pamphlet, in a manual of instruction, or in the pages of some survey, do the fragments exist out of which can be built a picture of the office, the status, prospects and remuneration of the clerk.

The period of economic development with which the old type of office was associated was that of individual enterprise capitalism. In banking as in railways, to be sure, the newer form of corporate business was established; and the enhanced functions of central and local government were also swelling the labour force of clerks. But by far their greatest representation was in commercial and industrial employment. Towards the end of the century corporate capitalism became the dominant form of enterprise in this field too, although the advantages of concentration which it afforded were only slowly exploited.[1] With incorporation, and the increased size of the normal establishment, came changes which revolutionized office administration. For the moment, however, we may confine our attention to the conditions prevailing before these changes came about.

We may assume that the office of the counting house was small,[2] the division of labour slight and intimate. The size of the office was restricted, not only by the scale of business operations,[3] but also by the nature of business accounting. During the period 1850 to 1880, office records tended to be considered primarily as legal documents

[1] B. C. Hunt, *The Development of the Business Corporation in England 1800–1867*, 1936, p. 79.

[2] 'The average number of clerks in commercial offices is four,' concluded Orchard from his survey of Liverpool in 1871. B. G. Orchard, *The Clerks of Liverpool*, 1871, p. 7.

[3] In 1851, there were 129,002 masters in the manufacturing trades of England and Wales, employing 727,478 men, or an average of 5·6 men per master. 41,732 masters had no man; so that the average for 87,270 masters was 8·3 men per master. More than half of the men were employed by masters who had 30 or more men; and more than one-quarter by 752 masters who had each 150 or more men. Merchants numbered 10,103 and commercial clerks 43,741. *Census of Great Britain, 1851*, Population Tables II, Vol. I, 1854.

and as a rule of thumb guide to business decisions, rather than a statistical basis for rational costing and sales, which was part of a later trend of 'scientific management'.[1] Central to the record system of the counting house was the ledger, which provided an account of the success of the enterprise as a whole, and the profitability of particular ventures and transactions. Work in the office was oriented to the meticulous keeping of such ledgers upon whose accuracy business decisions depended. The most simple division of tasks in the older office was that between the employer or partners, who made the important business decisions, the book-keeper-cashier, who dealt with financial records, and the ordinary clerk, who was responsible for correspondence, filing, elementary book-keeping entries and routine office matters.

Within such a work situation the relations between employers and clerks were inevitably personal; the meaning of clerical skills and the value of clerical labour are to be understood and evaluated in this context. 'The relations between the clerk and his employer,' wrote Charles Booth towards the end of the century, 'or between him and the work he undertakes are usually close and personal. No one man is to be replaced exactly by another. No two office boys are quite alike in the mistakes they make. This variety in value is true to some extent even if the work is of the dullest routine character; far more so I believe than is the case with even highly skilled artisans; and is beyond calculation when the work entrusted to the clerk becomes confidential and responsible. The value of a clerk's services thus depends closely and somewhat curiously on relations with the employer, that is to say, upon possibilities of combination in action between men who have learnt to know each other's ways and who suit each other. Such relations are usually formed gradually and are the essence of all high value in clerks' work.'[2]

The talents pre-requisite to a clerical career were consequently general rather than specific. 'A little instruction in Latin, and probably a very little in Greek, a little in Geography, a little in Science, a little in arithmetic and book-keeping, a little in French, with such a sprinkling of English reading as may enable a lad to distinguish Milton from Shakespeare are considered enough preparation for aught that may turn up in the way of employment.'[3] In other words, a superficial secondary education such as was within the reach of

[1] C. B. Leffingwall, *The First Half Century of Office Management*, 1930.

[2] Charles Booth, *Life and Labour of the People in London*, Vol. VII. 'Population classified by trades', 1896.

[3] Houlston's Industrial Library No. 7. *The Clerk: a sketch in outline of his duties and discipline*, London, 1878, p. 13.

aspiring artisan or lower-middle-class families. No doubt this standard was set higher than that actually achieved by many boys entering
the occupation, for the minimum essential qualifications were those
of quick and accurate arithmetical calculation, plus a legible hand.
Beyond this, 'the art of book-keeping is justly considered the
essential accomplishment of all clerks, speaking of them as a class:
and excepting those who are attached to a particular profession, as
to the law or to offices under government, it is the ordinary business
of their lives'.[1] But the acquisition of book-keeping knowledge was
something best accomplished within the confines of a particular
office, a method which employers often preferred. 'As our *élève* is
understood to have been educated with a view to commercial life,
he must have gone through a course of book-keeping. So different,
however, are the theories of the schools from the practice of ordinary
business—every establishment, too, having peculiarities of its own—
that much which he learned in the former will have to be unlearned
in the latter.'[2] It is undoubtedly true that many clerks were accomplished in other fields.[3] But these wider achievements which many
clerks prized—in painting, music, history, literary composition—
though appropriate to the status of an 'educated gentleman', were
definitely discounted by employers as of little significance in the
tough world of commercial negotiation. 'It cannot be too carefully
remembered by clerks that the education they require is that which
will be valued by the firms which they serve—knowledge of languages,
skill in accounts, familiarity with even minute details of business,
energy, promptitude, tact, delicacy of perception. These, not knowledge of ancient history or modern music, not skill in essay writing
or speech making, are the results of business education; and without
these a master is justified in regarding a young man as ignorant and
useless. Business is a definite, narrow pursuit for fixed ends, and
those who conduct it look in their clerks for *business* talent. Does he
know a bargain when he sees it? Is he a good mental calculator? Is
he brisk and plausible? Is he good at a push for rapid and accurate
work? Such are the questions asked—such the qualities sought.
These are the faculties which make clerks into merchants, and
merchants into millionaires; it is these which will enable the discontented clerk to earn more than eighty pounds a year.'[4]

[1] *Ibid.*, Chapter VII.
[2] *The Young Clerk's Manual: or Counting House Assistant*, London, 1848.
See later editions of this evidently popular book, e.g. *The Clerk's Instructor and
Manual*, London, 1862.
[3] The association of clerkdom and literature is well known: Lamb, Kaffka,
Maupassant and Bennett are only among the most outstanding examples.
[4] Orchard, *op. cit.*, p. 43.

The achievement of high economic and social status, the goal held out to clerks and certainly realized by some, was the result of a happy conjunction of appropriate talents with diligent, tactful and personal association in work with a particular employer. The dependence of the clerk on a particular employer, and the difficulty of mobility between firms once a mature age had been reached, were, in theory at least, counterbalanced by the opportunities for advancement through staying with one firm and gradually 'making oneself indispensable'.[1] It is thus possible to see that the particularism of the relationship between clerk and employer, the possibility of rising from the one position to the other, and the largely individual and informal training within the counting house, served to strengthen ties between individual clerks and individual employers and thereby weaken the common interests that existed among clerks as a body. Perhaps the most important factor is that such personal and particular relationships produced a bewildering lack of uniformity in clerical salaries, for not only did every establishment have its own scale, but practically every clerk his own price.

In approaching the question of clerical salaries and economic opportunities, what is striking is the immense range in the remuneration of functions that were termed 'clerical'. No doubt the term was used in a much wider sense in the world of the counting house than it is today, and many of the clerks mentioned at the earlier period were probably performing duties which would nowadays be classified as 'managerial'. Secondly, two classes of clerks seem to differentiate themselves in the latter half of the nineteenth century. On the one hand, banking, civil service, insurance and the more prosperous class of mercantile and business clerks were able to maintain a fairly respectable middle-class way of life without undue strain; on the other, the greater proportion of clerks whose salaries barely ran ahead of the wages of the artisante were never really a part of the middle class in an economic sense, but were always striving socially to identify themselves with it. Thirdly, in which of these two groups the beginner was likely to end up was determined partly by nepotism, personal recommendation by the influential, and privileged entry.

The range of remuneration in fields such as banking, insurance,

---

[1] *The Clerk, op. cit.*, p. 127: 'Though the path is difficult and tedious, the door is not closed, even to the moneyless and friendless clerk: his natural course to promotion is, as we have before hinted, by making himself indispensable to his employer; the head must, sooner or later, take the right hand into its confidence; and perhaps for one who has prospered by his own independent effort, twenty clerks might be quoted by any man versed in business, whether commercial or professional, who have risen to wealth and eminence as partners in the house where their years of clerkship were expended.'

government and commerce formed a pyramid-like structure in which the apprentice or routine clerks were found at the base earning anything between twenty and two hundred pounds a year, while at the apex the various grades of managing clerks earned salaries running into four figures. 'The man of experience,' says Booth, 'receives anything from twenty-five shillings a week to a thousand pounds a year.'[1] Between top and bottom came all grades of clerkly skill—correspondents, cashiers, book-keepers, secretaries—differing in their remuneration not only between trades, but within trades, even street by street. In some offices, especially those of lawyers, rates of pay scarcely equalled those of dock labourers,[2] while in banking and mercantile pursuits the very highest faculties found employment and their possessors could earn as much as the gentlemen who employed the law clerks.

On the whole, the largest salaries were paid in those businesses which did not directly lead to ultimate independence, that is to say, in banks, insurance offices and the civil service. Railway clerks were an exception. Although their tenure of office was fairly secure they did not enjoy a very high material status.[3] But 'in the usual course, a bank clerk at thirty earns about two hundred pounds a year, working hours being from 9.30 to 4 o'clock. These are excellent average salaries for superior clerks; they are made still more attractive by the social status which accompanies them, and by the ease with

[1] Booth, op. cit., p. 274.

[2] 'The Law, though in popular estimation respectable and mysteriously dreadful, is about the poorest grazing ground a clerk can feed on. Lawyers and law stationers do not need men of talent, nor do such go to them; for the work not done by the principals or the managing clerk is of the dreariest routine character, and the incomes earned by the legal gentlemen being, on the average, smaller than those that reward the enterprising exertions of employers in other businesses, it is only natural for them to save all they can in office expenses.' Orchard, op. cit., p. 35.

[3] 'The proportion of posts with work entirely routine and of low class is large, and the clerks employed are correspondingly inferior in education. The sons of artisans push into it, but for a lad who has been well brought up there is no prospect unless, by unusual good fortune, he commences under the eye of an influential man and thus from the first is encouraged and given opportunities for advancement.' Orchard, op. cit., p. 32. Giving evidence before the Playfair Commission on the Civil Service in 1874–5 Mr George Findlay, Chief Executive Officer of the London and N.W. Railway, gave the scale as £25 at entry age fourteen to a maximum of £300, although he admitted that there would be 'a great many who would never go beyond a clerkship of £80 a year' (para. 5164). According to the statistics presented by him on the salaried staff of the London and N. Western, 3,534 clerks earned less than £100 per annum and a further 892 earned more than £100 but less than £200, out of a grand total of 4,647, which included the chief officers of the company. Appendix to the First Report of the Civil Service Inquiry Commissioners, 1875, p. 203.

which anyone leaving a bank secures employment elsewhere.'[1] These were also the careers which once obtained gave greatest security, promotion being fairly regular and employment stable. Most such posts were filled through personal recommendation. Banking and insurance companies normally had waiting lists on which they entered the names of those recommended to them and commonly gave preference to the sons of clerks already in their employment.[2] In the civil service, where salaries compared favourably with those in banking, a mixture of open competition and patronage survived into the 1870s in several departments. This took the form of private nomination, subject to the provision that any candidate thus nominated must be fit by examination.[3] The situation in local government was chaotic, positions and promotions being largely determined by the 'cockpit of local politics'—a system which produced fantastically inefficient staffs.

Compared with these employments, the field of commercial and mercantile clerkdom stands out, not only by reason of the numbers employed therein, but also because of the sharp contrasts that existed there between the rewards to be reaped by the clerk-become-merchant and the miseries of those who were chained to their high stools for the rest of their days. Here the personal element was much more prominent. Here the sons of gentlemen and artisans sat side by side. The signs of success shone brightly. 'On every side are brokers, merchants, agents, who from the clerk's stool have been raised to the private room of the firm, because they deserved the promotion. Half the partnership firms in Liverpool twenty years old contain a partner who was once a clerk.'[4] On the other side, 'perhaps

---

[1] Orchard, *op. cit.*, p. 29. See also the conditions described in *The Clerk*, Houlston's Industrial Library, 1878. The Secretary of the London and Westminster Bank gave a salary list as evidence to the Playfair Commission. It showed that clerks entered at eighteen to twenty-one with a salary of £80 approx. The scale rose to a maximum of £400, roughly after twenty-five years' service, for first-class clerks. But he was unable to specify the chances of arriving at the latter figure for the general run of clerks, except that promotion was by merit alone and that the first-class grade was relatively smaller than the other three. On the question of social status, his replies are quite interesting. 'Q.4743 (Chairman)—Have you any objection to state what is the general social status of the clerks who enter; do they belong to the middle classes?—They belong to what I should consider the upper middle classes. Q.4745—The men whom you get are sons of professional men?—Yes, of clergymen, military and medical men and others. Q.4746—Are any of them sons of shopkeepers?—I should say none. We may have had one or two when we were not so rigid as we are now, but I should say that now, as a rule, we should not introduce the son of a shopkeeper.' *Appendix to the First Report of the Civil Service Inquiry Commissioners*, 1875, p. 183.
[2] Booth, *op. cit.*, p. 274.      [3] *The Clerk*, *op. cit.*, Chapter X.
[4] Orchard, *op. cit.*, p. 41.

only one man in twenty of those who enter the office or the counting house, as stipendiary clerks, ever attains the grade of principal',[1] and we hear repeatedly that financially the great mass of clerks were on a level with the great mass of artisans,[2] that the usual salary of a clerk until the age of thirty was 30s a week,[3] and of grey-haired old men who worked from nine to six all the year round for £130. The heights and depths of commercial clerkdom were the marks of a vocation in which there was great opportunity for those who rose and respectable poverty for the unfortunate. How equal in fact was the opportunity to rise? How far did merit go unrewarded?

'There is a wide distinction,' says one commentator, 'between the clerk by profession and the clerk in *statu pupillari*. The merchant, the banker, the solicitor, and the novice in almost any trade or profession, begins to learn his duty as a clerk—it is the only way in which he is initiated; in his case it is only a state of preparation, not even of probation; his station in life, his actual capital, or his influential connections, give him a *locus standi* before he is qualified to fill it: to enable him to fill it with credit and advantage, he must learn the elements of business; and therefore he is placed as a clerk at the desk, but only temporarily, till he can undertake the management of the same business in its higher departments. With such a man clerkship is, in fact, only another school, and he does not enter this school till he is supposed to have acquired that degree of knowledge which is essential to support the character of a gentleman and a man of property.'[4] And another viewpoint: 'Look for a moment to the youths who, by the aid of patronage or family influence—the crowning curses of clerkship—monopolize most if not all of the best appointments to which clerks aspire. They are usually the fortunate sons of parents who move in the upper middle class of society . . . with a few worthy exceptions they are the youths who lack either brains or taste for the course of study necessary to fit them for professional or scientific pursuits. These lucky gentlemen are to be met with in almost every town, and may easily be distinguished by the observant as, early in the afternoon, they saunter homewards, weary and languishing, thoroughly convincing the onlooker that they consider work "a horrid bore, you know".'[5]

In the cotton offices of Liverpool, too, 'we meet with the most striking development of that system which is the *bête noire* of every true clerk—the system of filling an office with numerous apprentices

---

[1] *The Clerk*, *op. cit.*, p. 49.      [2] Booth, *op. cit.*, p. 276.
[3] William Poole, *The Clerk's Grievance*, 1878.
[4] *The Clerk*, *op. cit.*, p. 49.
[5] Charles Edward Parsons, *Clerks: Their Position and Advancement*, 1876, p. 19.

at nominal salaries over which a few experienced and responsible men exercise painful supervision'.[1] Out of a total of 1,370 clerks employed by some 350 firms, only 420 were salaried clerks, while no less than 950 were apprentices, that is to say, 'usually lads of good family, and well supplied with pocket money, to whom, by virtue of their scanty pay, special facilities for learning the business are extended to the exclusion and disadvantage of the smaller body'. Again, some 400 brokers in the same city with 300 clerks and 1,000 apprentices 'are the great employers of unpaid clerks. Scarcely a general broker is without at least one. It is under this title that the various scions of the aristocracy who are learning business in Liverpool must be ranged'.

The presence of this advantaged type of clerk undoubtedly worked to narrow the opportunities, and at the same time cheapen the price to be paid, for clerical workers on the lower rungs of the ladder. 'The constant influx of newcomers who frequently work hard on the *noblesse oblige* principle, and will gladly work without salary to secure ulterior objects, cheapens labour (so that an independent position), like every other prize in the trade is singularly difficult of attainment by those (about four-fifths of the whole) who have only their talents to depend on.'[2] In other words, the 'clerk by profession' as our manual calls him, 'whether in public or private establishment stands in a very different position; he, too, may rise to be head of his department, but he is commonly destitute of capital or influence; he finds himself placed where he is, simply to secure independent and immediate subsistence and without any certain preferment in perspective'.[3]

This situation was markedly aggravated by the invasion of the clerical labour market by cheap labour from Germany and Scotland in the 1870s. 'The lower and middle class German and Scotch people are particularly addicted to these underbidding properties . . . thus prepared by their schools for commercial life they swarm to England and France in thousands, accepting duties at any salary they are offered, for the purpose of gaining practical experience, and of forming connections with a view to ultimate trading on their own account.' Consequently, 'in the daily newspapers of any of our large cities and towns can be found, for the trouble of perusal, a dozen or more advertisements by clerks offering their services without salary for the first three or six months, and as many employers seeking unremunerated assistance'.[4]

---

[1] Orchard, *op. cit.*, p. 32.      [2] *Ibid.*, p. 32.      [3] *The Clerk*, *op. cit.*, p. 49.
[4] Parsons, *op. cit.*, p. 16. See also *Clerks and Shop Assistants of Both Sexes. Their Grievances, Position and Advancement*, 1890. The competition coming from German clerks is noted and analysed in *The Clerk's Journal*, Vol. I, No. 1, issued at Liverpool, March 1, 1888.

The result of these combined forces seems to have been the creation of a relatively large group of clerks whose income barely exceeded that of artisans and whose prospects for advancement were exceedingly small.[1] Already in 1871, Orchard could distinguish two sets of clerks by income and opportunity. '£150 and £80 point to two distinct classes of clerks, distinct in their education, business prospects, and various other things, but chiefly in the social usages which custom has made the framework of their daily life. Each sum may be taken as the test of a class. Those in banks, insurance offices and other public companies, who, while living on their salaries, reside in a fairly genteel neighbourhood, wear good clothes, mix in respectable society, go sometimes to the opera, shrink from letting their wives do household work, and incur, as unavoidable, the numerous personal expenses connected with an endeavour to maintain this system. At 28 years of age they receive about £150 and hope someday to reach £350 or more . . .' while, 'below them and forming a much more numerous body come the young men who (if in many cases well read, well mannered and religious) still are not in society, place little value on gloves, lunch in the office on bread and cheese,

[1] A mid-century observer had already noted and deplored this fact as being against both the employer's self-interest and social stability. The familiar and no doubt true assertion, that the value of the clerk to the employer is not simply equal to the cost of replacing him in the market, is made. The author also points out that clerks hold responsible positions and that if they are to work with loyalty and enthusiasm in their employer's interest, they must not be subject to the impersonal competitive pressure of the market, which results in a lowering of salaries and the recruitment of 'rough and ill-bred' persons. The reason given for justifying the superior economic standing of the clerk over the manual worker is also interesting: 'It is in fact general, and almost unavoidable, that in all establishments clerks have more or less influence and direction over workmen or others employed in their different grades, such manual or other situations being generally accounted subordinate; and that this influence should arise would seem desirable, as being frequently a convenience, and a general help to due management. It is notwithstanding by no means uncommon for the pay of the latter to be strangely in advance of that of the former. Of course, the writer is better informed than to expect that in all cases a clerk should receive more than, or even as much as some workmen who may be employed; as with some houses, special workmen earn wages it would be quite out of the question that clerks generally, or perhaps even a managing clerk should have—he would however urge that there is in fact a general relative connection and should be a proportionate remuneration.' As regards the wider social effects of the depression of clerical salaries, 'the element of average stability and healthfulness in any country rests in there being an enlightened, numerous and increasing middle class', and one important section of the middle class—notably clerks—'is for the most part so circumstanced, as that its deterioration and absorption into the lower class are imminent'. J. S. Harrison, *The Social Position and Claims of Book-keepers and Clerks Considered*, 1852, p. 21.

clean their own boots, and are not alarmed by the prospect of doing without a servant when married, of lighting the fire each morning before they go out, and of never entering a theatre or buying a bottle of wine. These are they whose salaries, averaging £80, are unlikely ever to exceed £150.'[1] Needless to say, the income of the lower class of clerk was often supplemented by the wife's work, which, being predominantly done at home, formed a compromise between the husband's low salary, a forward-looking mentality and an over-riding sense of respectability. 'The home workers,' writes Booth, 'are to be found in every grade of society, among the wage-earning class; in the home of the middle class clerk and in the room of the dock labourer. The young wife of the clerk with regular employment but small salary takes sealskin capes home from the warehouse where she worked as a girl, because a good housewife has time to spare when she has only three rooms to keep tidy and only two people to cook for, and is glad to add something to the savings which may be useful someday when the children are being educated or started in life.'[2]

Although relatively worse off than the superior grade of clerk, and in many cases financially on a level with the skilled artisan, '£75 to £150 a year comparing with 30, 40, 50 and 60s a week',[3] the larger part of these clerks were socially on an entirely different footing than the artisan class. Their expenditure patterns were quantitatively different from those of the superior class of clerks, yet qualitatively they were the same, expressing a similar mentality and similar evaluations. 'From top to bottom clerks associate with clerks and artisans with artisans—but comparatively seldom with each other. A clerk lives an entirely different life from an artisan—marries a different kind of wife—has different ideas, different possibilities, and different limitations. A clerk differs from an artisan in the claims each make on society, no less than in the claims society makes on them. It is not by any means only a question of clothes, of the wearing or not wearing of a white shirt every day, but of differences which

---

[1] Orchard, *op. cit.*, p. 64.

[2] Charles Booth, *Life and Labour of the People*, 1891, p. 445.

[3] Charles Booth, *op. cit.*, 1896, p. 277. Orchard's figures for 1871 give a similar range for the lower class of clerks. The proportion of the working class whose incomes came within the £80–£150 range was quite small, perhaps 10–15%. Artisans earning more than 40s a week in the 1870s formed a highly select 'super-aristocracy'. See E. J. Hobsbawm, 'The Labour Aristocracy in 19th Century Britain' in *Democracy and the Labour Movement*, Essays in Honour of Dona Torr (edited by John Saville), 1954, p. 208. 'Mechanics earn as much as most ordinary clerks; they, of course, can live decently, not having the same appearance to keep up.' Poole, *op. cit.*

invade every department of life, and at every turn affect the family budget. More undoubtedly is expected from the clerk than the artisan, but the clerk's money goes further and is on the whole much better spent.'[1] In short—at least as one disillusioned clerk saw it—'foolish parents wish to see their sons in broadcloth instead of fustian; they think a clerk is a gentleman and an artisan not'.[2]

Thus, although there were sharp income differences within the clerical class, the common values which informed their behaviour seemed at once to unite them together and separate them from the wage-earning class.[3] One of the dominating features of the clerical consciousness at this time was the conception of the 'gentleman'. The ideal of the gentleman in the second half of the nineteenth century, being essentially defined as a state of mind and a corresponding mode of conduct, was an inexpensive luxury. Gentlemanliness was still within the reach of those clerks whose salaries would not support a proper middle-class style of life. It was also sufficiently vague as a value that gentlemanliness and respectability could become curiously confused in the lower-middle-class culture in which clerks played a major role. A few remarks concerning the function of the gentleman ideal as it affected the relationship between master and clerk may throw light on the way in which the striving for prestige only added to the other obstacles to collective action by clerks, despite the penurious condition in which many found themselves.

The relationship between clerk and employer was, as we have noted, in most cases a personal and particular one, strongly characterized by the exhibition of mutual trust in the form of unwritten, tacit expectations of conduct. In many cases it took the form of a 'gentleman's agreement'. Needless to say, this relationship was often exploited by the employer and great expectations frequently came to nothing. Nevertheless, the clerical notion of gentlemanly behaviour, at least in its lower-middle-class admixture with 'respectability', acted as a powerful social control over any intransigence or insurrection on the part of the clerk. 'Clerks are, as a rule, of decent address and gentlemanly habits, patient and long-suffering, not given to noisily "insisting upon their rights" and are possessed of some delicacy when requesting an advance of salary, not unnaturally believing that their

---

[1] Booth, *op. cit.*, 1896, p. 277.
[2] *The Clerk's Journal*, August 1, 1890, p. 2.
[3] This was also supported by the nature of their work. 'It would seem impossible to avoid allowing that a clerk's duties bear a greater similarity to those of the principal, and are of a more enlightening and improving nature than manual work; and also, that their tendency is not only to keep up, but decidedly to induce a more susceptible and sensitive state than rougher and less mental pursuits.' Harrison, *op. cit.*, p. 21.

employers ought to recognize their merits and reward their careful guardianship of trade secrets and the valuable information they frequently obtain, without requiring somewhat humiliating reminders.'[1] Gentlemanliness is here interpreted as an avoidance of disagreements about pecuniary matters within a relationship which is not to be valued in raw monetary terms.

Secondly, the privilege of appearing 'gentlemanly' in appearance, mannerism and work within the office,[2] must be counted, together with the possibility of mixing with the sons of gentlemen, as part of the clerk's reward in this period. 'The clerks in established and well-known merchants' offices yield to no one in gentlemanly deportment, cultivated proficiency and self-respect; and in appearance there is but little difference between many of them and the employers they serve.'[3]

Nevertheless, there was often a conflict between such aspirations and the actual condition of the clerk's servitude, dependence and low income which gave rise to frustration.[4] There seems to have been considerable dissatisfaction about the lack of correspondence between their social status and their actual rewards. They regarded their social standing as a ground for higher remuneration rather than as a reward in itself. But one shrewd employer, Benjamin Battleaxe, commenting on clerical discontent, singled out this predicament as deserving their special notice: 'But how comes it, if the pay is so miserably insufficient, that so many seek it; that clerks make their sons clerks; that warehousemen and farmers act similarly; and that the cry is "still they come"? Is it not because clerks are socially gentlemen—treated as such, and allowed to dress as such? Clerks, like officers in the army and navy, or like clergymen, have a position as well as salary. They pride themselves on that position. In virtue thereof they indulge in much liberty of action which other classes of servants do not enjoy. They call themselves their masters' equals, and demand recognition as such. And in dress, assumption, everything

---

[1] Parsons, *op. cit.*, p. 12.

[2] 'Between management and clerks there was loyalty and understanding. "I fully admit," said Mr Harben in reply to a complaint made by a shareholder, "that our clerks do read newspapers and chatter; but I have yet to learn that human nature can go on all day long without some little relaxation. I am not prepared as Manager of this company to be a nigger-driver." He added that he knew that, were they asked to do so, the staff would begin work at six o'clock in the morning and carry on until eight in the evening.' R. W. Barnard, *A Century of Service. The Story of the Prudential 1848-1948*, p. 24.

[3] Orchard, *op. cit.*, p. 33.

[4] 'Well-born and respectably-connected persons in this occupation have, much oftener than is commonly imagined, to pass their life for the most part amidst difficulties and perplexities.' Harrison, *op. cit.*, p. 21.

within their power, they follow this up, affording themselves much gratification, and realizing substantial advantage from the nature of their vassalage. Now, sir, let them consider this as part of their remuneration. Or if they object to do so, let them cease to put themselves forward as "educated gentlemen" assured that very soon there will be fewer labourers' sons forced into their ranks, and that by this reduction of their number they will obtain an increase in pay.'[1]

The derision and contempt which the 'poor, sad snob of a clerk' often evoked is understandable to a great extent in terms of the confusion between the form and the spirit of gentlemanliness which his behaviour often entailed. Because of the actual conditions of their employment, the dress, speech and outward mannerisms of clerical gentlemanliness were often an exaggerated and perverted form of the real thing.[2] And when it came to the spirit of the gentlemanly ideal, the clerk apparently compared unfavourably with the ordinary artisan, as the following extract is at pains to point out: 'It may appear paradoxical, but it is strictly true, that the manners of an English gentleman have much more in common with the manners of a labourer than with the manners of a mercantile clerk or a small shopkeeper. It is true that a gentleman's accent differs from a labourer's; he holds himself differently, and his features express altogether a different class of emotions and recollections, but the manner of the two men has a radical similarity which ought not to be overlooked by anyone who wishes to understand English society. The great characteristic of the manners of a gentleman, as we conceive them in England, is plain, downright, frank, simplicity. It is meant to be, and to a great extent it is, the outward and visible sign of the two great cognate virtues—truth and courage. It is the manner of men who expect each other to say, in the plainest way, just what they mean, and to stand to what they say, with but little regard either for the opinion or for the approbation of others, though with full respect for their feelings. This sturdy mixture of frankness when they do speak, with a perfect willingness to hold their tongues when they have nothing to say, is the great distinguishing feature of educated Englishmen, and is the one which always strikes foreigners with surprise. It is their incapacity to appreciate the qualities which it covers which makes their criticisms of us so wildly remote from the truth as they often are. This manner prevails much more amongst the labouring than among the shopkeeping classes. Their language proves it conclusively. A gentleman and a labouring man would tell the same story in nearly the same words, differently pronounced, of course,

---

[1] Quoted by Orchard, *op. cit.*, p. 44.
[2] See *The Clerk*, *op. cit.*, Chapter V, 'Affectation in Dress and Manner'.

and arranged, in the one case grammatically, and in the other not. The language of the commercial clerk, and the manner in which he brings it out, are both framed on quite a different model. He talks about himself, and constantly tries to talk fine. He calls a school an academy, speaks of proceeding when he means "going" and talks, in short, much in the style in which members of his own class write police reports and accounts of appalling catastrophes for the newspapers.'[1]

Frankness and forthrightness are functions of economic independence; unpretentiousness is a function of social independence. In both respects, the clerk generally lacked the necessary security. The conditions of his work and the orientations of his life very often brought the opposite qualities of obsequiousness, circumlocution and pretentiousness to the fore. Occupationally his future was tied to a particular firm and employer, economically he was almost on a par with the labouring classes, and socially he took his pattern of life and standard of values from the class above him. All contributed to form a 'gentleman' as different from the aristocratic gentry culture above him as from 'nature's gentleman' below him. His distinguishing mark was respectability.

It can be readily appreciated that despite the obvious economic pressure under which a great many clerks lived due to their social aspirations, there were many obstacles to their concerted action for improved economic status.

They were, as a class, fragmented and isolated in small groups in a great many offices and businesses. On the whole, the internal social relations of the office were such as to discourage that kind of impersonal appraisal of the situation which is the basis of group action. 'For clerks a trade union has no attraction. Its advantages are not apparent, the relationship between employer and employed being in this case essentially personal.'[2] Moreover, trade unions were the means by which the labouring class was beginning to raise its standard of living, and they were definitely not respectable in the eyes of most clerks. Their own ranks contained a diversity of elements, whose interests, backgrounds and connections had little in common. 'I fear that a combination of clerks for legitimate purposes upon a basis similar to that of the trade unions can never succeed; and this is because the vast army of clerks is recruited not from one, but from nearly every grade of society.'[3] A considerable proportion of their number was formed by the sons of employers or the nephews of employers who, by interest and sympathy, were not clerks, and who

[1] *The Cornhill Magazine*, 1862, Vol. V, p. 337.
[2] Booth, *op. cit.*, 1896, pp. 278–9.   [3] Parsons, *op. cit.*, p. 18.

would refuse to unite in any movement intended to restrain employers. Added to this the ablest clerks, those who alone could organize and conduct such a movement, were likely themselves to become masters or confidential and well-paid managers, so that they too had little sympathy for their fellows and had no desire to incur the odium or lose the time involved in making such exertions. The example of these successful clerks must have always been a spur to the individualistic strivings of the younger clerks, while for the older and unsuccessful ones yet another confirmation that their own lowly positions were due entirely to their own deficiencies. Moreover, the clerk growing old in the employ of a particular firm increasingly vested his future in it. If separated from its peculiar routine, acquired painfully through a lifetime's service, he was unlikely to be employed elsewhere. He would be most reluctant to risk dismissal, therefore, and the chance of some pension, however small, by joining a combination of clerks.

In the larger offices, in the civil service, in railways, banking and insurance, greater numbers of clerks were often concentrated in the same establishment. Some of the earliest active attempts to form protective organizations are to be found in these groups. 'Several attempts have been made by those engaged in railway and other large offices to form minor and purely local combinations, with the object of bringing grievances before their respective employers and for obtaining an improvement in salary, or the abolition of some objectionable system; but success has hitherto been very indifferent. Occasionally their petitions have been granted; but more frequently the leading spirits of each movement have received summary dismissal as the reward of their exertions.'[1]

More often clerks looked to friendly societies rather than to trade-union action in order to achieve some kind of economic security. 'A great many of them have always belonged to tontines, or to the Oddfellows, Druids, or some other of the great sick and burial clubs; of the clerks proper perhaps a fourth; of the married men a small proportion—perhaps a tenth—insure their lives.'[2] Sometimes there were local attempts to establish associations and provide sick, building and superannuation funds, and employers were frequently urged to take an interest. One writer in 1878, proposing such a venture, begged that 'since no association can be started without the co-operation of the influential, the writer looks to clerks to help him circulate *The Clerk's Grievance* among directors of large companies, heads of departments and all other influential gentlemen'.[3] It is very hard to assess the extent of such local and often ephemeral attempts

---

[1] *Ibid.*, p. 18.  [2] Orchard, *op. cit.*, p. 48.  [3] Poole, *op. cit.*

at association, but it is certain that the trade-union form of action, which manual workers were beginning to use to an ever greater degree outside the ranks of the skilled artisan class, was still very unusual among clerical workers, even at the end of the period under discussion.[1]

In understanding the failure of concerted action among clerks it is not to their economic position, narrowly conceived, that we must look, but principally to the motives and actions occasioned by their role in the division of labour of the office, and by their position in the hierarchy of social rank in society at large.

The world of the counting-house formed an environment which, despite the objective economic position of many clerical workers, was generally conducive to their estrangement from the mass of working men and to their identification with the entrepreneurial and professional classes. In these early years, many of those who went into blackcoated work were drawn from the middle class or from socially aspiring artisan families; they usually had more education than those who went into factory employment; their work was clean and involved the exercise of brain not brawn; their dress distinguished them from ordinary employees and approximated that of the master class, with whom they worked in a close and personal relationship; their skills and future were tied up with a particular employer and enterprise, and often they were entrusted with confidential matters and delegated authority over other employees; their salaries, if not always large, were generally secure and progressive; possibilities of advancement undoubtedly existed and, even when not

---

[1] The following estimate of the membership of various clerical associations, together with the dates of their establishment, is given in *The Clerk's Journal*, June 1, 1888, p. 4:

| | | |
|---|---|---|
| Liverpool | 1861 | 3,292 |
| Manchester | 1855 | 2,565 |
| London | 1871 | 2,600 |
| Newcastle | 1873 | 576 |
| Birmingham | 1883 | 284 |
| Belfast | 1878 | 150 |
| Dublin | 1873 | 242 |
| Glasgow | 1886 | 429 |
| Leeds | 1862 | 159 |
| Cardiff | 1887 | 168 |
| Lancashire, Yorkshire and London | 1883 | 600 |

Of course, friendly societies were in existence much earlier than this. The rules of a society established in Newcastle, for example, date back to the first decade of the century. See *The Articles and Rules of the Clerk's Society: A Friendly Society Established in Newcastle-upon-Tyne, 1st January, 1807.*

an actuality, continued to spur energies and imagination in an individualistic direction. If economically they were sometimes on the margin, socially they were definitely a part of the middle class. They were so regarded by the outside world, and they regarded themselves as such. At the same time, we see evidence of extensive nepotism in the more lucrative appointments and promotions, of clerks offering their services in return for experience or token salaries, of masters taking advantage of the over-supply of the market to pay their clerks less than it took to marry and maintain a respectable family. But for the most part these grievances were inarticulate because clerks were socially isolated from one another and dependent on the good will of particular employers.

# THE MODERN OFFICE:
# INTRODUCTION

THERE is no sharp dividing line between the counting house and the modern office. There is only a gradual development of the administrative unit in terms of size, equipment and mode of organization. The most noticeable index of change is to be found in the numerical increase of clerical workers themselves. In 1851 clerks formed less than 1% of the total labour force. Today rather more than one out of every ten workers is a clerk.

| Year | Clerks as percentage of Total Labour Force | Female Clerks as percentage of Total Clerks |
|------|------|------|
| 1851 | 0·8 | 0·1 |
| 1901 | 4·0 | 13·4 |
| 1951 | 10·5 | 59·6 |

The second major change is in the sexual composition of the occupation. The seventy or eighty thousand clerks of 1851 were almost entirely male—there were in fact nineteen women listed under the heading of 'commercial clerks' and a sprinkling in other fields. By 1951, clerks numbered well over two millions, and six out of every ten of these were women. By the mid-twentieth century, to be precise, we should no longer speak of the 'blackcoated', but rather of the 'white-bloused' worker.

The average size of the office increased concomitantly with the increase in the ratio of non-manual to manual workers in industry, and with the proliferation of 'non-productive' functions in commerce, finance, distribution and government. Scientific management brought in its train an obsession with the elaborate accounting of production costs and market demand. Scientific management initiated office mechanization; and office mechanization in its turn promoted further the recording of new types of data. Industrial concentration and amalgamation, born of joint stock enterprise, lead to the concentration and rationalization of office work and staffs. And the vastly enhanced functions of government in an industrial *milieu* called for increasingly more efficient administration. The field from which clerical workers were recruited was also widely

36

extended by the institution of compulsory elementary education in the last decades of the nineteenth century. Every literate person became a potential clerk, thus breaking the hitherto monopolistic position of the blackcoated worker.

The following chapters seek to trace the impact of these changes on the position of the clerk, in the market, at work, and in society at large. They aim further to demonstrate the relationships between changes in these spheres of his life and the development of blackcoated trade unionism and class consciousness.

# CHAPTER TWO

# THE MODERN OFFICE: MARKET SITUATION

'It should be remembered that, although by reason of their unorganized state, clerks suffer many economic disabilities, yet they have a great many economic advantages not enjoyed by manual workers. Among them may be cited permanency of employment, periodical increases of salary, payment of salary during sickness and holidays, comparatively reasonable hours of work, and in certain sections superannuation. These advantages, chiefly matters of custom and usage, constitute a powerful common interest among clerks, and should be an equally strong reason for protective organization.'

*The Clerk*, 1916

# THE MODERN OFFICE:
# MARKET SITUATION

DURING the century that divides the counting house from the office of the present day, the economic position of the blackcoated worker saw considerable change. In the counting-house era the clerk generally enjoyed a material status clearly removed from that of the mass of manual workers. His salary, hours of work and holidays were decidedly more favourable; and to be added to these were security of tenure, a greater chance of promotion, and the probability of a pension of some kind. All in all, these conditions gave the blackcoated worker a security and opportunity that distinguished him from other propertyless and contractual labour. Although he was in the same fundamental market situation as the fustian-clad workman by reason of his propertyless dependence, the economic consequences of propertylessness worked out rather differently in his case than in that of the manual wage-earner. He was somehow a privileged type of proletarian.

What changes have taken place in these features of the market situation during the rise of the modern office? Has the general economic position of the clerk approximated more and more to that of the manual worker? How far have income and other differentials been maintained between clerical and the various grades of manual employment? Is office work a more secure form of employment? Finally, to what extent is clerical work an avenue of mobility to supervisory and managerial positions? In short, how valid is the thesis of 'white-collar proletarianization'?

## INCOME

Reliable evidence relating to the remuneration of clerical labour has always been scarce. The following account refers to the period 1900–54, more particularly to the pre-1914, inter-war and post-war periods. It is built up around investigations made in the years 1909, 1924 and 1930, and thereafter is largely based on the surveys carried out by the Office Management Association since 1942. These statistical probes have been supplemented by data gleaned from the journals of the various clerical associations, and the resulting facts about blackcoated incomes have been compared with the available evidence on working-class earnings.

I. *The Pre-war Period, 1900–14.* The major source of information in this period is a paper read in 1910, before the British Association for the Advancement of Science at Sheffield, when the following statistics on the distribution of clerical earnings were presented.[1]

### TABLE I—PERCENTAGE OF MALE CLERKS EARNING MORE THAN £160 A YEAR BY INDUSTRIAL GROUPS[2]

#### 1909

| Industrial Group | Percentage of clerks earning more than £160 a year (61s 6d) a week | Average earnings of clerks earning less than £160 a year |
|---|---|---|
| Insurance | 46 | £85 |
| Banking | 44 | £90 |
| Civil Service | 37 | £95 |
| Local Government | 28 | £91 |
| Industry and Commerce | 23 | £80 |
| Railways | 10 | £80 |

These figures give the first representative picture of the blackcoated market situation as a whole and may be taken as roughly comparable with those available on average manual earnings in 1906. The latter, computed by Bowley, refer to men and boys in a wide range of manual occupations.[3] Between 1906 and 1909, the date of the clerical survey, there was little change in the money wage-rate; and we may safely assume that the average earnings of manual workers did not change very much between these two points of time.[4] Conversely, there is small reason to believe that the figures on clerical salaries in 1909 differed substantially from the average earnings of three years previously.[5]

---

[1] *Report on the Amount and Distribution of Income Below the Income Tax Exemption Limit,* by Professor E. Cannan, A. L. Bowley, F. Y. Edgeworth, H. B. Lees-Smith and Dr W. R. Scott, p. 170.

[2] The proportion of those clerks falling above the £160 limit is probably boosted slightly in these figures by the inclusion with 'clerks', strictly interpreted, of the class of 'officials' with whom they were grouped in the Census. Officials include the salaried officers of varying rank in banking, railways, etc., who stood immediately above the clerical grades proper. Clerical workers formed the vast bulk of the sample, however, and certainly they account for those falling below the income limit.

[3] A. L. Bowley, *Wages and Income in the U.K. since 1860,* 1937, Table XI, p. 51.

[4] E. H. Phelps Brown and Sheila V. Hopkins, 'The Course of Wage-Rates in Five Countries, 1860–1939', *Oxford Economic Papers,* NS, Vol. II, No. 2, June 1950.     [5] See Appendix A.

Bowley's estimate of the average actual earnings of manual workers in 1906 is 27s a week, ranging from 22·9s in textiles to 31·5s in coal-mining. Another, slightly later, survey of manual earnings gives the figure of approximately 29s a week as the average weekly earnings of men aged twenty-one and over.[1] The immediate impression conveyed by a comparison of clerical and manual earnings is that of the relatively high economic status of the blackcoated 'aristocracy' and the penuriousness of the mass of ordinary clerks. Almost one-half of the insurance and banking clerks, and well over one-third of the civil-service clerks earned more than 61s 6d a week. Those who fell below this line earned around 34s 6d a week. Commercial and railway clerks, the lowest ranks of the blackcoated brigade, were much less prosperous. Nine out of ten railway clerks and three out of every four commercial clerks earned on the average just under 31s a week. Railway and commercial clerks, therefore, lay precariously on the edge of the abyss. The situation of the railway clerk was particularly bad following the slow-down of railway expansion and the rationalization of railway administration.[2] The mass of industrial and commercial clerks weighed much more importantly, however, in the total balance; by 1911 they accounted for well over half of the total number of blackcoats. If about one-quarter of their number earned more than 61s 6d a week, the 'pound-a-week' clerk was a sufficiently familiar figure to the infant National Union of Clerks for it to devote much time and energy to his elevation in the immediate pre-war period and to the establishment of a 35s weekly minimum.[3] Compulsory elementary education was working with a vengeance. Thousands of young men and women equipped with the essential clerkly skill—literacy—were pouring into the market; and at a faster rate than even that rapidly expanding market could absorb. The practice of employing a succession of young boy clerks in routine 'dead-end' jobs had also become widespread by this time.

As a consequence, the clerical labour force was relatively youthful by comparison with the working population as a whole. In 1911 some 46% of commercial clerks were under the age of twenty-five as compared with 29% of the total male occupied population. This difference in age-structure is an important consideration in evaluating the above comparisons of earnings. There is no indication that

[1] Board of Trade, *Earnings and Hours Enquiry 1906–7*, Summary Tables, 1908, p. 14.

[2] *The Life of the Railway Clerk: Some Interesting Facts and Figures*, Railway Clerks Association, seventh edition, December 1911.

[3] Fred Hughes, *By Hand and Brain*, 1953, Chapter III.

43

allowance was made for this factor in the survey, and this means that the relationship between the average earnings of blackcoated and manual workers naturally reflects the disproportionate influence of the younger element in the former group. When we couple this fact with a second—namely, that the difference between the earnings of younger and older workers is generally greater for clerks than for manual workers—it is reasonable to conclude that about two-thirds of the clerks who earned 31s a week were relatively young men who would either leave the occupation or gradually progress to the more highly remunerated positions. A balanced comparison between the earnings of adult male clerks and manual workers over the age of twenty-five would probably have shown the position of clerical workers in a slightly more favourable light.

Nevertheless, it cannot be doubted that the blackcoated worker was experiencing lean years. Whilst the earnings of the worst-paid clerks were roughly on a par with the average manual worker's income, the ordinary adult clerk was not better off, on the whole, than the artisan, and his cost of living was conventionally higher.[1] Even the blackcoated 'aristocracy' of insurance, banking and certain civil-service clerks, who were somewhat removed from the plight of their less-privileged fellows by reason of their traditional status and more stringent selection, increasingly felt the pressure from below in the years immediately preceding the outbreak of the First World War.

II. *The Inter-war Period, 1919–39.* The rise in the cost of living which continued throughout the war reached its peak in 1921. The official index jumped from 97 in 1911 to 203 in 1918, and to 249 in 1921. After that date it fell steeply to 1923 and then more slowly, reaching its lowest point in 1933. The two dates for which there is adequate information on clerical salaries in the inter-war period are 1924 and 1930, that is, at points on the downswing of the economic cycle measured both in terms of cost of living and wage-rates. The general

---

[1] 'The earnings of the average clerk are not on the whole higher than those of the skilled artisan, whilst the necessity of keeping up a respectable appearance makes his cost of living much higher. By the age of 20 or 21 a man should be earning from 30s to 35s a week. By the age of 30 an ordinary clerk should be receiving a salary of about £130 per annum, at which level he frequently remains; a good correspondence clerk, or book-keeper, however, will often get £150–£180 a year. Confidential clerks may earn from £250 a year upwards. The above are the salaries paid by the best firms; but there are a large number who never pay more than 40s–50s a week.' *Commercial Occupations*, One of a Series of Handbooks on London Trades Prepared on Behalf of the Board of Trade, 1914, p. 3. See also Lady Bell, *At The Works*, 1911, p. 86.

relation between wages and salaries was such that between 1924 and 1928 salary-rates fell more than wage-rates; between 1929 and 1933 rates of salaries did not fall so much as rates of wages; whereas between 1934 and 1939 salary-rates made a slower recovery than wage-rates.[1] The surveys of 1924 and 1930, but especially the latter, give a picture of the market situation of clerical labour at periods when the relative movements of wages and salaries were slightly more favourable to the blackcoated worker. The periods immediately following the First World War and immediately preceding the Second were, on the other hand, times when the upward pressure of wages on salaries was most noticeable.

The 1924 survey deals with practically the same groups as the 1909 survey, clerks forming the vast majority of the sample.[2] The following table sets out the main results of this inquiry.

TABLE II—PERCENTAGE OF MALE AND FEMALE CLERKS
EARNING MORE THAN £150 A YEAR (57·7s A WEEK) BY
INDUSTRIAL GROUPS

1924

| Industrial Group | Percentage of clerks whose salary was over £150 a year | Average Weekly Income of Clerks below £150 a year |
|---|---|---|
| *Males* | | |
| Local Government | 87 | 34·6s |
| Industry | 78 | 35·0s |
| Banking | 75 | 39·0s |
| Insurance | 91 | 35·0s |
| Commerce | 75 | 31·1s |
| Railways | 80 | 39·6s |
| *Females* | | |
| Local Government | 47 | 37·3s |
| Industry | 12 | 35·4s |
| Banking | 69 | 49·2s |
| Insurance | 30 | 43·8s |
| Commerce | 14 | 34·6s |
| Railways | 17 | 39·0s |

[1] A. L. Bowley, *Studies in the National Income 1924–1938*, 1942, p. 94.
[2] A. L. Bowley and Sir J. Stamp, *The National Income 1924*, 1927, pp. 20–3.

45

The line of 57·7s is convenient because the average of manual earnings in 1924 is estimated at 57·6s, the range being from 70·7s in printing to 51s in textiles.[1] For the distributive trades the average wage was 48s 6d, in catering 52s 6d, in carting and warehousing 51s 7d. Seamen earned 62s, tram- and busmen 68s 6d, dock labourers 60s, and postmen 57s 6d.[2] The rates for skilled workmen in the same year are given as 55s 7d for shipwrights, 56s 6d for engineering fitters, and 73s 5d for bricklayers.[3] If rates bore the same relation to earnings in that year as in the previous one, the earnings of engineering fitters would have been approximately 69s.[4] Thus the average earnings in industry were well above the average for clerks earning less than 57·7s a week; but these, forming 25% of commercial clerks, 20% of railway clerks, and 25% of bank clerks, were probably the younger clerks. In all cases the majority of clerks fell above the 57·7s mark. How far above it is difficult to say. In the case of the railway clerk, the new agreement achieved by the Railway Clerks Association in 1919 had markedly improved his situation. In 1924 it was estimated that the average earnings of railway clerks, classes 5 to 1, was 84s 10d.[5] The following year, a railway clerk of twenty-eight was earning about 70s a week on the normal salary scale.[6] In the same year, the National Union of Clerks made an agreement with a Welsh brewery which gave the clerks 35s a week at twenty-one, general clerks a scale from 70s rising to 95s, first-class clerks a scale from 90s rising to 135s, and chief clerks from 110s rising to 140s.[7] The Brighouse Co-operative Society agreed to pay its clerks a salary of 60s at age twenty-one, rising to 75s at twenty-five.[8] A London accountant was paying minimum rates of 70s for twenty-one-year-old clerks, and his adult clerks got 80s, rising by 5s per week annual increments to 100s a week.[9] There were of course tremendous variations, especially in the commercial and industrial field, and if it is true to say that adult clerks could be found earning less than unskilled labour, it is also true that others were earning salaries which no manual worker could hope to equal. Although the facts do not permit accurate estimates to be made, it may be hazarded that only among working-class artisans did remuneration equal that of the average adult clerk. As for the elite of the occupation, a bank clerk

---

[1] A. L. Bowley, *op. cit.*, p. 51.
[2] Colin Clark, *The National Income 1924–31*, 1952, p. 58.
[3] *Twenty-Second Abstract of Labour Statistics, 1922–1936*, 1936–7, p. 824.
[4] K. G. J. C. Knowles and D. J. Robertson, 'Differences between the Wages of Skilled and Unskilled Workers, 1880–1950', *Bulletin of the Oxford Institute of Statistics*, 1951, p. 126.
[5] *The Railway Clerk's Journal*, 1925, p. 404.    [6] *Ibid.*, January 1925, p. 15.
[7] *The Clerk*, 1924, p. 108.    [8] *Ibid.*, 1924, p. 106.    [9] *Ibid.*, 1924, p. 35.

at twenty-eight could count on a salary of about 106s a week, a civil-service clerical officer on a fraction less, and the local government officer in the provinces on about 77s.[1] The earnings of female clerks bore more or less the same relationship to those of working-class women and girls. Industrial and commercial clerks were mostly earning around 35s compared with an estimated average of earnings for women in manual work of 27·5s.[2]

The survey of 1929–30 deals with clerical labour in London, and the relevant statistics on average earnings are set out in the table below.[3]

### TABLE III—AVERAGE WEEKLY SALARIES OF CLERKS IN LONDON IN FOUR INDUSTRIAL GROUPS

#### 1929–30

| Sex | Age Groups | Public Services | Industry and Commerce | Transport | Banking and Insurance |
|-----|-----------|-----------------|-----------------------|-----------|----------------------|
| | | s d | s d | s d | s d |
| Male | Under 25 | 40 0 | 35 0 | 35 0 | 42 6 |
| | 25+ | 100 0 | 85 0 | 87 6 | 105 0 |
| | All ages | 90 0 | 65 0 | 75 0 | 82 6 |
| Female | Under 25 | 40 0 | 35 0 | 35 0 | 40 0 |
| | 25+ | 70 0 | 57 6 | 60 0 | 65 0 |
| | All ages | 55 0 | 42 6 | 45 0 | 50 0 |

The investigators also compared clerical and manual earnings in London and came to the conclusion that the average money income of the adult male clerk was 'somewhat higher than that of the most skilled workman. The weekly rates for a number of skilled manual occupations show an average in the neighbourhood of 80s for workmen of twenty-one years and over, whereas the average for the male clerks aged twenty-five and upwards is 90s and for those aged twenty and upwards 82s 6d a week.'[4] The same relationship between the earnings of female clerks and manual workers also held. These findings are supported by the survey of social conditions in Merseyside during 1929–32.[5] The median weekly earnings of male clerks aged twenty and above was 60s; that of clerks aged twenty-five to

[1] Appendix A.   [2] Bowley, *op. cit.*, 1937, p. 51.
[3] *The New Survey of London Life and Labour*, 1934, Vol. VIII, pp. 272–309.
[4] *Ibid.*, p. 306.
[5] *The Social Survey of Merseyside*, 1934, Vol. II, p. 331.

thirty-four, 69s 6d; and that of clerks aged thirty-five and over, 74s. The median earnings of skilled manual workers and foremen aged twenty-two and over was almost 69s.[1] Taking both the London and Merseyside relativities into account, then, it would appear that in 1930 clerical workers had maintained their position of parity with the skilled manual worker, with the usual wide range between the more highly and lowly paid clerks themselves. After 1930, there were cuts in clerical salaries following the downward swing of the cost-of-living and the lead set by the Government with regard to civil-service salaries and wages. These cuts were not restored until the mid-thirties. Thereafter salaries lagged behind wages in the quickening recovery from the depression. This was the beginning of the gradual loss by the blackcoated worker of the economic position that he had largely maintained through the fluctuating fortunes of the first three decades of the century.

III. *The War and Post-war Period, 1939–56.* The war and post-war situation brought about a substantial narrowing of the income differentials between manual and non-manual work and between the higher and lower paid office workers themselves. Seers has shown that in the period 1938–49 wages increased more rapidly than salaries and that the percentage increases in salaries were greater in the lower than in the higher ranges.[2] In the case of clerks, the 'squeeze on salaries' has continued unabated until the present time. During the post-war decade, 1946–56, the median salary rates of most adult male clerks in industry and commerce increased by between 39% and 63%.[3] The average earnings of the adult male in industry increased by over 100% during these same ten years.[4] The younger male clerk, on the other hand, seemed to enjoy increases in pay proportionate to or even greater than those received by his manual worker counterpart in industry. The median rates of pay of the junior grades of male clerks rose by between 131% and 154%; the average earnings of youths in industry by 132%. For women, relativities moved in more or less the same direction. Most female clerks had increases of between 67% and 80% in their median rates of pay as compared with an increase of about 100% in the average earnings of women in industry. The younger female clerks enjoyed increases ranging

[1] This fits well with another estimate of the average earnings of skilled engineering workers for 1928 and 1931 as 71s 8d and 66s 5d respectively. Knowles and Robertson, *op. cit.*, p. 126.

[2] Dudley Seers, *The Levelling of Incomes Since 1938* (n.d.).

[3] Office Management Association, *Clerical Salaries 1956*, 1956.

[4] *Ministry of Labour Gazette.* The clerical figures relate to the period March 1946 to March 1956; the manual earnings to January 1946 to April 1956.

from 106% to 115% by comparison with an increase in the average industrial earnings of girls of 129%.

These comparisons are between median rates and average earnings, and the overtime earnings of clerks are not taken into account, but the gross change in income relativities is unmistakable. The main result of this change is that the average clerk is now very roughly on the same income level as the average manual worker, or perhaps even slightly below. The median salaries of the main adult grades of male clerks in March 1956 were 203s 10d, 223s 10d and 279s 11d. In April 1956 the earnings of the adult manual worker averaged 235s 4d.

Undoubtedly one major factor in this closure of the gap between the earnings of blackcoated and manual workers has been the boost given to manual earnings by bonus and overtime payments in a period of full employment and labour shortage. The increase since the end of the war in the average wage-rates of manual workers shows a much less drastic climb over the salary-rates of industrial and commercial clerks. Taking 1947 as 100, wage-rates for male manual workers stood at 165 by the end of September 1956, whereas the salary rates for most adult male clerks in April 1956 were between 139 and 163, if 1946 is taken as 100.[1] From the point of view of the blackcoated worker, however, we may assume that it is earnings rather than rates which count. Within an occupational universe of skill, differences in rates of pay are jealously guarded, even when they are obscured by actual earnings. The reasons are clear. The rate determines the number of hours which have to be worked in order to earn a certain sum. Of equal importance is the fact that rates symbolize status differentials accorded to gradations of skill in the occupation. Nevertheless, between occupations whose skills are not directly comparable, relative earnings seem to be more important than rates; especially when the earning capacity has socially observable effects, such as the income spent on recreation, drinking, smoking, clothing, etc. It may be of little comfort to the clerk to know that the manual worker has to work longer hours for his bulkier wage-packet. The various elements of a strict calculus of economic welfare are not so finely weighed against each other when inter-class comparisons are being made.

If we turn to another group of clerks—those employed in railway offices—the same broad picture presents itself (Table IV). Here we have a comparison between the rates of pay of various grades of clerks, and between salaried employees and selected occupations from the conciliation grades. Between 1939 and 1954 the salary rate

[1] *Ministry of Labour Gazette*, October 1956, p. 361.

increased by 80% among Class 1 clerks and 101% among Class 5 clerks. The only comparable group with such a low proportionate increase in the conciliation group was, significantly enough, the

TABLE IV—COMPARATIVE RATES OF PAY OF MALE SALARIED
AND CONCILIATION GRADES ON THE RAILWAYS FOR THE
YEARS 1939, 1948 AND 1954, SHOWING PERCENTAGE
INCREASES OF 1954 OVER 1939

| Grade | 1939 | 1948 | 1954 | Increase 1954 over 1939 |
|---|---|---|---|---|
| Salaried | Pounds per annum | | | % |
| Clerk Class 1 | 335 | 475 | 605 | 80 |
| Clerk Class 2 | 285 | 425 | 547 | 92 |
| Clerk Class 3 | 250 | 380 | 492 | 97 |
| Clerk Class 4 | 220 | 348 | 451 | 105 |
| Clerk Class 5 | 190 | 320 | 382 | 101 |
| Conciliation | Shillings per week | | | % |
| Goods Porter | 47 0 | 92 6 | 125 6 | 167 |
| Train Ticket-Collector | 60 0 | 109 6 | 142 10 | 138 |
| Drivers and Motormen | 81 0 | 131 0 | 177 3 | 108 |
| Engine Cleaners | 45 0 | 98 0 | 128 11 | 186 |
| Passenger Guard | 57 0 | 107 0 | 146 9 | 157 |
| Total Males (Adult) | 63 2 | — | 146 3 | 131 |

Source: For 1939 and 1948, *Report of a Board of Conciliation Appointed by the Minister of Labour and National Service to Assist in the Consideration and Settlement of Certain Problems Relating to Salaries, Wages and Conditions of Service of the Conciliation and Salaried Grades on the Railways*, 1949, Appendix 7; for 1954, *Annual Census of Staff*, British Transport Commission, 1954.

skilled grade of 'Drivers and Motormen'. Lower skilled groups had enjoyed much greater wage-rate increases and for the group of adult male railway employees as a whole the percentage increase in rate was 131. But if earnings rather than rates are compared (Table V), then the difference between salaried and conciliation grades becomes more marked. In 1954, most of the latter group were able to earn in addition up to a fifth or a quarter of their wage-rates. For the group of males as a whole, the average difference between rate and earnings worked out at 28% of the average rate of pay. For the lowest paid clerks, this figure was only 9·9%, for the highest, 4·3%. Taking earning relativities, we see that the earnings for all railway employees averaged 182s 10d. This was considerably higher than the average for Class 5 clerks who formed 40% of the total clerical group, and almost skirted the average earnings of Class 4 clerks who, together with Class 5, formed almost 70% of the total clerks employed. The skilled group in the conciliation grade earns on the average an amount equivalent to the salary of the next to the highest grade of clerk, Class 2, or the average salary of a bank clerk in his late twenties. The influence of this differential earning above the wage-rate proper—compounded of payments for piecework, bonus schemes, overtime, Saturday afternoons, Sunday and night duty—is clearly displayed when we consider that if average *rates* of pay only were compared, the whole clerical class would stand clearly above the average rate of pay for all male railway servants.

TABLE V—COMPARISON OF RATES OF PAY AND AVERAGE
EARNINGS AMONG THE SALARIED AND CONCILIATION
GRADES OF THE RAILWAYS IN 1954

| Grade | Average Rate of Pay | | Average Earnings | | Difference as Percentage of Rate |
|---|---|---|---|---|---|
| *Salaried* | s | d | s | d | |
| Clerk, Class 1 | 232 | 8 | 242 | 7 | 4·3 |
| Clerk, Class 2 | 210 | 6 | 220 | 2 | 4·4 |
| Clerk, Class 3 | 189 | 3 | 200 | 11 | 6·2 |
| Clerk, Class 4 | 173 | 7 | 187 | 1 | 7·8 |
| Clerk, Class 5 | 146 | 10 | 159 | 10 | 9·9 |
| *Conciliation* | | | | | |
| Goods Porter | 125 | 6 | 152 | 1 | 21·2 |
| Train Ticket-Collector | 142 | 10 | 183 | 0 | 29·8 |
| Drivers and Motormen | 177 | 3 | 220 | 3 | 24·3 |
| Engine Cleaners | 128 | 11 | 143 | 4 | 11·3 |
| Passenger Guard | 146 | 9 | 182 | 10 | 24·7 |
| Total Adult Male Conciliation | 142 | 6 | 182 | 10 | 28·0 |

Source: *Annual Census of Staff*, British Transport Commission, 1954.

What is true for the lower paid clerical worker is even more true of the blackcoated 'aristocracy' of bank and insurance clerks, as may be seen from Tables VI and VII. Again, the familiar pattern of the narrowing of differences within the group and between it and the wage-earning class. By 1955 the average bank clerk of twenty-eight was getting a salary only a little higher than the average manual wage for men; the civil-service clerical officer and the local-government clerk both got considerably less.

One development within the working class itself is rather important for the market situation of clerical labour. This is the fact of the narrowing differential between the economic status of skilled and unskilled workers.[1] As we have seen there has always been an overlap in the incomes of skilled manual and clerical workers. It was from the great unwashed, however, that the clerical worker felt

TABLE VI—A COMPARISON OF THE PERCENTAGE INCREASES
IN EARNINGS SINCE 1938 IN BANKING AND ALL INDUSTRIES
IN 1953

| Year | Percentage Increases in Earnings since 1938 (All Industries) | | | Percentage Increases in Earnings since 1938 (Banking) (Average) | | |
|------|------|-------|--------|------|-------|--------|
|      | Men  | Women | Youths | Men  | Women | Youths |
| 1946 | 75   | 101   | 78     | 20   | 64    | 85     |
| 1947 | 86   | 114   | 99     | 34   | 82    | 108    |
| 1948 | 100  | 129   | 125    | 37   | 86    | 112    |
| 1949 | 107  | 142   | 130    | 39   | 88    | 113    |
| 1950 | 118  | 154   | 144    | 45   | 97    | 126    |
| 1951 | 141  | 177   | 165    | 54   | 109   | 137    |
| 1952 | 159  | 196   | 187    | 82   | 135   | 178    |
| 1953 | 174  | 215   | 203    | 82   | 135   | 178    |

Source: *The Bank Officer*, June 1954.

TABLE VII—YEARLY SALARIES OF INSURANCE OFFICIALS AT
VARIOUS AGES IN TWO REPRESENTATIVE OFFICES IN 1938–9
AND 1954, SHOWING PERCENTAGE INCREASES (MALES)

| Office 'A' | 1938 | 1954 | Percentage Increase 1954 on 1938 |
|------------|------|------|------|
| Age |  |  |  |
| 20 | £110 | £275 plus 15% bonus | 187 |
| 25 | £210 | £385 plus 15% bonus | 111 |
| 30 | £300 | £570 plus 15% bonus | 118 |
| 35 | £400 | £690 plus 15% bonus | 98 |

[1] K. G. J. C. Knowles and D. G. Robertson, 'Differences Between the Wages of Skilled and Unskilled Workers, 1880–1950', *Bulletin of the Oxford Institute of Statistics*; H. A. Turner, 'Trade Unions, Differentials and the Levelling of Wages', *Manchester School*, September 1952.

| Office 'B' | 1939 | 1954 | Percentage Increase 1954 on 1939 |
|---|---|---|---|
| Age | | | |
| 20 | £105 | £252 plus 12·5% | 169 |
| 25 | £180 | £398 plus 12·5% | 149 |
| 30 | £285 | £509  5s plus 12·5% | 101 |
| 35 | £330 | £619 10s plus 12·5% | 111 |

Source: *Insurance Guild Journal*, December 1954, p. 249.

his material and social status most removed. The relative upward movement of the incomes of unskilled and semi-skilled workmen must have proved the most bitter pill of all for the blackcoated worker to swallow. It is not only the printer and the fitter who now rival his economic status, but also the dock labourer and the navvy.[1]

## OTHER CONDITIONS

In respect of hours, holidays, period of hire and superannuation the office worker has generally been in a better position than the manual worker, although the differences have been somewhat reduced in recent decades. The clerk worked, and still works, fewer hours for his income than the wage-earner. Traditionally, his holidays have been longer and with pay, the latter benefit only lately having been acquired by the mass of manual workers. The Committee on Holidays with Pay reported in 1938 that a week's holiday with pay ought to be the standard practice for industry.[2] In the 1920s about 1,500,000 wage-earners were entitled to such a holiday annually; by 1938, 3,000,000; and in 1939, following the Holidays Pay Act of 1938, some 11,000,000 workers enjoyed this right. Holidays with pay, mostly of a fortnight, had been fairly well established throughout the clerical field well before this.[3] But improvement in the wage-earner's situation, especially since the war, when the paid holiday has been extended, has gradually reduced the relative advantage of the clerk on this count.

The greater security of blackcoated work was generally reflected in the 'salary' of the clerk as opposed to the 'wage' of the manual

[1] A good example of the frustration to which this situation has given rise is evidenced in a correspondence in *Red Tape*, January 1954, p. 104, in which the salaries of a young labourer and a civil-service clerical officer are invidiously compared.

[2] C. L. Mowat, *Britain Between the Wars, 1918–1940*, 1955, p. 501.

[3] *The New Survey of London Life and Labour*, 1934, Vol. VIII, pp. 284–5.

worker, and this was associated with the further distinction between monthly and weekly, or even hourly, payments. But the weekly period of payment is now much more common among clerks than the monthly.

A recent survey revealed that upwards of 70% of firms outside London pay their clerks by the week.[1] For Britain as a whole 60% of clerks are paid weekly and 37% monthly. The higher proportion of monthly payments for London (47%) probably reflects a greater concentration of higher-grade clerical jobs. Despite these changes, the longer period of hire still gives the blackcoated a worker a general advantage in security, and symbolically in prestige, over the manual worker.

When we turn to superannuation arrangements the position of the office worker is still noticeably different from that of the ordinary wage-earner. Railway, civil service and banking clerks have long had pension funds. Local government officers achieved a legislative backing for their superannuation in 1922, although local authorities were not compelled to set up funds for this purpose. By 1931, however, some 80% of all local government officers were covered by the provisions of the Act.[2] On April 1, 1939, the Local Government Superannuation Act of 1938 became operative, bringing compulsory superannuation to all local government officers.

It is impossible to say with any exactness how many clerks in private industry and commerce were covered by pension arrangements in the course of the present century, but the situation in post-war Britain is illuminated by a survey of office conditions made in 1952. 'A remarkable trend revealed by this Survey is the development of Pension and Superannuation Schemes in industry. Before the war, many firms had no doubt made such provision, but a great advance has evidently been made since 1946.[3] In the country as a whole, 81% of the firms provided superannuation schemes for their male staff, and 75% for their female staff. Clerical workers are not, however, absolutely privileged in this matter of pensions, but only relatively to manual workers. No exact comparison is possible, but a recent survey of British incomes and savings gives details of the estimated participation of manual and non-manual workers in such schemes over a wide range of industries.[4] Forty per cent of the non-

---

[1] Office Management Association, *Office Administrative Practices*, 1952, p. 36.

[2] *Annual Report*, NALGO, 1931, p. 48.

[3] OMA, *op. cit.*, p. 36. The opinion of the New London Survey was that only a small minority of the whole body of clerks enjoyed the benefit of organized pension funds. The extent to which annuities were given on a private and informal basis is, of course, unknown.

[4] H. F. Lydall, *British Incomes and Savings*, 1955, p. 117.

manual workers, as opposed to 21% of the manual workers, were actually contributing to such schemes. The discrepancy between these figures and the ones previously quoted may be partly attributed to the fact that the higher percentage refers to firms in which superannuation schemes are available, the lower percentage to the actual number of persons participating in such schemes. Further, the 'non-manual' group in the latter survey not only included sales assistants who are likely to have fewer pension schemes available to them than clerks, but it also contained a high proportion of young female clerks who would be less likely to enter pension schemes than the men clerks. What is surprising and important, however, is the degree to which manual workers participate in such schemes—24% of the skilled and 15% of the unskilled were contributors—especially when we remember that the above figures refer only to schemes arranged by employers and do not include those run by trade unions and friendly societies.

### UNEMPLOYMENT EXPERIENCE

Briefs singled out liability to unemployment or insecurity of tenure as the distinguishing feature of the proletarian estate.[1] In this respect, clerical work has been characteristically different from wage employment. The general unemployment rate in this country between the world wars was such that being out of work was a normal situation for a high percentage of the working-class population. Unemployment increased in intensity in the early twenties and again more severely after 1930. Only in the late thirties did the situation begin slowly to improve.

Clerks engaged in public service, both central and local, as well as those in banking and on the railways hardly suffered from unemployment at all throughout this period. Among bank clerks there were only twelve or fourteen cases out of a total guild membership of 21,000 in 1932.[2] General or commercial and industrial clerks were rather less fortunate, but even then they were less seriously affected by unemployment than the mass of the workforce. In 1931 the proportion of unemployed male clerks was only 5·3% as against 12·7% in the total labour force. The corresponding figures for women were 4·3% and 8·6%. Generally speaking, those higher in occupational status suffered less acutely than those lower down. Thus, among the male clerks, only 1·6% of office managers were out of work, but 8·3% of typists.

Nevertheless, the experience of the thirties was something new in the annals of clerical employment. 'Prior to the war and the

[1] Briefs, G. A., *The Proletariat*, 1937.   [2] *Bank Officer*, June 1932, p. 7.

immediate post-war period, it was generally assumed that office workers could rely on being permanently employed, providing they were efficient and their character good; in other words, they could feel assured of regular employment in contra-distinction to the manual worker, whose employment might often be intermittent,' but now the General Secretary of the National Union of Clerks could report that 'the industrial depression which started in 1921 has completely altered this position. A wholesale dismissal of office workers took place then, and has continued down to the present; clerks with twenty, thirty and forty years' service to their credit have been dismissed, very often without consideration beyond receiving the notice to which they were entitled. Owing to the continued depression, this has meant that some of them have never again been employed as clerks, and others have never known regular employment since.'[1]

The situation of the older, senior clerk was particularly bad, because he often fell outside the National Insurance limit, and was thus devoid of state support in his distress.[2] This uninsured blackcoat unemployment persisted in the early thirties, and in 1934 it was estimated that some 300,000 persons in this category were out of work. Not all of these were clerks or office managers, of course. They included engineers, electricians, chemists, architects, surveyors and so on, many of whom joined the Institute of British Executives, or the 'Over-forty-fives Association', and some of course the Fascist Movement.[3]

'The greater number of these middle-class unemployed are over forty years of age—for businesses which are cutting down expenses are naturally inclined to dismiss the older men who are earning the larger salaries.'[4] These were the men who found it hardest to obtain another job, and their unemployment was in some ways more distressful than that of the manual worker. Once out of work, out of the 'careers run in a well-worn groove', the paradox of their situation as unskilled specialists was uncomfortably revealed and they very often had to take work much below their previous status and remuneration. Even where their recruitment had been more fluid, 'there is never

[1] Memo. submitted to the Royal Commission on Unemployment Insurance, 1931, by Herbert Elvin, *The Clerk*, October 1931, p. 46.

[2] *Report of the Unemployment Insurance Statutory Committee on the Remuneration Limit for Insurance on Non-Manual Workers*, 1936.

[3] 'Sweated or unemployed clerks and administrative workers, students graduating into a jobless world, ex-officers who cannot fit into civilian life, tradesmen and professional men suffering from intense competition; such men form the backbone of Fascist and similar movements in every country. 'Black-Coated Unemployment,' *The Spectator*, April 10, 1936, p. 653.

[4] 'The Middle-Class Unemployed,' *The Spectator*, March 9, 1934, p. 361.

the continual in-and-out movement as with manual workers, and while this means greater security for those employed, it also means, as Charles Booth said of the older clerks in his original Survey of London Life and Labour, that "those who drop out, drop under".[1]

Deprivation is also relative, relative to what a person has grown used to. In many cases the office-worker's standard of living and accustomed necessities had been based upon a career that was both secure and progressive. Many would have undertaken house purchase and payments for their children's education. Moreover, the unemployed clerk had a harder struggle to keep up appearances than the manual worker. If he was to get another job, he had to impress his prospective employers, and it was hard to be impressive in a black coat that was shiny and a white collar that was badly frayed.

Thus, although in bare quantitative terms the clerical and administrative worker was not affected by the depression as much as the average manual worker, those who were actually unemployed were sufficiently numerous to destroy the traditional association of security and blackcoat employment. They suffered as acutely as almost any other group due to the lack of communal provision for their plight and the conventional expectations of their position.

How far these experiences persist as memories and are potent in the consciousness of the present-day blackcoat is difficult to estimate. Even among manual workers, the characteristic sentiments of those workers who experienced the years of unemployment are not shared by their younger fellows, who benefit from the security, high wages and welfare provisions of the war and post-war world.[2] A considerable proportion of those clerks who suffered unemployment are retired or dead. Some of the unemployed also probably found employment in other occupations. Those with actual experience of unemployment can form but a small proportion of the total present-day office workers.

### OCCUPATIONAL MOBILITY

Clerical work has traditionally been associated with the opportunity to rise to better things, and although we have no quantitative proof, there seems to be evidence that mercantile success through clerkships was fairly common in the counting-house world. We also know that particularism played a large role in the career pattern of the clerk and that chances of success were not always related purely to merit.

How do the conditions of the modern office affect chances of

[1] *The Spectator*, 1936, *op. cit.*, p. 653.
[2] N. Dennis, F. Henriques and E. Slaughter, *Coal Is Our Life*, 1956.

upward occupational mobility? Again, we have no direct information on this point. One useful indirect indication of mobility, however, is the age structure of the clerical population as compared with that of the working population as a whole. 'Only 26·8% of male clerks live or continue as clerks after forty-five years of age', noted a black-coat journal in 1925. 'Where do they, like the flies, go in the winter of their lives? Do they simply, like old soldiers, fade away, do they die of the clerk's disease, tuberculosis, are they transferred into managing directors at that age, or have they realized by then that clerking is a hopeless job, and taken up stone breaking or something more lucrative than their own calling?'[1] Later evidence on the same lines, ostensibly to do with mortality rates, was presented in a government report.[2] 'The group of clerks loses to other occupations from age thirty-five onwards considerably more men than it recruits, as may be seen by comparing the Census populations at various ages after thirty-five with the numbers expected if the inward and outward movements were exactly balanced, that is, if the population of the group from twenty to thirty-five onwards continued to decline in numbers at precisely the same rate as does the population of all males. By the time fifty-five is reached nearly one-half of the surviving men who were occupied as clerks between the ages of twenty-five and thirty-five must have passed into other occupations, and an examination of the figures for higher clerical occupations on similar lines indicates that these can only have absorbed a small proportion'. The clerks unaccounted for, the report concluded, 'probably pass into occupations such as commercial travellers or proprietors of businesses'. There is, of course, another possible explanation; namely, that a considerable proportion of clerks are downwardly mobile to various kinds of manual work.

Both explanations seem to be corroborated by more recent evidence. A study of labour mobility in Great Britain between 1945 and 1949 presents the rather striking fact that of those who had begun their occupational life as clerks no less than 38% were in managerial and professional jobs at the date of the inquiry, while another 28% had passed into various kinds of manual work.[3] Only a third of those who began as clerks stayed on; another third was upwardly mobile, another third downwardly. In other words, if a boy became a clerk from school he would be just as likely to end up in managerial or

---

[1] *The Clerk*, December, 1925, p. 184.

[2] *The Registrar-General's Decennial Supplement*, England and Wales, 1931, Part IIa, Occupational Mortality, p. 148.

[3] Geoffrey Thomas, *Labour Mobility in Gt. Britain 1945–49*, an inquiry carried out for the Ministry of Labour and National Service, p. 29 (mimeographed).

manual work as he would be to remain a clerk. The same study showed that there was a substantial number of clerks recruited from other occupations. Thirty-eight per cent of all those who were clerks at the time of inquiry had started in some other occupation. Sixty-two per cent of the present clerks had started as clerks, but only 49% had been clerks all through their working lives, so that 13% of those who began as clerks and ended as clerks had, at some time, worked in other occupations.

The general picture of clerical work provided by this study, then, is one of an occupation that has quite high rates of inward and outward mobility, with a hard core of persons who probably remain as clerks throughout their working lives. Of special interest here is the fact that just about a third of those who started as clerks ended up in managerial positions. The precise significance of this statement is only clear when we consider that 'managerial' occupations were defined as including foremen, charge-hands, chief clerks and similar supervisory workers as well as owners and executives. Further, we cannot be sure whether those clerks who became managers did so directly from clerical work, or indirectly, by moving into manual occupations first, and then subsequently into supervisory posts. The managerial group as a whole was, in fact, recruited rather heavily from individuals who had been in manual work. This latter group was chiefly made up of skilled workers whose normal avenue of promotion would be to the 'foremen' group of management, and it is probably safe to assume that in most cases the upwardly mobile clerks advanced directly to supervisory and executive positions on the 'office' rather than the 'factory' side of management.

We may pursue further the question of the clerk's opportunity to rise by turning now to information on the occupational backgrounds of those who have risen. In a recent study of the occupational backgrounds of business leaders, it was noted that 'those who started as clerks come up near the top of the list—up with engineers and accountants'.[1] Some 22% of the directors had begun their working lives as trainees for executive posts, and 17% as engineers. Those who started as clerks formed 16% of the business leaders. 'In other words, a person without professional qualifications appears to have stood a poor chance of rising to the top of the industrial ladder if employed as a skilled or unskilled worker, but a much better chance if employed as a clerk.'[2] Nor was this to be explained by the fact that the sons of businessmen were introduced into a business career by a spell in their fathers' offices as 'clerks'. 'It might be thought that some of those who claimed to have started as clerks

[1] C. H. Copeman. *Leaders of British Industry*, 1955, p. 94.    [2] *Ibid.*, p. 94.

may have really started in the offices of which their fathers were directors. However, cross-classification has revealed that this happened in the case of only 5% of "clerks".' This, of course, does not rule out another, perhaps more common, practice of placing one's son in the office of a friend for the same purpose. In fact, when the parental occupations of the business élite are examined it can be seen that the majority of those directors who began as 'clerks' were the sons of businessmen, executives or professionals. Just under one-fifth had fathers who were either lower-salaried middle class or working class. Thus, although clerical work was, and is, one of the main avenues to business leadership, it is evident from this particular investigation that the clerks who have successfully risen have been drawn overwhelmingly from other than lower-blackcoated and working-class backgrounds. Of the group of directors studied, 16% began as clerks; and of these only 19% came from lower-middle or working-class backgrounds.

The same study also illustrates the declining opportunity to rise from the office to the boardroom. Of an older group of directors, aged fifty and over, the second largest proportion (18%) had begun their careers as clerks: while for the younger group, this origin took fourth place, though it still accounted for some 14% of the appointees. These figures would seem to indicate, and thus confirm the general impression, that clerical work as a source of occupational mobility in industry and business is being superseded by more formal training for management. This is probably even more true of coming generations of directors. On the other hand, even for the younger group of directors, clerical work seems to have represented a still quite important means of achievement; decidedly of much greater significance than mobility out of manual jobs.

The above statistics refer, of course, to the opportunities for clerks in the first three decades of the present century; and there is strong reason to believe that in more recent decades the university graduate is being increasingly drawn upon to build up the managerial cadres in commerce and industry. On the other hand, it should be remembered that the group which was studied is the very élite of the directors of British industry. Much more likely end-positions of clerical achievement are the numerically greater ranks of middle and lower management, and the multifarious grades of supervisory and inspectional jobs in industry. It is this type of mobility, of a more limited nature, which is probably more common among successful clerks.

Some insight into the recruitment of industrial management from clerical positions has been provided recently by a study which takes into account junior and middle management.[1] Management was defined as all staff above the level of foreman and those of equivalent rank in offices. Those managers who rose from clerical jobs formed about one-third of the total. Again, however, the long-run tendency is shown to be working gradually against the chances of the clerk and in favour of the management trainee. Of the managers who were between fifty-five and fifty-nine years old at the time of the study, 35% had begun as clerks and only 4·5% as trainees; of those under thirty, the corresponding figures were 12·2% and 25%. The figure of 12·2% for the under-thirty group is probably under-representative because clerks take longer to work their way up into managerial positions, and therefore it does not take into account those who are promoted later on. The next oldest age group, for example, still had 26% of its total number coming from clerical jobs and a trainee component of 18%.

The figures as they stand are, from a different viewpoint, a clear refutation of those who argue that clerical work no longer carries *any* opportunity to rise. These statistics were compiled from an investigation of firms employing more than 10,000 persons. What the situation is in the smaller firms, where a large proportion of clerks is employed, we cannot know, except that fewer trainee and graduate appointments are likely to obstruct the avenue of promotion for clerks. Some crude idea of the statistical 'chances' of clerical advancement to management may be obtained from the following facts. The median ratio of management—as defined in the above study—to total employees was in the order of 2·25%. The ratio of clerks to total employees in the same manufacturing industries roughly averages 9%, and women clerks—for whom there is little possibility of promotion—outnumber the men in the ratio of 13 to 9. This means that the male clerks form about 3·5% of the total employees, and it is from this relatively small group of blackcoated workers that a substantial proportion of managers is drawn.

As regards the clerical population as a whole, some abstract idea of their 'occupational chances' can be arrived at by comparing their number with the total number of persons in the various managerial grades to which they may reasonably aspire. In 1951 male clerks totalled 861,679 and the combined managerial trades totalled some 560,000.[2] If one out of every three such 'managerial' positions is

[1] Acton Society Trust, *Management Succession*, 1956.

[2] Including the following categories as 'managerial': Civil Service Executive and Higher Clerical Officers, Local Authority Administrative and Executive Officers, Secretaries and Registrars of Companies, Institutions and Charities, Heads or Managers of Commercial and Industrial Office Departments, Managers in Industry, Banking, Insurance, Railways, Bus Transport, Ship and Air Trans-

filled by an ex-clerk, then this means that one out of every four or five clerks is likely to rise into management.

Taking the above, rather scattered pieces of evidence into account, it may be argued that Lord Percy's statement that 'in nearly all industries the road to management and control lies through the office side; it is the clerk, not the man at the machine, who carries the marshal's baton in his knapsack'[1] is still true, to a lesser extent to be sure than when he made it, but to a greater extent than is often believed.

In general, there are three main determinants of the chances of promotion of clerical labour to supervisory or managerial positions: the rate of expansion of particular industries or undertakings, and more particularly the rate of expansion of the demand for clerical and managerial staffs; the ratio of clerical to managerial posts; and the degree to which internal recruitment or, alternatively, 'blocked mobility' prevails. In industry and commerce, to which the foregoing data refer, internal recruitment has tended to persist, and is only in recent (especially post-war) years being partially replaced by external recruitment. 'Recruitment of the managerial class is still effected largely through ownership in the actual business, but to an increasing extent by promotion from the operative or clerical side through the foremanship and other supervisory posts. Direct entry to the managerial grades . . . is still not very common . . . in the larger organizations there is a steady flow from the office staffs to the higher positions and it is the practice with some firms to accept for training suitable persons through this channel.'[2]

In other types of clerical work, the large-scale bureaucratic organization of railways, banking and central government has been associated, in varying degrees, with blocked promotion opportunities for the clerical grades. This has been due to the general reduction in the ratio of managerial to lower office positions that accompanies rationalization, and to the policy of recruiting persons for these superior positions from outside the clerical grades. Only in the civil service, however, has the latter process been carried to its fullest extent, and even there promotion from the lower grades has never been entirely blocked, as we shall see.

After the great expansion of railway activity in the nineteenth

port, Managers of Wholesale Businesses, Brokers, Agents, Factors, Sales and Advertising Managers, Buyers, and Entertainment and Sports Managers. Census 1951, *Occupation Tables*, 1956.

[1] Lord Eustace Percy, *Education at the Crossroads*, 1930. Quoted by Olive Banks, *Parity and Prestige in English Secondary Education*, 1955.

[2] Ministry of Labour, Careers for Men and Women, No. 25, *Industry and Commerce*, 1945, p. 4.

century, fewer opportunities for clerical promotion were provided as the expansion slowed down and large-scale amalgamations occurred towards the end of the nineteenth and at the beginning of the twentieth century.[1] This diminishing opportunity was reinforced by a policy of external recruitment from public schools and universities—the so-called 'probationers' and 'cadets'—and clerks of this kind were regarded as a major source of future management and were given greater opportunities than ordinary clerks to gain experience to this end.[2] The practical result was that only the exceptional clerk from the routine grades was likely to obtain promotion to supervisory and managerial positions; and to do this he had to make his mark quite early on in his career. The characteristic feature of the inter-war years was the 'stagnation' of promotion possibilities, even within the clerical grade itself.[3] Since nationalization, the situation has been somewhat improved. All employees, if under thirty years of age, are eligible for the 'traffic apprenticeships' which provide promotion to managerial posts. Those selected are given a tour through a large number of departments over a period of three years to widen their experience. In contrast with the practice of private

[1] *The Life of the Railway Clerk, Some Interesting Facts and Figures*, seventh edition, December 1911, pp. 9–12.

[2] See the evidence of Sir Frank Ree, General Manager of the London and North-Western Railway, in the *Fourth Report of the Commissioners*, Royal Commission on the Civil Service, 1914, Second Appendix, especially questions 35, 254–55, 267.

[3] In 1925, A. G. Walkden, General Secretary of the RCA, presented the following statistics on 'stagnation' to the National Wages Board; he emphasized that they probably underestimated the actual numbers of clerks waiting for promotion. These figures refer to stagnation *within* the clerical grade itself, and the number of clerks affected formed approximately one-quarter of the total clerks employed on the railways. *The Railway Service Journal*, 1925, p. 405.

CLERICAL STAFF STAGNATING AT CLASS MAXIMA

|  | Over 2, under 3 years | Over 3, under 4 years | Over 4, under 5 years | Over 5 years | Total |
|---|---|---|---|---|---|
| Class 1 | 76 | 41 | 53 | 494 | 664 |
| Class 2 | 121 | 95 | 109 | 1,281 | 1,606 |
| Class 3 | 275 | 187 | 211 | 3,055 | 3,728 |
| Class 4 | 439 | 278 | 376 | 5,949 | 7,042 |
| Class 5 | 540 | 346 | 402 | 4,051 | 5,339 |

This is a situation highly favourable to strong unionization, and able leadership. The present General Secretary of the TSSA was promoted from the fifth class to the fourth class of clerks only in his late thirties.

companies who relied mainly on entrants from the public schools, three-quarters of the vacancies under this scheme are reserved for candidates from within the industry, the remainder being recruited from university graduates. The higher administrative posts are normally filled by the clerical grades.'[1] On the whole, the policy of nationalization has tended to favour the pattern of internal recruitment and reduce privileged entry to managerial posts from outside the industry.

In banking, many opportunities of promotion at quite early ages were provided by the depletion of bank staffs during the First World War and the post-war expansion in banking which persisted until the middle and late nineteen-twenties. Thereafter, with positions filled and a curtailment of the previous expansion, a considerable blockage of promotion was created for men of mature age. By the early nineteen-fifties, this blockage was quite acute and is still a feature of the present situation.[2] As regards external recruitment to managerial positions, entrants from public schools and universities have not been particularly important in the total picture, though increased recruitment from these sources has frequently been proposed and discussed. 'There is not a very wide field in banking for graduates, but both the Bank of England and the Joint Stock Banks do from time to time accept entrants holding a university degree, mainly for specialist posts.'[3] 'In the past,' promotion from within to senior positions, 'has not been rapid, and although men have occasionally been appointed to managership or assistant-managerships at about thirty-two it has generally taken considerably longer to attain this status. The present policy of a number of leading banks to encourage young men of personality and ability by giving them special training, will probably result in appointments being made at an earlier age than heretofore. The more highly paid appointments are, in fact, made to men who have graduated from the rank and file. In general, a man of ability who applies himself conscientiously to his duties and studies may be reasonably assured of reaching a position of responsibility after twenty to twenty-five years' service.'[4] The 'promotion prospects are considered to be good for young bank clerks today in comparison with promotion prospects in some other

[1] Acton Society Trust, *op. cit.* See also Acton Society Trust, 'Promotion in British Railways', pp. 78–9 of *Training and Promotion in Nationalized Industry*, 1951.

[2] *The Bank Officer*, April 1954, p. 21.

[3] Ministry of Labour, Careers for Men and Women, No. 42, *University Graduates*, 1945, p. 7.

[4] Ministry of Labour, Careers for Men and Women, No. 46, *Banking*, 1950, p. 144.

organizations which have clearly marked barriers between "staff grades" and ordinary clerks', one report concludes.[1] And in 1956, the Westminster Bank, no doubt calculating upon a reduction of the ratio of 'promoteable' staff to managerial positions with further rationalization and mechanization of the industry, asserted that 'one out of every two or three young men entering the service of Westminster Bank *must* reach Managerial or high Executive positions'.[2] The Bank Officers Guild, giving evidence to the Royal Commission on Equal Pay in 1944, acknowledged that 'men are given opportunities of training and are, in fact, trained for promotion to posts as Security Clerks, Cashiers, Chief Clerks, Assistant Accountants, Accountants, Clerks in Charge, Inspectors, Managers, Heads of Departments, General Managers, etc.'.[3] This does not apply, of course, to many of those bank clerks whose advancement was blocked during the earlier period, for very often when their opportunity came they were too old to take advantage of it. As was noted, this blockage still persists, though less acutely, and the prospects for younger men are decidedly better.

The recruitment of civil service staffs after the 1920 reorganization was attuned to the educational structure. Gradually the Administrative, Executive and Clerical grades were filled by persons with degrees, higher school certificates and school certificates respectively. Although recruitment from below, from the Clerical to the Executive, and from Executive to Administrative grades has never, in theory, been closed, in actual fact mobility has been effectively curtailed for a considerable part of the period.

Before 1920, the class of Assistant Clerks had little opportunity as a whole for promotion to the Second Division. In 1913, their promotion opportunities were being unfavourably compared with those existing for clerks outside, in railways, insurance and industrial undertakings.[4] We learn that 'on the average of the years 1902–11 inclusive, about twenty Assistant Clerks were promoted each year to the Second Division. The percentage therefore of the whole class who may in existing conditions expect advancement in this manner is small, and the number so promoted form a small percentage of the whole Second Division'.[5] Dissatisfaction with promotion remained

[1] Office Management Association, *Clerical Salaries Analysis*, 1952, p. 21.
[2] *Manchester Guardian*, March 28, 1956.
[3] Memo. of the Bank Officers Guild, p. 165 of Appendix XII to *Minutes of Evidence* taken before the Royal Commission on Equal Pay, December 14, 1944.
[4] Vol. XIV of Evidence given before the Royal Commission on the Civil Service, 1913, especially questions 33,655, 33,924, 34,019, 34,020, 34,107, 34,421 and 34,246.
[5] *Red Tape*, April 1914, p. 8.

a dominant theme after 1920[1], and has continued until the present time. Throughout the inter-war years, the normal promotion for clerical officers was to Higher Clerical Officer positions, and a certain number of Executive Officer posts were filled by internal promotion. The outbreak of war, and the consequent expansion of civil service departments, opened up further opportunities for promotion for clerks. In 1947 many of the Higher Clerical grades were given Executive Officer rank, thus increasing the chances of Clerical Officers to become Executive Officers. In 1954 evidence on promotion opportunities was given before the Royal Commission on the Civil Service: 'During 1953 it was estimated that the total number of promotions of Clerical Officers to Executive Officer and Higher Clerical Officer posts would be 1,000. This figure can be regarded as roughly representing the average prospect in a normal situation. With a Clerical Officer grade totalling nearly 80,000 the prospects of promotion beyond the grade are extremely limited, particularly for older entrants whose seniority dates from the time of establishment.'[2] A system of 'pooling' promotion chances has equalized, but not increased, possibilities of advancement.[3] The present-day position is that approximately two-thirds of vacancies in the Executive Officer grade are filled by promotion from the Clerical grade, the rest being filled by direct entry. Of these two-thirds, eight out of ten promotions are made from the Clerical Officers aged twenty-eight and over, and two are made from Clerical Officers under twenty-eight who sit an open competition. On the whole the Clerical Officer today may look for promotion to Higher Clerical or Executive Officer after a shorter lapse of time from his entry into the service than was usual in the inter-war period.[4] At the same time, for a large proportion of older men now in the Clerical Officer grade chances of promotion are very slim. As regards

[1] Between 1920 and 1927, there were promotions to the Executive Grade for only 2% of the total Clerical Grade. *Red Tape*, 1929, p. 297; also 1928, p. 605, and 1929, p. 468.

[2] *Minutes of Evidence* before the Royal Commission on the Civil Service, 1953, fourth and fifth days, p. 104. Many of these 80,000 are older persons who entered the service during the war and were established between 1946–50, and they are unlikely to get promotion now. 60,000 is probably a more reasonable population from which promotions are likely to be made. In 1953, 52% of male clerks were over forty years of age.

[3] Bernard Newman, *Yours for Action*, 1953, p. 174.

[4] Chances of promotion are likely to increase in the near future because a high proportion of Executive Officers are now reaching retiring age. But once these positions are filled by fairly young persons, the upward mobility of subsequently recruited Clerical Officers will be blocked unless there is an expansion of the service. For this fact I am indebted to Mr Wines, Deputy General Secretary of the CSCA.

promotions to the administrative class, about 35% of the persons in this class today were recruited from lower grades, but mainly from the Executive class.

## CONCLUSION

Looking at the period 1900–55 as a whole[1] we may summarize the main changes in the 'market situation' of the blackcoated worker as follows:

As regards income relativities, the clerical worker more or less kept his position *vis-à-vis* the wage-earner until the late thirties. Wages probably rose more sharply than salaries during the First World War and immediately afterwards, but by 1925 the increases in most blackcoated fields of employment since 1905 had kept pace with increases in manual earnings. The exception was the bank clerk who seems to have lost ground between these two dates. During the depression years, salary cuts followed the fall in the cost of living, but on the whole salaries did not decline so much as wages. By 1935, there was still no noticeable narrowing of manual and non-manual differentials. The squeeze on salaries which occurred during the Second World War and after took the form of reduced differentials between manual and non-manual workers; between more highly paid and poorly paid sections of blackcoated work (such as between banking and railway clerks); between the higher and lower grades of clerical workers, which was partly a result of the reduction of the differentials between older and younger clerks, and between male and female clerks.

In terms of actual income, we have seen that in the years prior to 1914 the ordinary adult clerk was roughly on a par with the skilled worker. Through the inter-war period the blackcoated worker managed to maintain this parity, but during the war and post-war years differentials between manual and non-manual employment were gradually reduced, so that by 1956 the mass of clerks were roughly on the same income level as the average manual worker. Even the aristocracy of blackcoated labour—the banking and insurance clerks—are no longer enjoying an economic status clearly distinct from the wage-earning classes. There has always been an overlap between the earnings of blackcoated and manual labour, even in the era of the counting house, but until the last two decades the mass of clerical workers were relatively better off in income terms than the mass of manual workers. Today this is no longer true. Although the closing of the differential between manual and non-

[1] See Appendix A.

manual labour has been partly due to an increase in wage-rates, it has also been caused by the boost given to manual earnings by piece work, bonus and overtime additions, which are in turn a result of the continuing full employment since 1940 and the contemporary emphasis upon incentives and productivity. Thus the process of the equalization of rewards for blackcoated and manual work has been achieved by the economic improvement of the working class rather than by the sinking of the non-manual worker into the ranks of the 'proletariat'.

While no such differences are absolute, the clerk has been generally better off than the manual worker with regard to hours of work, conditions of work, security of tenure, pension schemes and similar benefits above and beyond income. The depression of the thirties demonstrated that the blackcoated worker was not immune from the hazards of the market in extreme situations, and that the unemployed clerk could often find re-employment only at a lower remuneration and status. In quantitative terms, however, the clerk was not so badly hit as the working class as a whole.

The possibility of advancement, which Hilferding considered to be the basic factor making for the individualistic outlook of the blackcoated worker,[1] is something about which it is very hard to generalize for clerks as a whole throughout this period. If pressed, one might say that clerks have, as a group, enjoyed, and continue to enjoy, greater chances of rising to managerial, quasi-managerial and supervisory positions than wage-earners. These chances have varied from time to time and from employment to employment. Railway clerks and banking clerks had their chances reduced by the slowing down of business expansion in the inter-war years and by amalgamations. Civil-service clerks and railway clerks have had their chances reduced by the policy of recruiting from outside to fill managerial posts; and this factor is probably curtailing the chances of clerks in industry and commerce today, with the increased number of graduates entering management-traineeship schemes. In the civil service, wartime expansion increased the chances of promotion for clerks, as did the nationalization of the railways. One of the major features of the modern office—the employment of women in routine clerical jobs—has meant increased chances for male clerks because few women starting in the lower grades either choose, or are chosen for, promotion.

[1] Rudolf Hilferding, *Das Finanzkapital*, 1927, pp. 444–8.

# CHAPTER THREE

# THE MODERN OFFICE: WORK SITUATION

'The business by which a person earns his livelihood generally fills his thoughts during by far the greater part of those hours in which his mind is at its best; during them his character is being formed by the way in which he uses his faculties in his work, by the thoughts and the feelings which it suggests, and by his relations to his associates in work, his employers or his employees.'

ALFRED MARSHALL,
*Principles of Economics*

'No doubt many of the faults of the clerk may be traced to the artificial atmosphere in which he works and the false values which influence his life. Conversely, it is probable that he is deterred from displaying many of the robuster qualities of the manual worker by the powerful anti-social forces by which he is usually surrounded. We may frankly admit these difficulties of our colleagues without losing faith in them or thinking hardly of them, because it is not in ordinary human nature to withstand more than a certain amount of pressure.'

*31st Annual Report of the
National Union of Clerks*, 1922

# THE MODERN OFFICE:
## WORK SITUATION

THE office of the counting-house era was small, the clerk was closely bound up with his employer in a personal and particular work relationship, and clerks were isolated from each other by a lack of any really impersonal standards of common identification. Clerks were thus impotent as a collective force—dispersed in small groups, dependent on their employers and divorced from each other. We have already seen how the clerk was distinguished from the manual worker by the security and opportunity inherent in his economic position. Here too—in the environment of his daily working life— the clerk was differently situated from the workman who was being marshalled into the workshops of the new factory system of production. If he was 'propertyless' like his fustian-clad fellow in the factory, he was not exposed to the same kind of life experiences as those which dominated the consciousness of the manual wage-earner. For, with the rise of modern industry and the development of the labour market, the work-relationship of master and workman was progressively and radically transformed. The establishment of machine production in factories and the rationalization of organization which this entailed created a working environment which was highly conducive to the emergence of class-conscious action. Productive relationships in the factory separated management from the worker as they simultaneously united workers with one another in cohesive groups. Physical separation and concentration were reinforced socially by the impersonal discipline and standardized relationships of the factory bureaucracy; and these were further generalized through the operation of the labour market. In this way the factory became, in Michels' phrase, a model school of working-class solidarity.

How did the blackcoated worker fare in this respect during the rise of the modern office? Were the relationships of administration transformed in the same direction, to the same extent? How far did office workers become concentrated together in large units of administration? In what ways have the internal relations of the modern office fostered unity or disunity among clerical employees? To what degree have the impersonal standards generated by bureaucracy and labour market provided a common point of reference for blackcoated workers, transcending their physical dispersion? Finally,

71

how has office mechanization affected the work situation of clerical labour?

## INTERNAL OFFICE ORGANIZATION

'In general, there has been much less systematic and scientific organization of personnel in offices than in factories, although there is no reason why this should be so.'

*Office Organization and Practice*,
British Standards Institute, 1943

The rationalization of administration involves the establishment of standard procedures and the specialization of functions within the office. This does not necessarily involve the mechanization of work: the bureaucratic re-organization carried out in the civil service and in banking just after the First World War is an example of the way in which work may be rationalized without the introduction of machinery. We shall, therefore, consider rationalization and mechanization separately, though they often go together in fact.

The basis of administrative rationalization is the growth in the average size of the office. Between the counting house and the modern office lies a period of great industrial and commercial expansion. There has been a growth in the average size of the unit of production and administration in almost every field. The ratio of non-manual to operative workers has increased as 'scientific management' called for more and more precise recording and analysis of business data. Amalgamations have added to this process by allowing administration to be centralized in head offices that are often comparable, in terms of numbers employed and conditions of work, to large-scale factory production.[1] The concentration of whole armies of clerks in these large-scale organizations draws most attention, of course, and tends to distort the facts of office size.

What, in fact, is the degree of physical concentration of clerical labour? There are, unfortunately, no statistics on the varying size of offices in different industries. At the same time if we wish to understand the forces determining clerical consciousness, it is essential to know certain basic facts. What proportion of clerks work in large units of administration? What is the average number of clerks employed in concerns of varying size?

[1] The Ministry of National Insurance centre employing 7,000 office workers in one huge establishment in the north of England, working largely on machines and routine filing operations, is probably the largest of its kind. See *Times Survey of Office Equipment and Machinery*, 1950.

A rough answer to this problem can be attempted in the case of the manufacturing trades.[1] In the Census of 1931, and then only, are statistics on the distribution of the occupied population classified according to functional divisions of industry.[2] These include clerical employees in relation to total employees for each of the manufacturing trades. (See Table VIII.) We find that for the manufacturing trades as a whole there were 424,332 clerks out of a total of 6,330,118 employees. That is, clerks formed 6·7% of total employees in these trades. A higher proportion of clerks to total employees was found in chemicals and allied trades, in metal manufacturing, engineering, shipbuilding, vehicles and metal goods, and a relatively low proportion in textiles, clothing and the manufacture of wood and cork.

TABLE VIII—PROPORTION OF CLERICAL TO TOTAL EMPLOYEES
IN MANUFACTURING INDUSTRY, 1931

| Industry 1949 | Classification 1931 | Total Employees | Clerks | Clerks as Percentage of Total |
|---|---|---|---|---|
| III | iii2 | 60,863 | 2,660 ⎫ | 4·0 |
|  | iv | 214,479 | 8,394 ⎭ |  |
| IV | v | 217,244 | 31,610 | 14·5 |
| V | | | | |
| VI | | | | |
| VII | vi | 2,185,136 | 185,721 | 8·5 |
| VIII | | | | |
| IX | | | | |
| X | vii | 1,185,778 | 39,925 | 3·3 |
| XI | viii | 85,653 | 4,286 | 5·0 |
| XII | ix | 833,148 | 27,737 | 3·3 |
| XIII | x | 616,539 | 50,450 | 8·2 |
| XIV | xi | 275,788 | 10,303 | 3·7 |
| XV | xii | 444,427 | 40,482 | 9·1 |
| XVI | xiv | 211,063 | 22,764 | 10·8 |

| Total Manufacturing Industry | | 6,330,118 | 424,332 | 6·7 |

[1] These trades in the 1949 classification are as follows: III treatment of non-metalliferous mining products other than coal; IV chemicals and allied trades; V metal manufacturing; VI engineering, shipbuilding and electrical goods; VII vehicles; VIII metal goods; IX precision instruments, etc.; X textiles; XI leather goods and fur; XII clothing; XIII food, drink and tobacco; XIV manufacture of wood and cork; XV paper and printing; XVI other manufacturing industries. The comparable 1931 classification is shown in Table VIII.
[2] *Census of England and Wales*, Industry Tables, 1934, pp. 701–3.

These statistics may be compared with those given in the Census of Production of 1930 on the proportion of administrative, technical and clerical staffs to total employees in the same factory trades.[1] For the larger establishments (those employing eleven or more persons) the salaried group of administrators, technicians and clerks formed 11·9% of total employees. If all units of production are taken (including those employing up to ten persons) the salaried group formed 13·8% of total employees. This obviously means that there was a higher proportion of salaried to total employees in the smaller firms, which had 10% of the total employees in the factory trades. Very roughly, then, we may assume that, if clerks formed 6·7% of total employees in the manufacturing trades and the salaried group 13·8%, clerks formed about half the salaried employees in this area of economic organization.

In order to try to relate these facts to the analysis of production of 1949, we have to take into account the expansion of the administrative, technical and clerical group in relation to other employees. Between 1930 and 1949 the salaried group had grown from 11·9% to 16·6% of all employees in the case of the larger establishments, which employed 95% of the total workforce in the manufacturing trades by 1949.[2] If we assume that clerical employees formed the same proportion of the salaried group as in 1930, clerks would form approximately 8·3% of total employees in 1949. The figure of 16·6% on which this calculation is based refers to salaried staffs in the larger firms. If the smaller firms had a relatively higher proportion of salaried staff to total employees, as they did in 1930, then the average ratio of salaried staff to total employees would probably be slightly higher than 16·6%, though not so much higher, because the smaller firms accounted for only 5% of total employees in 1949, whereas they accounted for 10% at the earlier date.

The figure of 8·3 as the percentage of clerks to total employees in the manufacturing trades for 1949 is, therefore, not to be taken as anything but a crude approximation, subject to all the foregoing qualifications. It does, however, appear to be compatible with other estimates which can be made. Clerks formed roughly 10% of the total occupied workforce in 1951. This is a larger proportion than the one arrived at for manufacturing trades, but this is consistent

---

[1] *Final Report of the Fourth Census of Production of the United Kingdom*, 1930, Part V, General Report, pp. 84 et seq.

[2] *Censuses of Production for 1950, 1949 and 1948*, Summary Tables, Part I, 1953. There were 58,094 firms, employing 11 or more persons, who employed a total of 7,063,274 persons, and 79,138 firms, employing 10 or less persons, who employed a total of 368,027 persons.

with the higher proportion of clerks employed in commercial, banking, insurance and government undertakings. Similar confirmation of the reasonableness of the estimate for manufacturing trades is provided by a survey of office administrative practices.[1] This survey showed that the proportion of office staff (which means 'supervisory office staff' as well as clerks proper) to total employees for several manufacturing trades was 10·7. However, those trades which are known to have a relatively high proportion of clerks per total employees were heavily represented in the range of trades for which information was available. The inclusion of supervisory staff with clerks also probably boosted the ratio to total employed.

If it is assumed that clerks make up approximately a half of all non-operative workers, and this would seem to be a reasonable assumption in the light of the foregoing evidence, then it is possible to arrive at an estimate of the degree of concentration of the clerical labour force. Without claiming to be anything but a very rough analysis, Table IX shows the total and average numbers of clerks per establishments of varying size in manufacturing trades. The information on the distribution of total employees and of administrative, technical and clerical workers is taken from the Census of Production for 1949.

The figures have to be interpreted with great care. They are an estimate of the average numbers of clerks to be found in different sizes of establishments in *all* types of manufacturing industries. But, in fact, as was shown above, certain industries have a higher ratio of office workers to total employees than others. For example, 777 establishments, in each of which are employed between 400-499 workers, have an estimated total of 27,664 clerical employees, or an average of 36 per establishment. But establishments of this size in the textile industry will probably employ less than the average number of clerks, and those in the chemical industry considerably more than the average. In this sense, the figures on the average numbers of clerks by size of establishment abstract from these industrial variations.

The degree of concentration of clerical labour does not appear to be very great. Half the total number of clerks employed in manufacturing industry were probably working in establishments in which the average number of clerks was 26 or less, while 68% of the total were to be found in establishments in which the average number of clerks was 80 or less. Only 32% of the clerks were employed in units in which the average number of clerks was greater than 80. By contrast, 75% of all workers in manufacturing industry were employed

[1] Office Management Association, *Office Administrative Practices*, 1952, p. 7.

TABLE IX—DISTRIBUTION OF CLERKS BY SIZE OF ESTABLISHMENT
IN MANUFACTURING INDUSTRY, 1949

| Size of Establishment (No. of Employees) | Number of Establishments | Total Employees | Total Administrative, Technical & Clerical Workers | Total Clerks (estimated) | Average No. of Clerks per size of Establishment (estimated) |
|---|---|---|---|---|---|
| 10 or less | 79,138 | 368,027 | — | 33,122 | 0·42 |
| 11–24 | 17,371 | 299,358 | 53,843 | 26,921 | 1·5 |
| 25–49 | 15,436 | 540,391 | 88,742 | 44,371 | 2·9 |
| 50–99 | 10,707 | 748,578 | 112,327 | 56,163 | 5·2 |
| 100–199 | 6,899 | 964,973 | 142,736 | 71,368 | 10·3 |
| 200–299 | 2,651 | 644,699 | 95,110 | 47,555 | 17·9 |
| 300–399 | 1,346 | 464,283 | 69,431 | 34,715 | 25·8 |
| 400–499 | 777 | 347,477 | 55,328 | 27,664 | 35·6 |
| 500–749 | 1,001 | 612,151 | 101,227 | 50,613 | 50·6 |
| 750–999 | 417 | 359,339 | 66,795 | 33,397 | 80·1 |
| 1,000–1,499 | 365 | 441,882 | 86,923 | 43,461 | 119·1 |
| 1,500–1,999 | 185 | 319,855 | 58,755 | 29,377 | 158·8 |
| 2,000–2,499 | 112 | 247,737 | 46,156 | 23,078 | 206·0 |
| 2,500–2,999 | 74 | 201,758 | 37,515 | 18,757 | 253·5 |
| 3,000–3,999 | 61 | 208,402 | 39,751 | 19,875 | 325·8 |
| 4,000–4,999 | 31 | 129,962 | 27,339 | 13,669 | 440·9 |
| 5,000–7,499 | 32 | 191,358 | 40,206 | 20,103 | 628·2 |
| 7,500–9,999 | 19 | 149,444 | 28,764 | 14,382 | 756·9 |
| 10,000 plus | 12 | 190,620 | 38,620 | 19,310 | 1,609·2 |

in establishments with a hundred or more employees. To be sure, these figures represent office sizes much greater than those associated with the period of the counting house, but in relatively few instances do office sizes approximate the workforce concentration that is typical of factory production.

As for clerks employed in non-manufacturing industry, distribution and commerce, the situation is difficult to estimate. The proportion of clerks to total employees is probably higher on the whole, but the unit of production smaller, than in manufacturing industry. Insurance and banking have very high ratios of clerks to total employees, but again there is considerable physical dispersion in branches.

Yet physical concentration and dispersion is only one, and perhaps not the most important, aspect of the work situation of the blackcoated worker. In order to get a rounded picture of his environment, we have to fill in the statistical framework with what is known of the internal social relations of the modern office.

Since many of the social relationships of the counting house persist in the smaller office today, we may direct our attention to the large-scale establishment. Here, the original, simple division of functions to be found in the counting house is barely recognizable in the complex hierarchy of departments and offices-within-offices. Although the increased size of office has meant that more office workers than ever before are now brought together in the same unit of administration, it has also involved a greater specialization and subdivision of tasks. As a result, clerical workers are not usually all concentrated in one department, but are dispersed among a number of different departments within the administrative hierarchy. 'Clerical workers are arranged in units or clusters at every stage of managerial organization. An executive or supervisor does not delegate work solely down the line; the duties of his position may require the services of a number of immediate assistants whose work is clerical.'[1] The actual working group, then, by reason of the organization of most office work, tends to be small. 'As a rule the working group in an office is a smaller one than in industry. Offices which conduct a quite important business are themselves frequently small units. Even the large office itself is frequently an aggregation of small units.'[2]

Such functional specialization can be seen in embryo in the division of labour of a medium-sized office employing about thirty people. As described in a contemporary manual on office organization, the work of some twenty-six clerks is directly controlled by four or more persons of managerial or supervisory rank, including the office manager. These supervisors manage the eight distinct sections into which the office is divided: costing, accounts, cashier, stock control, wages, sales, typing, machine calculation. The greatest number of clerks in each section does not exceed five. 'Normally, one person cannot effectively supervise the work of more than about six persons, unless the subordinates are engaged on simple routine. Thus it follows that in an office employing, say, a staff of thirty, the office manager may have five or six assistants, each of whom in turn may control some five or six clerks.'[3] An additional noteworthy feature is that the clerks within the different sections are distinguished from each other by considerable degrees of skill and responsibility, passing all the way from unskilled to quasi-managerial positions in a small, integrated work hierarchy.

[1] Wilbert E. Moore, *Industrial Relations and the Social Order*, 1947, p. 158.
[2] F. J. Tickner, *Modern Staff Training*, 1952, p. 53.
[3] *Office Organization and Practice*, British Standards Institute, 1943, p. 41.

77

Over wide areas of industry and commerce, the work situation of clerical labour must approximate such a pattern. In larger offices essentially the same conditions hold. The prevalent form of administration is the line-and-staff organization.[1] Functions are merely subdivided, there is a multiplication of managerial and supervisory positions, and a finer splintering of clerical work-groups. Only in the case of very highly standardized machine and typing operations is the 'pooling' of clerks, resulting in the formation of an isolated class of operatives, a typical phenomenon of office organization. Naturally the larger the office the greater the technical possibility of simplifying and standardizing clerical tasks or reducing them to a form suitable for mechanical manipulation. Even then, as we shall see, the number of clerks employed in this type of work forms only a very small proportion of the total. In the large firm, as in the small, much clerical work is specific, non-repetitive, requiring a modicum of skill and responsibility and individual judgement. Apart from these technical obstacles to a thoroughgoing rationalization of work, there are well-known resistances on the part of managers and clerks to the anonymity which inevitably results from any attempt to run the office like a factory.

One consequence of such small, tightly knit work-groups is that the management of clerical work is not carried out with the same kind of impersonal discipline that is a common feature of factory organization; on the contrary it tends to be performed in a social context which must of necessity be fairly intimate in all but the very largest offices. The division of labour not only splinters the workforce among departments and through occupational differentiation, but also brings clerical staffs into relatively close and enduring relations of co-operation with managers and supervisors.[2] This human aspect of the work situation is undoubtedly further increased

---

[1] Moore, *op. cit.*, Chapter VI.

[2] This may be contrasted with Michels' characterization of the work situation of the factory worker: 'The mechanized factory and large-scale enterprise robbed the employer of his previous function as fellow-worker, overseer and adviser. Personal contact and conversational intimacy were also lost. Where the latter persisted it was not the expression of a working community but of class distinction and class distance. By the workers it was regarded as arrogance and insolence, and answered in the same spirit, even occasionally by the staging of strikes. Direct control over the work process was delegated to intermediaries. The employer became invisible to his employees. Shut away in closed, not always easily accessible offices, absorbed in matters of accounting, he became a stranger to his workers, with only the superficial ties of the labour contract to unite them. The relationship between employer and employee became unreal and impersonal.' R. Michels, 'Psychologie der antikapitalistischen Massenbewegungen', *Grundriss der Sozialökonomik* IX, 1926.

by the typical age and sex divisions of clerical work.[1] The supervisor or manager of an office is normally an older man and his assistants younger women; and whether the ensuing relationship is a paternalistic, petty tyrannical, or sexually exploitative one, it is essentially personal.[2] What is decisive here is that, from the point of view of the ordinary clerk, at no juncture is the chain of command an impersonal one. There is no radical break between management and clerks corresponding to that between the 'office' and the 'works'. He co-operates with management and supervisors in a day-to-day routine, and is not simply directed by them. For a hundred years the manuals of office procedure have suggested that you do not get the best out of your clerks by ordering them about bluntly. At every point, the working contact between manager and supervisor, between supervisor and clerk, introduces a personal and continuous element into office organization and obviates the harsh, impersonal and purely instrumental character of the command which industrial sociologists are beginning to single out as an important source of latent hostility on the part of the factory worker.[3] The rationalization and routinization of work and the disciplined impersonality of the superordinate and subordinate relationship go together. Office work is most frequently not of the character that can be subjected to factory-work rhythm, and office relations form a social system in which work has traditionally been maximized by personal, rather than by impersonal command.

Not only are clerical staffs separated physically to a great extent among departments and thrown together into small working groups with managers and supervisors, but they also tend to be separated individually from each other by the authority and status hierarchy

[1] E. G. MacGibbon, *Manners in Business*, 1954. This book brings out very well the functional and dysfunctional consequences of personal attachments in a formally impersonal administrative work situation. See also Carl Dreyfuss, *Beruf und Ideologie der Angestellten*, 1933, pp. 77–80, 'Sexuelle Beziehungen im Geschaftsbetrieb'.

[2] 'To a very great extent women are employed on forms of work such as shorthand-typing, which brings them into personal contact with their employers or their managements. Women are capable of giving great loyalty to those whom they serve and this is why they make such excellent secretaries and personal clerks. It is not difficult to call on this loyalty as a reason why support should not be given to a trade union.' *The Clerk*, September 1954, p. 108.

[3] The peculiar role of the foreman, like that of the non-commissioned-officer, often requires the incumbent to transmit orders to subordinates without fully understanding the reason behind the command. This leads to the execution of the order in a spirit of undue harshness (e.g. violent swearing) as a reaction to his own lack of comprehension and conviction, and thus alienates those working under him, not simply in a personal sense, but also as the visible representative of 'them up there'.

of the company. 'The work and interests of office and clerical workers are more likely to reflect the differences in position and function of their immediate supervisors than their own low official position. This dispersion of clerks and secretaries throughout the managerial hierarchy gives to these persons a reflected status based upon the relative rank and authority of the administrators for whom they work. In fact, the whole official hierarchy may be in large measure duplicated by the unofficial distribution of privilege and rank in the clerical staff.'[1] This situation is further reinforced in its effects by the concern with status which is known to be unusually highly developed among office staffs, especially where the organization of positions, merit criteria and seniority is not consistent and explicit. 'Within the office group itself, there is usually a high development of status symbols. With office people the symbols of status are often a major concern and changes in them create terrific disturbances. To account for such emphasis is difficult, but we may present two possible hypotheses. In the first place, the office and supervisory groups probably contain more people trying to get up in the world, who want to improve their status. And these people naturally want to display evidence of any gains; they want people to know where they belong. At the same time, the nature of office work is such that all jobs look alike from a distance; people sitting at desks, writing and shuffling papers may be either important executives or the most unimportant clerks. For that reason, it becomes important that the superior people acquire symbols to distinguish them from the rest.'[2] The proliferation of office titles is recognized by those expert in the human relations of the bureau as an inexpensive way of keeping staff content, through satisfying prestige needs and by furthering individualism. A recent advocate of this policy argues that 'the bestowal of an office title is usually welcomed for its "prestige" value, even where little or no financial considerations are involved', and, 'wisely used, these office titles pay dividends both to employer and employee. They lift the latter out of the common rut, stimulate his interest in his job, and make for healthy competition within the firm itself'. This is true even of the most routine positions, for 'every shorthand-typist would prefer to be called a secretary, and though frequently this cannot be arranged, particularly in offices where the "pool" system is in force, it is policy to permit a girl to call herself a secretary wherever possible.'[3]

[1] Moore, *op. cit.*, p. 185.

[2] Burleigh B. Gardner, *Human Relations in Industry*, 1946, p. 21.

[3] 'What's in a name?' *Office Magazine*, October 1955, p. 477. Take the case of Mr Bloggs—'It may well be that the duties of Mr Bloggs—an employee of many years' standing—are, strictly speaking, those of a senior clerk, but it will

In all these ways—physical distribution, organization of work-groups, occupational differentiation and status differences formally and informally established within the hierarchy of the office—the work situation of clerical labour forms a social context in which officer workers tend to be separated from each other on the one hand, and closely identified, as individuals, with the managerial and supervisory cadres of industry on the other. Some of these factors, of course, are also to be found in the work situation of factory labour, but it may safely be asserted that they operate more powerfully in the environment of the clerk than in that of the bench-hand.

The converse of the working co-operation of clerks and management is the social isolation of the office worker from the manual worker. The completeness of the separation of these two groups of workers is perhaps the most outstanding feature of industrial organization. Because of the rigid division between the 'office' and the 'works' it is no exaggeration to say that 'management', from the point of view of the manual worker, ends with the lowest grade of routine clerk. The office worker is associated with managerial authority, although he does not usually stand in an authoritarian relationship to the manual worker, the orders governing the labour force being transmitted from management through the foreman rather than through the clerical staff. Naturally there are degrees of isolation and contact between clerks and manual workers. Groups such as warehouse, railway, docking and colliery clerks are obviously more likely to be brought into contact with manual workers than are banking, insurance and civil service clerks. Finally, the administrative separation of the office worker from the operative, which is based primarily on the conception of the secret and confidential nature of office work, is completed by the separation of the works canteen from the staff dining-room.[1]

do his firm no harm, and need cost them nothing, to confer an "Inspectorship" upon him. And it will probably do Mr Bloggs' morale a power of good to sign his name above such a title, not to mention enabling his wife to hold her own in conversation with that odious Mrs Jones whose husband, as she never allows one to forget, is Manager of Makepeace and Farraday's Export Branch. It will also provide Bloggs junior with a more "face-saving" reply to such questions as "My father's a Director—what's yours?" These reactions of Mrs and Master Bloggs are not so completely divorced from the firm's interests as might at first sight appear, since anything that conduces to father's prestige in the home tends to make him a more contented man, and a contented man is rarely a problem in the office.'

[1] F. Zweig, *The British Worker*, p. 202: 'A lead press cable maker described to me what he regards as the greatest difference between a working-class chap and an "office man" in his workplace: ". . . he eats in the staff dining-room and has a better served meal which he calls lunch, while we eat in the general dining-room and call it dinner." '

## LABOUR MARKET AND BUREAUCRACY

Above and beyond these features of office organization, however, there is another dimension of the work situation of the office worker which may be interpreted as a further influence making for his social isolation. This has to do with the nature of clerical work itself, and the degree to which it is peculiar to the individual enterprise.

There is a sense in which the 'market situation' of clerical labour is not really a market situation at all; at least for many clerks. The prime social characteristic of a labour market is its impersonal nature. Insofar as a labour market exists, there is a tendency for skills and remuneration to be standardized. In this way, we can speak of a 'class' of operatives, such as fitters or turners. Labour power is thereby made homogenous and comparable, and is divorced from the setting of a particular firm. A fitter means much the same thing in firm A as in firm B; he is a worker with recognizable skills and standard remuneration. Manual workers have thus been identified with one another through the emergence of a market for their labour and the concomitant growth of such common standards of skill and payment.[1]

Well into the present century, and over wide areas of commercial employment, the typical clerk was not really in the market at all in this sense. His initial engagement was secured through the personal contact of relative, schoolmaster or friend. It contained the implication that he would stay with his employer and perhaps become a partner himself, or at least a chief clerk, in due course. Moreover, the highly individual nature of business methods introduced him to a routine peculiar to the firm in which he started his career. He definitely acquired skills, but it was difficult to say exactly what they were, or to compare them with those of other clerks. His maturing experience would be peculiar to his own firm, often highly valuable to his particular employer, but relatively worthless outside.[2] Promotion was given and responsibility added, not by virtue of his progressive certification, but in accordance with his employer's estimation

[1] Of course, the creation of standard conditions in the market is partially a function of trade unionism itself. See Sidney and Beatrice Webb, *Industrial Democracy*, 1913, Part II, Chapter V, 'The Standard Rate'.

[2] 'It may be noted that while an artisan often improves his skill and experience by moving from one master to another, a clerk, after the preliminary stages of his work, can, as a rule, only rise to a responsible post by remaining in the firm with whose affairs he has grown familiar.' *Commercial Occupations*, One of a Series of Handbooks on London Trades prepared on behalf of the Board of Trade, 1914, p. 4.

of his merit and worth—in other words, by the value of a particular clerk to a particular employer in a particular business routine. Needless to add, all this could, and often did, redound to the clerk's disadvantage.

The importance of the particularism of clerical skills can be seen in the fears and actual experience of men suddenly jettisoned on the market. In *Howard's End*, Forster describes the predicament of Leonard Bast, the clerk who has lost his job: 'Leonard was near the abyss, and at such moments men see clearly. "You don't know what you're talking about," he said, "I shall never get work now. If rich people fail at one profession, they can try another. Not I. I have my groove, and I've got out of it. I could do one particular branch of insurance in one particular office well enough to command a salary, but that's all." '[1] The goal of the ambitious clerk was a lifelong career of devoted effort in the enterprise of a particular employer culminating in his eventual 'indispensability' and ultimate recognition. This was all highly precarious, highly individual and the source of high hopes and self-help. The market had little to do with it. When he was put on the market he became an unskilled specialist. 'There is no more helpless figure in the ranks of unemployment than the out-of-work clerk. Paradoxically he is both specialized and unskilled labour.'[2] In the social survey of Merseyside it was found, in studying unemployment among clerks, that 'the majority of clerks who have "got on" also possess knowledge which can be classed as skilled, but it has little value outside the particular firm they have served. In seeking new work they often have to start at the bottom again or content themselves with temporary employment.'[3]

The lack of standardization of clerical training and skills can be traced to the undervaluation of formal preparation and to the emphasis placed on particular experience: 'In selecting book-keepers and clerks there is a good deal to be said in favour of requiring certificates in such subjects as book-keeping and shorthand, although it should not be imagined that the possession of these certificates indicates that their holders are trained men of business. Employers are often inclined to complain of our system of commercial education, and that there is room for improvement may be readily admitted. It is, however, useless to expect that any conceivable system of scholastic training can take the place of actual experience, and the danger is that, if the opposite be assumed to be true, the first duty of

[1] E. M. Forster, *Howard's End*, 1910, p. 212 (Penguin edition).
[2] *The Bank Officer*, April 1931, p. 6.
[3] *Social Survey of Merseyside* (edited by C. Caradog-Jones), 1934, Vol. II, pp. 328–9, 336–7.

a new entrant to an office will be to unlearn a good deal of what has been inculcated outside. What is wanted is a good foundation of general knowledge—supplemented by an acquaintance with common commercial terms and general routine—and a receptive mind.'[1] These are qualities not unlike those which employers demanded seventy years previously.

How far a real market for clerical labour is emerging at the present time is difficult to estimate.[2] But there can be little doubt that hitherto the lack of universally acknowledged standards of grading office work has weakened common identification and solidarity among commercial and industrial clerks. This deficiency has been frequently noted by the Union concerned with their organization.[3]

'The present low standard of qualification among clerks is a handicap to the Union by lowering respect for the craft among employers and workers alike . . . with better qualification and grading will come greater craft consciousness . . . there are today many excellent facilities for training in many branches of clerical work, but they lack co-ordination and recognized standards. No authoritative body has ever bothered to put down in black and white what qualifications should entitle a person to call himself a clerk.'[4]

As late as 1947, Thomas found that clerical workers ranked only above unskilled workers in terms of occupational training received.[5] Training is usually received on the job in clerical work, and this

TABLE X—THE ASSOCIATION BETWEEN OCCUPATION AND
TRAINING RECEIVED (MEN)

| First Occupation | Apprenticeship, Articles and Prof. Training (%) | Other Systematic Training (%) | None (%) |
|---|---|---|---|
| Professional and technical | 72 | 20 | 8 |
| CLERICAL | 6 | 23 | 71 |
| Manipulative | 80 | 14 | 6 |
| Operative | 8 | 23 | 69 |
| Unskilled | 0 | 8 | 92 |

[1] L. R. Dicksee and H. E. Blain, *Office Organization and Practice*, 1936, p. 7. See also *Factors in Industrial and Commercial Efficiency*, Committee on Industry and Trade, 1927, p. 221.

[2] See O. G. Pickard, *The Office Worker: A Study in Labour Economics and Organization*, unpublished Ph.D. Thesis, University of London, 1956.

[3] *The Clerk*, 1915, p. 109. 'The Unions and Professional Education'.

[4] *Ibid.*, January to February 1945. 'What is a Clerk?'

[5] Thomas, *op. cit.*, p. 48.

training is rarely analysed systematically, or rationalized so as to make clerical work comparable to any great extent. In a survey recently carried out by the Office Management Association into office administrative practices, it was found that, even among firms with large clerical staffs, only 43% used any kind of job-rating system, and only 24% used any form of merit rating for purposes of promotion. In most cases, decisions on promotion were left to the office or departmental manager's judgement. Nor was there any pressure for uniformity from without, for 75% of the firms fixed salary scales without reference to organizations representing their staff.[1] It is only since the war that the Office Management Association has promoted rationalized systems of job and merit rating for inter-firm comparisons, but it is difficult to say with what success they have met.[2] In machine operation, as well as in typing pools, some kind of standardization of performance is possible, but together they constitute but a small fraction of clerical functions.

Insofar as common standards are not instituted in office work, then, the clerical work force is not only physically scattered, but also socially separated into isolated units, between which there is little comparability in terms of work, skill and remuneration.

In fields other than industry and commerce, notably in the civil service, in railways, banking and to a lesser extent in local government, large-scale organizations have emerged in which many thousands of clerks are employed. In such administrative units, the rationalization of the work situation has been achieved other than by the creation of a labour market for clerical work. Through the introduction of uniform scales of remuneration, through the rigid classification of jobs, through the establishment of explicit criteria of merit, through the articulation of the individual career with prescribed examinations and certificates, through the facilitation of mobility within the organization—in short, through bureaucratization—the equivalent of a market situation has been brought about. The market and the bureaucracy are alternative modes by which the labour relationship may be rationalized. But in both cases, the ensuing relationship has the same basic character; the individual worker is related to his fellows through uniform and impersonal standards.[3]

---

[1] OMA, *Office Administrative Practices*, 1952. 323 firms were investigated, employing a total of 108,547 office workers. This is an average of 336 per firm.

[2] OMA, *Job Grading*, 1952.

[3] With the institution of open competition, the situation of the civil-service clerk was transformed; 'He knows that he exists officially, not as a favour, but as a necessary cog in a huge machine. He realizes that his progress is bound up with that of his whole grade, so he organizes himself accordingly.' *Red Tape*, October 1913, p. 4.

Such a work situation possesses features which differ substantially from those to be found in less rationalized structures of administration. In a bureaucracy positions are defined as clearly as possible, and the amount of skill, responsibility, income, status and authority going with them is made transparent. Competition for advancement between clerks is regulated in an orderly fashion through seniority and merit systems which are explicit and do not admit of exceptions to the rules. Such a situation may be contrasted with that in which the job is tailored to fit the man, in which promotion is left to the discretion of the supervisor, in which office titles are proliferated indiscriminately to satisfy prestige cravings. Both types of system encourage individualism; but the one through impersonal, the other through personal, criteria.

These differences, to be sure, are relative. Some large industrial and commercial undertakings may be highly bureaucratic in their staff organization; on the other hand even the most formally established bureaucracy never works according to blueprint. Between the small-scale paternalistic administration of a private firm and the large-scale 'civil-service' bureaucracy of a public organization come admixtures of both types. A quasi-bureaucratic form is to be found in banking for instance. The various large banking concerns form a system in which there is a high degree of comparability of administration as between one bank and another, but not complete identity. Strong loyalties on the part of the staffs of the rival houses are encouraged deliberately, and clerks are not allowed to move from one bank to another in the wider system. Within the banks, such features as incomplete grading of jobs and secret reports on office staffs cause their internal administration to fall short of the pure bureaucratic form. The practical result is to create a working environment in which the common identification of bank clerks, both between banks and inside banks, is less than it would be were their mobility unhindered and their positions unambiguously defined. This relation between incomplete bureaucratic organization and lack of staff solidarity is recognized in the programme of the National Union of Bank Employees, which clearly presses for a complete rationalization of the work situation: 'Emphasis should be on grading the job rather than the man. It is too easy to give a dog a bad name. The grade of each job should be laid down, together with the salary range it attracts. The qualifications for each job should be laid down. Each employee should know the grade of his or her job and should be able to ascertain as a right the jobs in other grades and the qualifications considered necessary for them. Each employee should be able to know as a right if (and if so, wherein) he or she falls short of these requirements. An employee who disputes the correctness of the grading of a job should have the right to appeal for revision. Without these conditions there would be no safeguard against discrimination and nepotism; unexpected promotions and rises could still occur. There would be the added dignity of release from the paternalism that is a characteristic of employer-employee relations in banking today.'[1]

The degree to which administrative relations take on a purely bureaucratic form, therefore, is a crucial factor in the work situation of the blackcoated worker. In principle there is no difference between the impersonal and standardized relationships of the bureaucracy and those of the factory.[2] But in most areas of private industry the small size of the office workforce relative to the total number of employees, and the very diversity of competitively related firms, set narrow limits on the establishment of highly bureaucratic forms of administration. It is in the public or quasi-public organization whose labour force is predominantly clerical that bureaucratic administration flourishes, and is indeed imperative.

## MECHANIZATION

Early to bed and early to rise
Is really very little good
Unless you mechanize.

*The Clerk*, April 1937

Mechanization is a process affecting clerical work that is distinct from rationalization, although the two often go together. Thus machinery was first introduced to meet the rapidly growing demands that were being made on office staffs, and then extended with the aim of reducing the cost of clerical work.[3] It is, however, fallacious to argue, as is so often done, that the mere introduction of 'machinery' into offices reduces the status of the clerk to that of a factory opera-

---

[1] *The Bank Officer*, April 1954, p. 21. Also July 1934, p. 9.

[2] 'Bureaucracy implies conditions similar to those found in the mechanized factory. Looked at objectively, bureaucracy implies a similar reduction of all social functions to their basic elements, and a similar rational and formal regulation of these precisely differentiated parts. From a subjective point of view, it implies similar psychological consequences—arising out of the separation of work from the individual abilities and needs of those who perform it—and a similar rational, inhuman division of labour.' G. Lukacs, *Geschichte und Klassenbewusstsein*, 1923, p. 110.

[3] Raphael, Frisby and Hunt, *Industrial Psychology Applied to the Office*, 1934.

tive. The meaning of mechanization, the different types of office machinery, the relation between the organization of machinery and the administrative division of labour, and the actual extent of office mechanization—all have to be examined before we can determine the degree to which the work status of clerical employment has been affected by the introduction of office machinery.

The machine proper 'is a mechanism that, after being set in motion, performs with its tools the same operations that were formerly done by the workman with similar tools. Whether the motive power is derived from man, or from some other machine, makes no difference in this respect. From the moment that the tool proper is taken from man, and fitted into a mechanism, a machine takes the place of a mere instrument.'[1] The most simple form of machinery, then, consists in taking a single working tool out of the hands of the worker and fitting it into a mechanism which is then set in motion through some transmitting device. More complex machinery combines either a greater number of similar tools, or a variety of different tools within the same mechanism, and employs extra-human motive power. Complex machinery of this kind which is organized in a system and driven by a single source of power, brings about the qualitative change in the division of social labour which is characteristic of factory production. The division of labour within the system of factory production is determined by the demands of the machinery itself. Human labour becomes ancillary to the machine instead of the machine being ancillary to human labour. Here is a vital difference between factory and office mechanization.

A classification of modern office machinery clearly demonstrates that it is chiefly used to reinforce and support existing clerical functions.[2] Machinery, such as the electronic computer, which is introduced to *replace* existing clerical functions, is clearly comparable in its revolutionary effects with the most advanced factory mechanization. But so far this degree of mechanization is highly unusual.[3] Throughout the period under discussion, the majority of office machinery has belonged to a relatively simple stage in the development of machine technology and the machine organization of production. Insofar as the role of the machine operator is concerned,

[1] Karl Marx, *Capital*, Vol. I, 1906, p. 368. Marx's discussion of the social impact of mechanization in Chapters XIII and XIV is still one of the most penetrating.

[2] See H.M. Treasury, Organization and Methods Division, *Machines and Appliances in Government Offices*, 1947. Machines are chiefly used for preparing and producing documents by recording data; duplicating data; analysing data; performing calculations with data; transmitting messages; finding and filing data.

[3] See 'LEO, Lyon's Electronic Office', *Office Magazine*, April 1954.

three degrees of mechanization can usefully be distinguished on the basis of (*a*) the degree of specialization in relation to the machine, and (*b*) the degree of discretion or automaticity involved. First, there are those machines which facilitate part of some complicated work, such as for instance the calculator used by a cashier. In his work, the machine is not used full-time, but is really an ancillary device which takes over the mental drudgery involved in routine addition, subtraction, multiplication and division. Secondly, there are those machines which are not used continuously, but where the operator really directs them after having thought out certain details of the performance. Typing is a good example of this kind of work; the typist is usually specialized in relation to the machine, but the work involves discretion, and the tempo of work is her own. Thirdly, there are those machines which are merely supplemented by the operator, the latter becoming really a cog in the machine. This is the role of the operator of an automatic duplicating machine, for example. It is really in this third type of operation that the clerk is reduced to the status of a machine-minder, which for Marx and Veblen was the distinguishing characteristic of modern factory labour. Thus the number of office machines which subordinate the work of the clerk to the tempo of the machine, which take over the larger part of the discretion involved in the operation, and which require full-time, specialized attendants, is extremely small.

Although machines have been limited in their impact upon the actual nature of clerical functions when compared with their influence in factory production, the rationalization of work procedures in relation to machinery have produced social consequences similar to those in the factory, especially in large-scale and central office departments where there is a continuous demand for the recording and analysis of data. In such offices, the standardization of methods of work, of the size of forms, and of the ways in which these are to be set out, etc., have been the main factors in speeding-up and simplifying work for machine processing. They have also led to considerable improvements in the methods of grouping and supervising office workers. We may briefly consider the social consequences of this kind of work situation.

One of the main changes in the division of labour has been the appearance of the specialized, semi-skilled office employee who is responsible for the 'processing' of data. The actual division of tasks very often preceded mechanization, but machinery has speeded up the trend by which a small group of executives, who make decisions about the selection and analysis of data, are separated from a mass of subordinates whose functions less and less justify their classification as brain workers. 'The nature of the work tends to isolate the machine worker, and affords little opportunity for her to gain a general knowledge of the undertaking in which she is employed, which might lead to promotion into other grades of work. Continuous employment over a period of years on one process tends to create a rigidity of outlook which militates against the assuming of responsibility. This is true of all monotonous employment but the additional danger as far as machine workers are concerned is the fact that their work isolates them and creates of them a class apart.'[1] 'Office workers, therefore, are now divided into classes. The managerial staff is being more and more sharply distinguished from the subordinates, and the standardization of duties and the fixing of salaries within narrow limits have placed the latter category in a position similar to that of factory workers. Before mechanization, on the contrary, duties were not so exactly defined, and the level of earnings was not subject to any uniform scale; consequently office workers, whatever their duties, did not feel a sharp distinction from one another.'[2] To the extent that mechanization of this kind has taken place in large undertakings, the sense of separation from management through the impersonal relations of the work situation, which as we have seen is one of the main factors in the growth of working-class consciousness, is reproduced in the work situation of the office worker. 'Another psychological consequence of new organization methods in offices is that the division of labour and specialization have meant the loss of the power to satisfy what *de Man* has called the instinctive desire for importance. In the old-fashioned office, even the office boy felt that he was somebody, simply by belonging to the undertaking; but the invoice clerk who now works a book-keeping machine all day is nothing but an impersonal unit. In workshop and yard there has always been a considerable number of nameless hands; but these are undoubtedly a new feature of office work.' Further, 'the development of methods of selection has undoubtedly contributed towards the present feeling of inferiority among subordinate staff. One of the reasons why the office-boy of the old days thought himself an important person was the fact that no impassable barrier separated the lower from the higher grades, and many cases of a rise from one to the other did occur. But in selecting staff by modern methods for well-defined mechanical

[1] Joint Consultative Council for Promoting Equality of Opportunity for Men and Women, *Report on the Effects of Mechanization on the Salaries, Status and Promotion Prospects of Women in Offices*, 1936.

[2] 'The Use of Machinery and its Influence on Conditions of Work for Staff,' *International Labour Review*, 1937, Vol. XXXVI, p. 512.

duties, the employer runs the risk of eliminating those who have not the physical qualifications for the use of certain machines, but have on the other hand the gifts of intelligence and character which would permit them to reach the higher rungs of the ladder. The inverse is equally true: owing to such methods, the employee employed as a machine operator receives a strong impression that he is meant exclusively for this unimportant function and must remain his whole life in an inferior post.'[1]

Such a division of labour affects also the age and sex composition of office staffs. 'Visits to big mechanized undertakings will suffice to show that young persons of either sex between sixteen and twenty-five are very commonly used to work and supervise machines.'[2] In the civil service, the introduction of machinery was accompanied by a large increase in the proportion of women in the machine-operating grade.[3] The same was true of banking[4] and

[1] *Ibid.*, p. 513.

[2] *Ibid.*, p. 511.

[3] The expansion of this group between 1928 and 1934 can be seen from the following figures:

| Government Staffs | Jan. 1, 1928 | | April 1, 1934 | |
|---|---|---|---|---|
| | Men | Women | Men | Women |
| Administrative | 1,131 | 19 | 1,210 | 25 |
| General Executive | 4,002 | 137 | 4,034 | 225 |
| Other Executive | 10,243 | 480 | 11,123 | 519 |
| General Clerical | 27,442 | 6,961 | 32,938 | 8,007 |
| Other Clerical | 19,206 | 2,503 | 18,319 | 3,480 |
| *Writing Assistants* | — | 4,914 | — | 7,336 |
| Typing Grades | 120 | 6,980 | 76 | 8,904 |

Taken from F. W. Fox, 'Introduction of Office Machinery into Government Departments', *Institute of Public Administration*, 1936.

[4] The following figures are from the *Report of the Intelligence Committee of the Bank Officers' Guild on Mechanization of Banks*, October 1935.

Yearly average numbers of insured persons, with salaries of £250 and under, employed in banks.

| Year | Men | Women | Boys | Girls | Total |
|---|---|---|---|---|---|
| 1924 | 26,190 | 12,645 | 2,838 | 114 | 40,787 |
| 1926 | 26,797 | 11,877 | 1,953 | 120 | 40,747 |
| 1928 | 27,454 | 12,060 | 1,610 | 242 | 41,366 |
| 1930 | 26,409 | 13,057 | 1,225 | 444 | 41,135 |
| 1932 | 25,212 | 13,388 | 370 | 202 | 39,172 |
| 1934 | 23,064 | 14,031 | 733 | 316 | 38,144 |

The changing pattern of recruitment, during the years of heavy mechanization, is clearly shown here. The trend was, of course, influenced also by the depression.

railway[1] office staffs during the inter-war years. Since the war, this development has speeded up, so that the machine-operating grades are almost exclusively filled by young girls.

When the mechanization and rationalization of office work has proceeded to the extent that relatively large groups of semi-skilled employees are concentrated together, separated from managerial and supervisory staffs, performing continuous, routinized and disciplined work, often rewarded in accordance with physical output, with little chance of promotion—then clerical work becomes, in terms of social and physical environment, extremely like that of the factory operative. The sense of isolation, impersonality, the machine-dominated tempo of work, the destruction of the unitary nature of the product, are all reproduced in varying degrees.[2]

It remains to discuss the extent to which these conditions are present in clerical work, and how far office machinery has revolutionized office relations. It is extremely easy, and very common, to overestimate the degree to which this process has occurred. Again, the most advanced developments in the field are likely to divert attention from the normal division of labour. In most cases, the size of the office and the nature of clerical work set narrow limits to the application of 'production-line' methods. The introduction of com-

---

[1] The following figures are taken from *The Clerk*, June 1938, p. 260:

*Railway Clerks*

| Year | Men | Women | Year | Boys | Girls |
|------|--------|--------|------|-------|-------|
| 1914 | 75,900 | 1,100 | 1922 | 4,464 | 384 |
| 1919 | 73,000 | 12,000 | 1928 | 2,030 | 1,035 |
| 1935 | 61,800 | 11,500 | 1935 | 1,450 | 949 |

[2] 'On the correspondence side, the introduction of the dictaphone has led to similar results. The girls do not in such cases work for one or two individuals taking shorthand notes and typing them back their own work. They are attached to a typing pool with 20, 30 or 100 other typists. To this pool come all the dictaphone discs from all departments which are then distributed among the typing staff. The girls sit at their machines all day, with headphones over their ears, typing back from the dictaphone discs.' *Women in Offices*, Labour Publications Department, 1936, p. 10. This naturally raises the question of unionization, which will be dealt with in detail in Chapter V below. The division and separation of office employees into upper and lower categories, which is the result of mechanization, might be considered a factor favourable to unionization. On the other hand, clerks employed in such office 'factories' are mostly young women who regard the work as 'stop-gap' which they are glad to leave as soon as a favourable opportunity—marriage or other work—can be found. Also, the turnover rate for such workers is known to be high. This is facilitated by the precise nature of their skills and the present high demand for their work, which together increase their chances of mobility. The result of these factors is that, as a group, such office workers are less solidary than might be imagined.

plicated statistical and accounting machinery, such as for example the Hollerith machine, on which employees are to be continuously employed, is an expensive decision which only large establishments, such as government departments and the central statistical offices of private firms, can make. As we have seen, the distribution of clerical employees by size of firm would seem to indicate that machine pools of this kind are the exception rather than the rule in business organization as a whole. In the majority of cases—affecting the greater proportion of clerks—machinery is probably used in a small way, largely ancillary to clerical work, as in the use of calculators, adding machines, addressing machines and so on. These machines are used occasionally by different employees to take out of their work much of the mental drudgery with which it was once associated. Of the other office machines, the typewriter is at the same time the most extensively used and least mechanized. But, as the discussion on the division of labour indicated, typing is an operation that is likely to be dispersed throughout the administrative hierarchy, except in the largest offices where the standardization of procedure permits the economy of typing pools.[1]

As far as the statistics go, they tend to support these considerations. The clerks listed in the Census of 1951 as 'machine operators'[2] formed only 5·5% of women clerks, and something like 3·4% of total clerks. In addition, 9% of women clerks were listed as 'typists' and although this indicates specialization, the condition of work (i.e. whether working singly or in pools) is unknown. About 30% of the women were 'shorthand-typists' and 'secretaries' (other than company secretaries), and an even larger group simply 'clerks'.

[1] Typing pools have motivational disadvantages which are not always taken into account at first when assessing their economic advantages. A recent study showed that many executives preferred to have a particular typist of their own and that many typists preferred to be attached to a particular officer. Management Practice Report No. 7, *Typing Pools*, British Institute of Management. Again, 'many offices are now realising that typists and shorthand-typists, whether or not they are allowed to call themselves secretaries, like to identify themselves with a particular individual or department, since advertisements in the situations-vacant columns not infrequently add, as an inducement, "No Pool"'. *Office Magazine*, October 1955, p. 478.

[2] Occupational Category 894, including 'Accounting Machine Operator, Adding Machine Operator, Advertising Clerk, Book-keeping Machine Operator, Burrough's Operator, Calculating Machine Operator, Comptometer Operator, Comptometrist, Duplicating Machine Operator, Duplicator Operator, Elliott Fisher Operator, Gammeter Operator, Gestetner Operator, Hollerith Operator, Machine Assistant, Machine Operator, Multigraph Operator and Setter, Multilith Operator and Printer, Powers Samas Machine Operator, Roneo Operator, Rotaprint Operator, Senior Machine Operator, Sumlock Operator, Supervisor (Office Machine Operator)'.

We may conclude, then, that mechanization, though comparable in its most advanced effects to factory mechanization, is, on the whole, a factor affecting the social relations of office work to a much smaller extent than is often imagined.[1]

The automation of office work is an important new development whose future effect on office workers is very difficult to assess. It is a subject on which it is easy to cross the frontier between fact and fiction. So far, the application of fully automatic office machinery has been limited by the size of business operations—for only large firms or organizations can effectively use the capacity of such machinery—and by the nature of clerical work itself. As regards the latter point, one expert considers the prospects of automation in the office to be 'extremely limited by the simple fact that, although some people would deny it, the clerk often has to think for himself, is constantly meeting new sets of circumstances and his raw material is information. No electronic device has yet been designed which will read a letter written by a member of the public, realize what the letter is about and start off the necessary chain of actions required to answer it.'[2] Work such as salary- and wage-sheet preparation, which involves a great deal of computation and is standardized and repetitive week-by-week, is best suited to the main tool which the electronics engineer has so far produced—the automatic digital computer. This is always provided that the job is on a large enough scale to warrant the investment in a machine costing anything between £15,000 and £100,000.

As regards the office division of labour, the likely effect of such electronic devices will be the further development of the staff organization discussed above. 'So far as we can see, when an office is fully automatic, it will need four main groups of clerical personnel —the 'input' group, to scrutinize and quantify the basic data before it is fed into the process; the 'operations' group, people operating the appliances; the 'output' group, people to translate the results into something the manager can understand; and lastly, the con-

---

[1] Indeed, Klingender's assessment, made in the early thirties, is rather extravagant: 'It is this process (mechanization) which completes the technical proletarianization of clerical labour. Just as in industry the former craftsmen were first brought together in the large-scale "factories" of the manufacturing period, before the nature of their work was revolutionized by the advent of modern machinery and they themselves transformed into proletarians in the modern sense, so it is the advent of the office machine, after the establishment of the office factory, which vitally transforms the work of the clerks and finally destroys the former craft basis of their trade.' F. D. Klingender, *The Condition of Clerical Labour in Britain*, 1935, p. 61.

[2] *Red Tape*, October 1956, p. 358.

ventional group of normal office workers who will continue the clerical processes that either cannot easily be made automatic (for instance we need not consider for many years the automatic production of a typed letter from the spoken word), or would take longer to prepare for automatic processing than to complete the job, such as keeping a small petty-cash account. The 'input' group would probably come from the junior staff working on existing clerical procedures, the 'operations' group would comprise the present machine operators, and the 'output' group would consist of senior clerks and junior executives. The 'input' group would be the largest of all. But 'all this, of course, would not happen overnight. It will probably be five to twelve years before there is widespread office automation of the larger concerns, and longer for smaller ones'.[1] The carrying of automation into the smaller concerns largely depends upon the development of cheaper machinery, and on the possibility of 'pooling' more expensive machinery.

## CONCLUSION

Although the above account by no means exhausts the topic, it may safely be asserted that the rationalizing tendencies of modern office administration have by no means completely swept away the personal and particular relationships of the counting-house work environment. The following appear to be the main reasons why this is so. (1) In most fields of blackcoated work the average size of the unit of administration, and the resulting physical concentration of clerical workers, is still small relative to the unit of production. (2) The division of labour inside the office normally tends to separate office workers from each other by department, job grade and status, and to distribute them in small working groups where they are in personal and co-operative contact with management. (3) There is a relative lack of universally accepted criteria for the standardization of clerical skills and qualifications. In other words, the rationalizing influence of a labour market for clerical work has been but weakly developed, though in the case of certain large-scale organizations an alternative rationalization of the work situation has been produced, in varying degrees, by the growth of bureaucratic administration. (4) The intensive mechanization of clerical tasks, though comparable

---

[1] From a report of the speech to the TUC Non-manual Workers' Advisory Council by Mr D. W. Hooper, Chief Organizing Accountant of the National Coal Board. *Transport Salaried Staff Journal*, February 1956. See also, 'Automation. What Is It?' *Red Tape*, October 1956.

in its most advanced form to factory mechanization, has not played a particularly important role in the rationalization of the work situation because its application has so far been narrowly limited by the size of the administrative unit and the nature of clerical work itself.

# CHAPTER FOUR

# THE MODERN OFFICE: STATUS SITUATION

'From the lowly unskilled labourer to the highly skilled artisan and professional worker, the degree of loyalty allies itself to the law of diminishing returns. The higher up the social ladder one moves the less degree of loyalty, worker to worker, is displayed. As a man climbs socially, the more his sense of comfort, selfishness and ego is aroused and accentuated.'

*The Bank Officer*
November 1934

# THE MODERN OFFICE:
## STATUS SITUATION

THE black coat of the mid-nineteenth-century clerk symbolized his middle-class status. The broadcloth he wore was, however, only one mark of his distinction from the working-class man. Running deeper than this sartorial claim to status was the social gulf between the manual worker and the rest. Working with one's hands was associated with other attributes—lack of authority, illiteracy, lowly social origin, insecurity of livelihood—which together spelt social depreciation. The dominant values underlying differences in social worth were those of the entrepreneurial and professional middle classes. The most widely influential criteria of prestige therefore were those which expressed the occupational achievement of the individual. The education required for the job, the rewards and responsibilities it offered, the fact that it was clean and non-manual, and therefore 'respectable', gradually established themselves as the key determinants of a person's social standing over a wide range of the society. The practical result was that the exclusion of the manual wage-earner from middle-class society further intensified the already strong class-conscious feeling that sprang from the experience of the worker in the factory and labour market. In a word, status consciousness inflamed class consciousness, and social distinctions reinforced economic distinctions.

Among blackcoated workers, on the other hand, status consciousness worked rather to dampen any incipient feeling of identification that they might have had with the manual worker. The clerk, less than a master but more than a hand, was poised precariously between the middle and working classes proper. Yet everything in his environment contrived to strengthen his attachment to the sentiments and way of life of the classes above him. His economic position made him forward-looking, striving and individualistic. His working life brought him into close contact with members of the middle class and from them he borrowed the prestige that surrounds authority. The family from which he originated was middle class, if not in substance then at least in spirit. The basic skill of literacy which he possessed set him apart from the working man and gave him a foot-hold on the lowest rung of the middle-class ladder. In all, the pull of the middle-class world was too strong for him to evade. And in any case he was a willing captive.

Yet he was not unequivocally middle class in social terms. He lacked the necessary independence. He lacked the necessary income also in most cases. He was a marginal man; and the frequent accusation of 'snobbishness' levelled at the clerk was founded in his exaggerated assertion of his middle-classness which in turn was a product of his marginality. Because he was insecure socially he sought to maximize the social distance between himself and the class immediately below him. And because this exaggeration jeopardized the very respect which he sought, his insecurity was redoubled. Moreover, the working class had values of its own—masculinity, assertiveness, group loyalty—and against these the clerk very often did not measure up too well. Therefore, just as his natural impulse was to orient himself to the middle class, this very act of identification produced reactions from the working class that reinforced his attachment to the former and his alienation from the latter. Thus, although the status position of the clerk has never been entirely unambiguous, among no other class of the population has the image of status operated so powerfully to inform the behaviour of its members.

The social and economic changes of the present century have made increasingly tenuous the association of blackcoated work with middle-class status and thereby revealed more clearly than ever before the marginal social standing of the clerk. Before turning to the manifestations of this 'status ambiguity' some of the main causative factors behind the declining prestige of blackcoated work may be briefly examined.

## REWARDS AND PRODUCTIVITY

The tie between economic position and social status is a close and obvious one. What is often forgotten, however, is that the relationship is frequently a reciprocal one. Economic advantage does not simply confer social status; in many cases traditional social status is a ground for the perpetuation of economic differences. This has certainly been true of clerical work. The differential in the reward of blackcoated and manual work, which was established in those decades of the counting-house era when literate workers were scarce and manual labour plentiful, gave substance to the general claim of the clerk to a superior social standing. The status and advantage that had been won through scarcity was perpetuated by tradition and proved extremely resistant to change. Indeed, as we have seen, it is only in the last two decades that the rewards of manual labour have gradually overtaken those for clerical labour. And the narrowing monetary differential has been all the more keenly felt because the other principal advantage of blackcoated over manual labour—job-security—has been largely neutralized in a full-employment economy. This change in relative economic advantage is attributable to the enhanced bargaining power of organized labour in a situation of labour scarcity and to the accent on productivity and manual skills in an economy whose balance depends heavily on competition in international markets. Thus the status of clerical labour which had its origin in a phase of economic development in which the bargaining power and scarcity value of manual labour were low has come heavily under fire in a situation where these conditions are reversed.

The result of this change has been a definite fall in the desirability and prestige of clerical work in the eyes of other occupational groups. In a recent survey, in which people were asked to state the job they would like to see their own son take up, professional and skilled manual jobs were most frequently chosen, while clerical work came low down on the list.[1] The attitudes of the manual worker reflect an increased consciousness of his augmented value and status and its obverse—a heightened contempt for the lower non-manual worker. This was well expressed on the occasion of the decision of the National Union of Mineworkers to press for a special investigation into administrative efficiency in the National Coal Board in 1951. 'All miners,' it was said then, 'and some other men and women who earn their living by hard work, under strict rules, feel suspicious, resentful and jealous of those chaps who sit on their you-know-whats in offices, and push pens. The administrators, technicians and clerks recognize this and feel a little nervous, ashamed or defiant about it, according to how their minds works. Actually the clerk is an unskilled labourer under modern conditions, and there is no reason for treating him any differently from any unskilled labourer. Usually the qualifications on which he gets his first job are a good appearance and address, and manners—the qualifications appropriate to a footman or a flunkey.'[2] This type of sentiment is not new in the annals of industrial relations.[3] There has always been a continual guerrilla warfare between these two groups which has simply been intensified

---

[1] F. M. Martin, 'Some Subjective Aspects of Social Stratification', being Chapter III of *Social Mobility in Britain*, edited by D. V. Glass, 1954, p. 69.

[2] *The Bradford News*, organ of the ILP. Quoted in *The Clerk*, September 1951, p. 246.

[3] 'You may not perhaps have realized,' the President of the NUC told the assembled delegates in 1910, 'that clerical work is very generally looked upon as "unskilled" work, not only by employers, but by the skilled artisan as well.' *Annual Report*, 1910, p. 7.

or weakened by the fluctuating level of employment and wages. In general the prestige of non-manual work in the eyes of the manual worker has varied inversely with the security of his own position. Since 1940, the maintenance of full employment, and the value set on output and skill, first in the war years and later in the period of post-war austerity, have provided an occasion for the re-awakening of old jealousies and the questioning of traditional social distinctions. For the most part the revaluation of work and rewards proceeds quietly in a piecemeal manner and is seldom so explicitly argued as in the following extract from a recent submission by the Union of Post Office Workers. 'The wages paid for clerical work,' the report concludes, 'appear to have been related not so much to the value of the work performed, as the social standing of the worker. For many years the wages system appeared to concede that certain classes were entitled to a standard of living as a class. The "working-class" manual workers, general labourers and skilled craftsmen such as engineers, bricklayers, carpenters, etc., appear to have had their wages related to a given standard of living as a "working class" rather than to the productive value of their labour. In more recent years the important place of the manual worker in society has been more widely recognized than hitherto; there has been a trend to give the craftsman and the technician that importance in industry which their value clearly justifies but without a revision of the pay relationship with the "white-collar" class. That the clerical workers have better conditions and higher pay than their operating counterparts is due, in the union's submission, to the policy of paying "white-collar workers" more than other workers, and not to the respective value of the work performed.'[1] Here we have a rare example of manual workers supporting a claim for pay increases by confronting traditional conceptions of social status with new formulations of social worth. The tables are turned on the blackcoated worker. The economic rise of the advance guard of the working class in those industries directly concerned with physical production and exports has already been secured and consolidated to the disadvantage of the clerk, and the new relativities are being interpreted as a revaluation of comparative social standing in terms of which a group of less 'productive' manual workers, who have lagged somewhat behind the general upward movement, can claim an improvement in their economic position.

[1] *Submission by the Union of Post Office Workers to the Royal Commission on the Civil Service*, 1954. See also the interchange between this union and the Civil Service Clerical Association, *Red Tape*, December 1955, and 'Clerical Carping' in *The Post* for January 1954.

The reaction of the non-manual worker poised on the verge of this landslide has varied. The narrowing differentials have not been accepted without considerable resentment and dismay in the black-coated camp. Perhaps the most striking decline in status has been experienced by the bank clerk. Prior to the Second World War he enjoyed a middle-class style of life. Among the conventional necessities of his existence were included not only the sartorial and housing standards of the suburban salariat, but also frequently private education for his children and perhaps even a motor car.[1] In social status he ranked himself fairly high. As one bank clerk saw it: 'The strata of society appear to me to be like this: First of all you have the country squire, with whom the vicar consorts, and the lawyer when it is necessary. Then you get the doctor—perhaps a doctor is on all fours with the lawyer—and just after him the bank clerk, who may, on special occasions, hob-nob at church bazaars and on the village greens.'[2] Since the war the signs of status decline have been too obvious to ignore. 'Not long ago banking was held in very high esteem. It was comparatively easy for anyone so employed to obtain entry into almost all branches of society. In recent years—and particularly in post-war years—this position has changed completely. It has now become customary to ridicule bank staffs both on the stage and in the films, and latterly in the columns of the daily press where, apart from vilified criticism of bank services and charges, the staffs are now categorized as "shop assistants". I believe the fundamental reason for the fall in the bankman's "status" is that he cannot now afford to live up to his pre-war standards, whereas the general standard of living of almost every group of employees has rightly improved in the last few years.During the past twelve years, salaries and wages in almost every industry have levelled income up to, and in some cases beyond that of bank staffs—with consequent loss of respect to the latter.'[3] There is in particular an acute consciousness of disrespect from the working class which occasionally manifests itself as in the following letter: 'A member of the staff of one of the Big Five, being hard up and wanting a quick lunch, went into a workman's café. At his table were two men, obviously manual

---

[1] See the *Bank Officer*, June 1927, p. 30, for examples of the budgets of bank clerks. Also May 1933, p. 9: 'The Council School, however good the education which it provides, is an institution of which few bank clerks will avail themselves save under stress and misgiving.' Also November 1920, p. 10: 'At fifteen years' service a man is usually up against the problem of his children's education. Such a salary leaves to a man's child no option but the Council School. We have no complaint against the curriculum of State education, but it does not pay a bank man to send his children there.'

[2] *Ibid.*, July 1933, p. 10.   [3] *Ibid.*, April 1953, p. 8.

workers. Our banking colleague pricked up his ears when he heard one say to the other—"What's happened to that bank clerk who used to come in here?" "Oh, I believe he got shifted to another branch or something." "Perhaps his manager didn't like him coming in here for his dinner. Make me laugh these bank clerks, all dressed up in their best clothes and haven't two half-pennies to rub together!" '[1]

What is felt by bank clerks is felt to a greater or lesser degree throughout the office-working population. Although in some cases the dismay and resentment of the blackcoated worker has taken on rather a savage form and been directed in an undisguised manner at the trade union movement,[2] the organized sections of the clerical world have on the whole tended to face up to the fact that there is involved here, as one of them put it, 'a necessary reassessment of labour values.' 'You and I,' emphasized the President of NALGO at the 1948 Conference, 'have been brought up in a world which recognized without question the social ascendancy of the white collar over the worker's muffler and its undisputed right to a preferential salary. Have we realized that that world has gone for ever—buried in the avalanche of two catastrophic wars—that the late President Roosevelt's phrase "the age of the common man" is literally true and that, whether we like it or not, it involves a complete revaluation of the worth of human work? The clerk and the collier are being weighed in the scale of social value, and who tips the scale is for us, as the largest union of blackcoat workers, a matter of supreme importance. Stripped of our former privilege, we have to weigh ounce for ounce in the social value of human endeavour, and our reward for clerical

[1] *Ibid.*, December 1954, p. 14.

[2] In a Gallup Poll (1956) roughly one out of every three clerks who were interviewed on the causes of recent strikes and on the policy of the government should take in this situation gave answers which clearly demonstrated their conception of the working class and trade unionism as a threatening and dangerous force which should be repressed. Typical of the answers of this group were the following: 'Stupidity among the strikers—Bring in the Army, do not allow nation to suffer—Ban all strikes for fifteen years—People should be appointed to overcome the strikers—Fight for the narrowing of classes got out of hand—Bring in the Troops—Imprison leaders—Trade Unions too anxious to exploit hold on country—Alter law to make strikes impossible—Stupidity on part of the working masses—Greed—Trample on these strike-mongers and make it a national offence—Organized Labour has become drunk with power and is finding it can press any claim by holding country to ransom.' (From the files of the British Institute of Public Opinion.) See also 'The Unions and the Middle Class', *New Statesman and Nation*, June 9, 1956. These notes of hostility are reminiscent of the blackcoated vision of the working class just before the First World War, vividly described by C. F. G. Masterman in his *Condition of England*, 1909.

work will be measured accordingly—no more and no less.'[1] The cult of productivity in the national interest has gone a long way to replace the cult of a leisured class as a symbol of social worth. The official standard of emulation for the blackcoated worker is now the skilled workman in the export industry, not the rentier in his seaside resort. Productivity has acquired the universal and disinterested appeal of a common norm against which the relative worth of occupations can be measured. Witness the social and economic rise of the miner. But the work of the clerk is not physical and does not seem very productive. 'In these days the understandable emphasis upon productive industry, and its vital importance to the national economy, the non-manual worker is too often disregarded, his role dismissed as that of a non-productive worker because there is no discernible "end product" to his labour.'[2] Nobody appeals to the clerk. If he is mentioned at all it is in connection with a demand to cut overheads and inefficient bureaucracy. In this new struggle for rewards the blackcoated worker is definitely at a disadvantage. But in claiming status he must conform to the rules, he must measure himself up against the new standards of social worth. 'We hear a great deal nowadays about the productive workers in manufacturing industry, and particularly in the export trades, and we are told that without their labours we could not continue to exist. That is true—but it is equally true that without our labours they could not exist. . . . As we are dependent on the productive worker, so he is dependent on us. And as he is entitled to a fair reward for his labours so we are entitled to an adequate recognition of ours.'[3] In this and similar demands we may clearly discern the change in underlying values that has accompanied the narrowing of the differential in the rewards of manual and blackcoated work over the last two decades.[4] And here, as in other situations of social change, there has been an interplay between facts and values. Just as the actual changes in reward have occasioned a revaluation of work, so the new standards of prestige have been used as the basis of further demands for changes in rewards.

[1] *Report* of the Annual Conference of NALGO, 1948, Presidential Address.

[2] President of the National Federation of Professional Workers at the 34th Annual Conference, reported in the *Insurance Guild Journal*, June 1954, p. 115.

[3] President of NALGO in his address to the Annual Conference, 1949, *Report*, p. 21.

[4] 'The Town Hall Young Men Are Producers Too,' *Local Government Service*, June 1952; 'Brain and Brawn,' *The Clerk*, November 1949; 'Look to the Future,' *Red Tape*, June 1955.

## SOCIAL ORIGINS AND INTERMARRIAGE

The social status of an occupation depends in part on the social origins of the individuals who enter it. The fact that an occupation recruits its members from higher social strata of the population is at once an index and a cause of its social standing. It follows that one manifestation of declining social status is the degree to which working-class recruitment to an occupation comes to replace middle-class recruitment. By this measure, too, clerical work has suffered a fall in status.

In the period of the counting house the majority of clerks were recruited from middle-class families—frequently from the homes of clerks themselves—for these were the families which could best provide their sons with the education and respectability necessary for blackcoated work. This was also true of the first women who entered office work in the later decades of the nineteenth century.[1] And as late as 1907 the President of the National Union of Clerks could say that 'as a rule clerks come from the middle class, a class opposed to the principles of trade unionism. In a middle-class family there are two sons, one goes as a clerk, the other as a teacher.'[2] It was increasingly the case, however, that by the turn of the century working-class boys were entering the occupation. They were largely the sons of skilled manual workers, notably the brightest pupils from the elementary schools. 'Where the father is a skilled workman,' ventured Rowntree in 1902, 'his sons will generally be apprenticed to the same or to some other skilled trade. Frequently they become clerks, but are seldom brought up as mere labourers. From the social standpoint "clerking" is looked upon as an advance, but the social prestige thus obtained is sometimes purchased at the cost of diminishing income.'[3] Clerical work not only had prestige, but also, and perhaps this was the more important consideration, security. At any rate, more and more children from the homes of aspiring working-class families found their way into this work. By the first decade of the present century the attractions of clerical work were also drawing 'a large and ever-growing stream of girls from the sources that fed the channels of domestic service, dressmakers' workrooms, and even factories and shop counters'. Not only had the middle-class family discovered respectable employment for its daughters, for now 'the

---

[1] 'Women As Civil Servants,' *The Nineteenth Century*, 1881; 'How Poor Ladies Live,' *ibid.*, 1897.
[2] Sixteenth Annual Conference of the NUC, 1907, *Report*.
[3] B. S. Rowntree, *Poverty, A Study of Town Life*, 1902, p. 72.

half-educated, half-trained and underbred elementary schoolgirl' began to swell the stream of aspirants.[1] By the early thirties Klingender established that one out of every three London clerks under the age of twenty-five came from a working-class family.[2] At the same time in Liverpool it was concluded that 'clerks are very mixed in origin. Many are themselves children of clerks. A few boys and a much larger number of girls come from the professional classes. But the great majority of clerks, the males in particular, are the children of shopkeepers, shop assistants, insurance agents, school teachers, or they come from the skilled and semi-skilled sections of the working class, the latter forming a high percentage of the whole.'[3]

That the growth of the modern office has been accompanied by an increase in the proportion of clerks whose social origin is working class is tolerably clear from the scattered evidence available. What is obscure is the exact degree to which this has occurred. An approximate answer to this question is made possible by data collected in an inquiry undertaken by the Government Social Survey on behalf of the London School of Economics and the Ministry of Labour in 1947.[4] Included in the random sample of adults aged eighteen and over for England and Wales were 708 clerks, namely 214 men and 494 women.[5] Data on the occupations of the fathers, spouses and fathers-in-law of these clerks were abstracted from the original schedules. These facts allow us to form a statistical picture of the

---

[1] M. Moyston Bird, *Women At Work*, 1911, pp. 126–8. Middle-class girls were apparently still preferred, however. One reason was that they were thought to be less likely to permit advances from their male colleagues. 'Those who are anxious to maintain the respectability of their offices,' reports one observer, 'engage girls of a higher social status than their male clerks, as they see the improbability of a "lady" permitting disrespect from men of less breeding than herself.' A. M. Royden, *Downward Paths*, 1916, p. 179.

[2] F. D. Klingender, *The Condition of Clerical Labour in Britain*, 1934, p. 64.

[3] *The Social Survey of Merseyside*, edited by D. Caradog-Jones, 1934, Vol. II, p. 335.

[4] This inquiry is described in detail in Chapter IV of *Social Mobility in Britain*, edited by D. V. Glass, 1954.

[5] The age distribution of this sample of clerks is as follows:

| Age-Group | Males | Females |
|-----------|----------|----------|
| 18–29 | 27% (30) | 46% (57) |
| 30–44 | 36% (35) | 32% (25) |
| 45 plus | 37% (35) | 22% (18) |

The figures in brackets represent the age distribution of clerks in the Census of 1951. The fact that the sample on which the present facts are based shows a distribution in favour of the older worker, especially in the case of women, has to be borne in mind when generalizations are made about the group as a whole.

social origins and marriage patterns of the contemporary clerical labour force. In the tables that follow, the analysis of the material has been carried out in terms of an occupational classification that involves ten elementary categories:

1. Professional occupations, owners of large businesses (employing more than fifty persons), middle and higher management, officers in armed forces.
2. Lower professions, such as teachers, nurses, qualified technicians, etc.
3. Self-employed persons with small businesses. including farmers; also lesser management in shops, offices, etc.
4. Office workers, clerks, shorthand-typists, book-keepers, secretaries, cost clerks, wages clerks, etc.
5. Salesmen and commercial travellers.
6. Shop assistants.
7. Foremen, lower inspectional and supervisory workers in industry, non-commissioned officers in armed forces, policemen, etc.
8. Skilled manual workers.
9. Semi-skilled manual workers.
10. Unskilled manual workers.

In some of the tables, however, it is necessary to use a rather coarser

TABLE XI—MALE CLERICAL WORKERS DISTRIBUTED ACCORDING TO FATHER'S OCCUPATION

*Father's Occupation  Percentage of Male Clerks*

|  | Father's Occupation | Percentage of Male Clerks |
|---|---|---|
| 1. | Professional, etc. | 5·6 |
| 2. | Lower professional | 1·4 |
| 3. | Small business, etc. | 17·3 |
| 4. | Office workers | 10·3 |
| 5. | Salesmen, etc. | 6·1 |
| 6. | Shop assistants | 1·0 |
| 7. | Foremen, etc. | 16·9 |
| 8. | Skilled manual | 29·6 |
| 9. | Semi-skilled | 5·2 |
| 10. | Unskilled | 6·6 |
|  |  | 100·0 |

system of categories in which these occupations are grouped as follows:

| 1 | Upper middle class |
| 2, 3, 4, 5 | Lower middle class |
| 6, 7 | Intermediate group[1] |
| 8, 9, 10 | Working class |

Any such classification is bound to involve a certain degree of arbitrariness. This particular one makes no claim to be a final and authentic portrayal of the social class system. It merely serves the purpose of allowing certain exact relationships to be established that are of interest in the present context.

Taking male clerks first, Table XI shows the proportions of all male clerks who have fathers in the various occupational categories.

The distribution may be shown in rather a different fashion in diagram form, using the broader status classification:

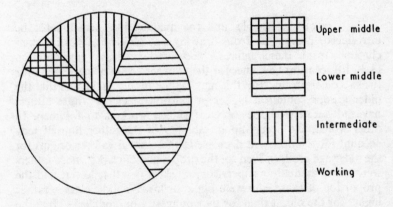

It can be seen that approximately one-third of the clerks hail from lower-middle-class backgrounds, while about 40% have fathers who are working class by occupation. In terms of the exact occupational status of the fathers, clerks are drawn predominantly from the homes of skilled workmen, small self-employed businessmen, foremen (who make up the mass of category 7) and lower office workers. The proportion coming from families whose heads are minor professionals or shop assistants is negligible. The remainder is drawn from the families of professional, sales, semi-skilled and unskilled workers.

Are there any important differences in the social origins of the younger and older clerks? The following table shows the social origins of male clerks in three different age groups.

[1] Cf. John Bonham, *The Middle Class Vote*, 1954, p. 57.

TABLE XII—MALE CLERICAL WORKERS DISTRIBUTED ACCORDING
TO FATHER'S OCCUPATION, BY AGE GROUPS

| Father's Occupation | Age Group | | |
|---|---|---|---|
| | 18–29 | 30–44 | 45 plus |
| | % | % | % |
| 1 | 3 | 4 | 11 |
| 2, 3, 4, 5 | 39 | 32 | 38 |
| 6, 7 | 10 | 20 | 16 |
| 8, 9, 10 | 48 | 44 | 35 |
| | 100 | 100 | 100 |

The size of the sample, and the qualifications which must be introduced, prevent us from drawing anything but tentative conclusions from these figures. The working-class representation (8, 9, 10) seems to be higher for the younger group of clerks than for the two older groups. But this may be due simply to the fact that the older groups contain a higher proportion of clerks whose fathers have advanced from positions of skilled workers to foremen. In other words, the occupational mobility of the father himself may account for the apparent decrease in the manual worker origins for the older age groups. Even so, the proportion of clerks whose fathers were either manual or supervisory workers is rather lower, and the proportion of those who were upper or lower middle class is rather higher for the oldest than for the youngest group of clerks. But the opposite might have been expected. For, if, as seems probable, owing to their superior educational status, the 'middle-class' clerks were more likely to have been promoted out of the clerical grade than the 'working-class' clerks, we should expect to find them forming a smaller proportion of the older age group. Since they form a larger proportion, this may indicate that the clerks entering the occupation up to 1920 were still drawn heavily from 'middle-class' families. It is also conceivable that had clerks under the age of eighteen been included in the survey, the trend towards increased working-class recruitment might have been even more pronounced.

We may now turn to the group of women clerks. In the following table they are divided according to the occupational status of their fathers.

TABLE XIII—FEMALE CLERICAL WORKERS DISTRIBUTED
ACCORDING TO FATHER'S OCCUPATION

| Father's Occupation | Percentage of Female Clerks |
|---|---|
| 1. Professional, etc. | 5·3 |
| 2. Lower professional | 2·2 |
| 3. Small business, etc. | 22·4 |
| 4. Office workers | 10·8 |
| 5. Salesmen, etc. | 2·9 |
| 6. Shop assistants | 1·6 |
| 7. Foremen, etc. | 9·4 |
| 8. Skilled manual workers | 28·9 |
| 9. Semi-skilled manual workers | 7·9 |
| 10. Unskilled manual workers | 8·6 |
| | ——— |
| | 100·0 |

Or, diagrammatically, thus:

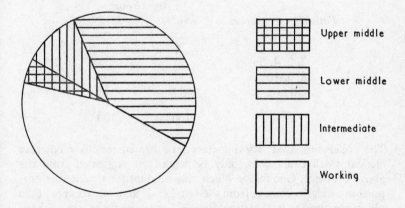

The pattern is almost the same as that for male clerks. Female
clerks derive almost equally from the working and lower middle
classes, with a slight balance in favour of the former group. The
proportion coming from families whose heads were minor professionals or shop assistants is again small.

The following table gives the same kind of distribution for three
age groups.

111

TABLE XIV—FEMALE CLERICAL WORKERS DISTRIBUTED
ACCORDING TO FATHER'S OCCUPATION, BY AGE GROUPS

| | Age Group | | |
|---|---|---|---|
| Father's Occupation | 18–29 | 30–44 | 45 plus |
| | % | % | % |
| 1 | 4 | 4 | 7 |
| 2, 3, 4, 5 | 32 | 44 | 45 |
| 6, 7 | 9 | 14 | 12 |
| 8, 9, 10 | 55 | 38 | 36 |
| | 100 | 100 | 100 |

Here also there seems to be an increase of 'working-class' clerks in the younger age group. This appears even more pronounced if the group 18–29 is further divided:

TABLE XV—FEMALE CLERICAL WORKERS DISTRIBUTED
ACCORDING TO FATHER'S OCCUPATION, BY TWO AGE GROUPS

| | Age Group | |
|---|---|---|
| Father's Occupation | 18–24 | 25–29 |
| | % | % |
| 2, 3, 4, 5 | 27 | 35 |
| 8, 9, 10 | 59 | 49 |
| Other | 14 | 16 |
| | 100 | 100 |

The conclusion that working-class girls are increasingly entering clerical work can, again, only be tentatively suggested from the above evidence. One factor which may account for the smaller proportion of clerks coming from the families of manual workers in the older age groups is that 'middle-class' women clerks are perhaps more likely to return to clerical work after marriage than are 'working-class' clerks, for whom factory work is a real alternative. Until such differences can be investigated, it would be unwise to claim too much for the figures as they stand.

We may conclude that, by the middle of the present century, approximately one out of every two clerks stems from the home of a manual wage-earner; and that if the definition of the working class is extended to include foremen, shop assistants and similar groups this proportion is considerably higher. These facts add precision to our general impressions about the changing social composition of clerical work and lead to the conclusion that in this respect also the social standing of office work has become increasingly marginal in the course of the century. In terms of social origins it is impossible to say that the present-day clerk is typically either working or middle class. As an individual it is equally likely that he is drawn from the higher ranks of the working class or the lower ranks of the middle class.[1]

Apart from social origins, we have a useful index of the social homogeneity or heterogeneity of a group in the degree to which its members marry within or outside the group.[2] How far do clerks marry clerks, and how far do they take spouses whose occupations and social origins are different from their own? The following table sets out the data relating to married male clerks. It shows the proportions of the wives of these clerks who have, or had, middle- or working-class occupations,[3] and the proportions of the fathers-in-law of male clerks who have middle- or working-class occupations.

Fifty-two per cent of the wives of male clerks have occupations which may be called 'middle class'. Predominant among these are office work and the lower professions. Only 28% hold distinctively working-class jobs. The wives of clerical workers seem to be drawn rather more heavily from the homes of 'middle-class' workers, though clearly many are 'working class' in origin, as measured by the occupations of their fathers. If we next divide the married male clerks, according to their origins, into 'middle' and 'working class', the following tables show that 'middle-class' male clerks are more

---

[1] The results of this analysis compare almost exactly with those given by Croner for Sweden in 1944. The group studied by Croner was that of the *Angestellten*, which is an occupational grouping much wider in composition than that of clerical employees as defined in the present work. But, allowing for this difference in terminology, and making the comparison with certain constituent groups, very similar conclusions were reached with regard to the proportions recruited from different strata and the increase in those coming from the working class among the younger office employees. For example, among the *Industrie-Angestellten* 51% of the women and 38% of the men were working class in origin; and among the *Handels-Angestellten*, 40% and 37% respectively. Fritz Croner, *Die Angestellten in der Modernen Gesellschaft*, 1954, Pt. IV, Chapters XIX–XXVI.

[2] J. A. Schumpeter, *Imperialism and Social Classes*, 1951, p. 141.

[3] The figures probably under-represent the actual proportion of wives 'not working', since it is not clear from a certain number of schedules whether the past or present occupation of the wife is recorded. From the present point of view this presents no difficulty, since the aim is not to determine the proportion of wives who are actually working, but rather the kind of jobs they held when working.

TABLE XVI—DISTRIBUTION OF WIVES AND FATHERS-IN-LAW
OF MALE CLERKS ACCORDING TO THEIR
OCCUPATIONAL STATUS

| Occupation of Wife or Father-in-law | Wives % | Fathers-in-law % |
|---|---|---|
| 1, 2, 3, 4, 5 | 52 | 48 |
| 6, 7 | 7 | — |
| 8, 9, 10 | 21 | 40 |
| Domestic service | 7 | — |
| Not at work | 13 | — |
| Unknown | — | 12 |
| | 100 | 100 |

likely to marry women who hold 'middle-class' jobs than are 'working-class' male clerks, although a substantial proportion of the latter do choose wives in 'middle-class' occupations.

TABLE XVII—OCCUPATIONAL STATUS OF WIVES OF
MALE CLERKS WHOSE FATHERS WERE IN
OCCUPATIONAL CATEGORY 2, 3, 4 or 5

| Wife's Occupation | Percentage of Wives of 'Middle-class' Clerks |
|---|---|
| 2, 3, 4, 5 | 65 |
| 8, 9, 10 | 13 |
| Other | 22 |
| | 100 |

TABLE XVIII—OCCUPATIONAL STATUS OF WIVES OF
MALE CLERKS WHOSE FATHERS WERE IN
OCCUPATIONAL CATEGORY 8, 9 or 10

| Wife's Occupation | Percentage of Wives of 'Working-class' Clerks |
|---|---|
| 2, 3, 4, 5 | 45 |
| 8, 9, 10 | 44 |
| Other | 11 |
| | 100 |

The same kind of analysis for women clerks is presented in the following tables.

TABLE XIX—DISTRIBUTION OF HUSBANDS AND
FATHERS-IN-LAW OF FEMALE CLERKS ACCORDING TO
THEIR OCCUPATIONAL STATUS

| *Occupation of Husband or Father-in-law* | *Husbands* | *Fathers-in-law* |
|---|---|---|
| | % | % |
| 1, 2, 3, 4, 5 | 55 | 41 |
| 6, 7 | 9 | 11 |
| 8, 9, 10 | 36 | 39 |
| Unknown | — | 9 |
| | 100 | 100 |

Thus rather more than half of the married women clerks married husbands whose occupational status was 'middle class', although a smaller proportion of the husbands seem to have come from 'middle-class' homes. There is, again, a marked difference in the status of the husbands of female clerks, according to whether the latter come from 'middle-' or 'working'-class homes themselves.

TABLE XX—OCCUPATIONAL STATUS OF HUSBANDS OF
FEMALE CLERKS WHOSE FATHERS WERE IN
OCCUPATIONAL CATEGORIES 2, 3, 4 or 5

| *Husband's Occupation* | *Percentage of Husbands of 'Middle-class' Clerks* |
|---|---|
| 2, 3, 4, 5 | 62 |
| 8, 9, 10 | 20 |
| Other | 18 |
| | 100 |

TABLE XXI—OCCUPATIONAL STATUS OF HUSBANDS OF
FEMALE CLERKS WHOSE FATHERS WERE IN
OCCUPATIONAL CATEGORIES 8, 9 or 10

| *Husband's Occupation* | *Percentage of Husbands of 'Working-class' Clerks* |
|---|---|
| 2, 3, 4, 5 | 35 |
| 8, 9, 10 | 55 |
| Other | 10 |
| | 100 |

On the face of it, women clerks tend to 'marry down' less than they 'marry up' as measured by the occupations of their fathers and husbands. Thus 35% of women clerks who came from 'working-class' homes married 'middle-class' husbands; while only 20% of women clerks from 'middle-class' homes married 'working-class' husbands. We cannot know, however, what proportion of women clerks married 'working-class' men, and then took up 'working-class' jobs themselves. The tentative conclusion that clerical work is an avenue of upward social mobility for women coming from 'working-class' homes, though in accord with general social impressions and studies of the aspirations of school-leavers, is subject to this qualification.

We find, therefore, that in general the spouse of the clerk is quite likely to have come from a working-class family or to hold a working-class job. Clerks as a group are definitely not endogamous. Because of the numerous marriage ties they establish with working-class individuals and families it becomes difficult to draw a clear social division between clerks and manual workers. This evidence, by illustrating another facet of class inter-relationship, may be taken as adding weight to the findings on social origins and to the general thesis of the social marginality of clerical work.[1]

## EDUCATIONAL STATUS

The degree to which formal education played a role in demarcating status groups was very greatly increased by the process of industrialization in the nineteenth century. The relative social standing of clerk and manual worker has its foundations in this development. The demand for competent pen-men in industry, commerce and government rapidly increased with the expansion of the mid-Victorian period. A premium was set on their basic skill of literacy which for several decades gave them a privileged position in relation to other employees.[2] Clerks were largely drawn, as we have seen, from the middle classes who could afford to provide their sons with

[1] With regard to the occupations of the offspring of clerks (information was recorded for the first- and last-born), the numbers involved were quite small, and the results do not deserve to be more than mentioned. It is interesting, however, in the light of what is said below on aspirations, that 74% of the children were employed in occupations 2, 3, 4 and 5 and only 17% in 8, 9 and 10.

[2] Reading ability was much more widespread than that of writing; it is principally with respect to the latter that we speak of the clerk's 'literacy'. See Robert K. Webb, 'Working Class Readers in Early Victorian England', *English Historical Review*, Vol. LXV, 1950, pp. 333–51. Also R. D. Altick, *The English Common Reader*, 1957.

an education and—perhaps equally important—actually secure openings for them in commercial life. In this way the educational status of the clerk was reinforced by its association with social origin and the expectation of upward mobility. It was not until 1870 that this monopoly of literacy was broken by the first national provision for the rudiments of reading and writing to be taught to the masses of working-class children.

The demand for clerical labour was such that the introduction of compulsory elementary education in 1870 did not immediately affect the market for this labour. But by the end of the century signs of over-supply in the clerical labour market were clearly visible. With the oncoming generations came successive waves of potential clerks. It was in this period that the derisive phrase, 'any fool can be a clerk', began to be repeated more frequently, although the social and economic advantages of non-manual work were still not to be despised by the sons of working men. But the clear effect of the change was that certain employers took advantage of the overstocking of the market to bid down the price they paid for the labour of their clerks. 'What is the reason for the low wages and miserable conditions under which the City clerks work?' asked Sir George Kekewich in 1909, 'Why, the overstocking of the market. How are you going to get rid of the overstocking of the market? It is due to that national system of education that we are so abominably proud of. It is a bad system, directed at turning out a nation of clerks.'[1] The pronounced social superiority of the literate over the illiterate was clearly at an end, and what had previously been exceptional now become a commonplace. Of all the blows struck at the status of the black-coated worker this was perhaps the most severe, closely linked as it was with economic disadvantages.

The national system of secondary education inaugurated in 1902 meant, however, that a new distinction in educational status could be drawn, and that employers could tap a new source of more highly qualified labour. From the inception of the grammar-school system until the outbreak of war in 1939 almost half the boys leaving such schools went into minor professional and clerical work, mostly into the latter. Since the end of the war this proportion seems to have fallen considerably, the latest figure being only 26·7% in 1947.[2] On

[1] *The Clerk*, 1909, p. 6.

[2] O. Banks, *Parity and Prestige in English Secondary Education*, 1954. Roughly a quarter of the leavers without two advanced passes in the 1946 intake went into clerical jobs, according to the survey carried out by the Ministry of Education (*Early Leaving*, 1954, p. 85). Of course, the intake to the grammar schools has increased since the inter-war period. If we take the average number of entrants over the years 1927–30 (34,455) and compare it with the average number for

the other hand, the proportion of girls entering commercial occupations from grammar schools has steadily increased over the same period. Nevertheless, those attending grammar schools remained a small proportion of the population. In 1949 only 12% of the adult population had been through such a secondary education. Indeed, one authority has argued that, 'before 1944, only those who attended grammar schools regarded themselves, and were generally accepted as having had, properly speaking, a secondary education at all'.[1] The grammar school was the main gateway to superior blackcoated employment, and it has been suggested that, 'on admission to a secondary school depended a child's chances of leaving the ranks of the wage-earners and obtaining a secure, clean and therefore "respectable" job'.[2] Because a grammar-school education carried, and increasingly carries, considerable prestige, it may be reasonably argued that the clerical worker has been able to maintain a superior educational, and therefore social, status over the manual worker insofar as he has been recruited from such schools rather than from the elementary system of education which has become the property of all. How many clerks have in fact acquired such a superior education?

Fortunately material exists which can provide a fairly clear answer to this question. The following statistics on types of schools attended by clerks are drawn from the data described in the previous section. The occupational categories used are the same as those defined there.

Among the male clerks aged eighteen and over in 1949, less than one out of two had attended a grammar or boarding school. Even so, three times as many clerks enjoyed such an education as did the male population as a whole. Allowing for the higher occupational groups included in the latter category, clerical workers must have had an even greater advantage in this respect than the mass of skilled and unskilled workers. The younger group of male clerks,

1945–8 (47,342) there is an increase of approximately 37%. Against this must be set the fall in leavers going into clerical work of about 14%. Since 40% of the 1927–30 average figure of grammar-school entrants is roughly 13,800 and 27% of the 1945–8 figure is some 12,800, it is fairly clear that the *actual* number of boys going into clerical work from grammar school has certainly not increased, but has in all probability decreased. At the same time, the number of males employed in clerical work has increased by about 6% between 1931 and 1951. This is only crude reckoning, but it would appear that the proportion of male clerks recruited from grammar schools has decreased since before the war.

[1] J. E. Floud, 'The Educational Experience of the Adult Population of England and Wales', being Chapter V of *Social Mobility in Britain*, edited by D. V. Glass, p. 101.
[2] *Ibid.*, p. 105.

TABLE XXII—TYPES OF SECONDARY EDUCATION OF
MALES AGED 18 AND OVER, 1949

|  | Secondary Modern or equivalent | Secondary Grammar | Secondary Boarding |  |
|---|---|---|---|---|
|  | % | % | % |  |
| All male clerks | 58·4 | 38·5 | 3·1 | (100) |
| All males | 85·4 | 12·7 | 1·9 | (100) |

aged eighteen to twenty-nine, seems to be drawn slightly more
heavily from the grammar schools than the group as a whole. But
this is probably partly due to the fact that in the older age groups
those with grammar-school education have been upwardly mobile
out of clerical work more frequently than those without.[1]

TABLE XXIII—TYPES OF SECONDARY EDUCATION
AMONG YOUNGER MALE CLERKS

|  | Secondary Modern | Secondary Grammar | Secondary Boarding |  |
|---|---|---|---|---|
|  | % | % | % |  |
| Male clerks aged 18–19 | 50·0 | 44·5 | 5·5 | (100) |

There are also differences in the chances of clerks having a grammar-
school education according to their social origin, measured in terms
of father's occupation. Of those clerks coming from 'middle-class'
homes twice as many had been to grammar or secondary boarding
school as those from 'working-class' backgrounds.

TABLE XXIV—TYPES OF SECONDARY EDUCATION OF
MALE CLERKS BY SOCIAL ORIGIN

| Father's Occupation[2] | Secondary Modern | Secondary Grammar | Secondary Boarding |  |
|---|---|---|---|---|
|  | % | % | % |  |
| Middle class | 44·3 | 50·6 | 5·1 | (100) |
| Working class | 71·2 | 27·4 | 1·4 | (100) |

[1] This is corroborated by taking the corresponding figure for female clerks,
for whom it is known that there is less possible mobility out of the clerical grades
proper. See Table XXV on the following page.

[2] In this and the following tables, 'middle class' is made up of groups 1, 2, 3, 4
and 5, and working class of groups 8, 9 and 10 as listed on p. 108.

But even among the middle-class group only a bare majority had attended grammar or boarding school. Of the male clerks as a whole, only 22% had taken School Certificates.

Among the female clerks those who had attended a secondary modern school were in a clear majority.

TABLE XXV—TYPES OF SECONDARY EDUCATION OF
FEMALES AGED 18 AND OVER

|  | Secondary Modern | Secondary Grammar | Secondary Boarding | |
| --- | --- | --- | --- | --- |
|  | % | % | % | |
| All females | 85·9 | 11·6 | 2·5 | (100) |
| All female clerks | 64·3 | 32·6 | 3·1 | (100) |
| Female clerks aged 18–29 | 61·5 | 36·8 | 1·7 | (100) |

Female clerks with a middle-class background were more likely to have had a grammar-school or boarding-school education than those with a working-class background, though less often than middle-class male clerks. In all, 14·1% of the female clerks had School Certificates.

TABLE XXVI—TYPES OF SECONDARY EDUCATION OF
FEMALE CLERKS BY SOCIAL ORIGIN

| Father's Occupation | Secondary Modern | Secondary Grammar | Secondary Boarding | |
| --- | --- | --- | --- | --- |
|  | % | % | % | |
| Middle class | 53·6 | 41·3 | 5·1 | (100) |
| Working class | 69·0 | 31·0 | — | (100) |

These statistics give us the distribution of clerks among the different possible educational backgrounds, and to round off the picture we may compare the distribution of clerical workers by the age at which they completed their education with that of other workers.[1]

[1] Census of Population, *One Per Cent Sample Tables*, Part II, 1952, Table VIII, p. 5.

TABLE XXVII—PROPORTION OF PERSONS WHO TERMINATED THEIR EDUCATION AT DIFFERENT AGES, BY OCCUPATION

| Occupation | Age of Terminating Full-time Education | | | | | |
|---|---|---|---|---|---|---|
| | Under 15 | 15 | 16 | 17–19 | 20 plus | |
| (1) *Males* | % | % | % | % | % | |
| All occupations | 76 | 10 | 7 | 4 | 3 | (100) |
| Clerks | 48 | 17 | 22 | 12 | 1 | (100) |
| Skilled manual | 80 | 12 | 6 | 2 | | (100) |
| Unskilled manual | 90 | 7 | 2 | 1 | | (100) |
| (2) *Females* | | | | | | |
| All occupations | 66 | 16 | 9 | 6 | 3 | (100) |
| Clerks | 41 | 26 | 21 | 10 | 2 | (100) |
| Skilled manual | 89 | 8 | 2 | 1 | | (100) |
| Unskilled manual | 85 | 13 | | 2 | | (100) |

Thus, while 92% of skilled manual male workers had left school by age fifteen, some 35% of male clerks stayed at school until sixteen or after. By the age at which the mass of skilled and unskilled manual workers had completed their education, just over one-half of the clerks were still at school. The same pattern appears for female clerks, but in a more pronounced degree. By the age at which almost 90% of skilled and unskilled manual workers had left school, only 41% of female clerks had gone, and of the remainder the greater number stayed on until sixteen years of age or later.

We may conclude, then, that although clerks have lost that monopoly of literacy and education which was their distinguishing mark in the period of the counting house, there are still important differences between clerks and manual workers with respect to the quality and the length of their education. The transformation of such an absolute advantage in educational status into a relative one is a process that has markedly reduced the social status of clerical work. At the same time, however, the recruitment of a considerable proportion of clerks from grammar schools has probably worked in the opposite direction to strengthen the association of clerical work and a superior educational status. As a result, we may say that the changes in education have helped to produce status ambiguity, by making the educational advantages of the clerk over the manual worker less distinct but without completely removing them.

## INTRODUCTION OF WOMEN

One of the most striking features associated with the rise of the modern office is the gradual increase in the proportion of young women employed in clerical work. This change in the sexual composition of the occupation has had its due effect on the social status of that work. Just as the social standing of an occupation is affected by the rewards and opportunities it offers, as well as by the education and social origins of those whom it attracts, so it is also influenced by the age and sex of its members. Age and sex are two generally operative determinants of status within the family and in the society at large, and although their effect on the prestige of office work has perhaps been more subtle than the factors previously discussed, it has been none the less effective.

The counting house was exclusively a male concern. But as early as 1870 this exclusiveness was being broken down by women who were establishing themselves in the civil service and, to a lesser extent, in commercial firms. They were the cause of a certain mild amusement on the part of their male colleagues, but of no real concern. Their work was peripheral to the main activity of the office and they were not competing directly with men. By the turn of the century women were firmly entrenched in certain types of clerical work. In telephonic and telegraphic offices they formed 45% of all employees, in local government 29%, and in the civil service 25%. In commerce they were still a small minority, and in banking, insurance and law there was strong resistance to their employment. But the first inroads had been made, and in the years immediately before the First World War the white-blouse invasion of blackcoated work was well under way. By 1911, one out of every three commercial clerks was a woman, and even one out of ten insurance clerks, although in banks and railways the woman clerk remained an unfamiliar figure. The war added greatly to the change that was going on. One reliable source estimated that some 200,000 women became clerks after the outbreak of war, and many of these stayed on permanently.[1] The inter-war years saw a rapid expansion of clerical work and in this widening market women clerks came into their own. In absolute numbers they increased from approximately 185,000 in 1911 to almost 580,000 in 1931, and by 1951 they numbered over 1,200,000. In 1911, women had formed only 24% of all clerks. By 1951 they outnumbered men by three to two. Between 1921 and 1951 the number of women clerks increased by almost 200%, while the

[1] *The Clerk*, October 1916, p. 130.

corresponding figure for men was only 14%.[1] This steady feminization of the clerical labour force meant that by 1951 clerical work had become one of the women's foremost occupations. One out of every five working women was employed in an office, and one out of every four single working women was a clerk. The woman clerk is moreover a relatively youthful worker. In 1951 some 28% of ordinary clerks and 35% of typists were under the age of twenty as compared with 18% of the female working population as a whole, while, on the other hand, 47% of all women workers were over the age of thirty-five, but only 32% of ordinary clerks and 15% of typists.

What effect has this revolution in the sexual composition of the occupation had on the social status of clerical work? In the first place we must recognize that clerical work was stigmatized as 'unmanly' even before women entered the occupation in large numbers. Although male clerks enjoyed many obvious social and economic advantages over manual workers, their status in terms of social values, such as masculinity, assertiveness and constructiveness, was decidedly low. 'Doing a man's job' had definite prestige value, especially among manual workers who were generally disposed to regard office work as 'soft' and 'cushy' by comparison with their own. This attitude was understood, and even shared by clerks themselves. 'Don't we lose our manhood?' asks the blackcoated hero of an early-twentieth-century novel as he reflects on his job. 'What do we see of real life? What do we know of the world? We're a small breed. We aren't real men. We don't do men's work. Pen-drivers—miserable little pen-drivers—fellows in black-coats, with inky fingers and shiny seats on their trousers—that's what we are. Think of crossing t's and dotting i's all day long.'[2] We find the same attitude in the letter from a clerk who, deploring the secondary and passive nature of his work, speaks of 'this very unmasculine calling', of his colleagues 'born to be men and condemned to be clerks', of their isolation from reality—'He can admire the loftiest buildings he has seen and say, "I never put one brick upon another"; he can watch the superb liner ploughing the high seas and say, "I never touched one with a tarbrush"; and he can witness the engine of an express train and say, "I never touched one with a hammer". But if he says, "I played my part concerning these things; I invoiced so much cement, etc.", one feels more sad still.'[3] Or again, the concern with

---

[1] The statistics for 1921 and 1951 are not strictly comparable because of the changing categories of the respective Censuses. They are only intended to be illustrative of a trend.

[2] S. F. Bullock, *Robert Thorne: London Clerk*, 1907, p. 276.

[3] 'Shall Our Sons Be Clerks?', *The Clerk*, April 1925, p. 51.

masculinity is manifested in the invidious comparison of the clerk's physique with that of the manual worker—'The office slave boasts a waist and slender figure, while the navvy rolls along, a fully developed man of bone and muscle. A young navvy at work is a sight for the gods to envy, the bowed figure of the young clerk at work must make the gods weep.'[1] These are not isolated, but rather recurring and consistent themes. That clerical work is unmasculine and character-debilitating is a universal comment. Even Alfred Marshall, noting the growing tendency of able and thrifty workmen to seek to put their sons into office work, affirms that 'there they are in danger of losing the physical vigour and force of character which attaches to constructive work with the hands, and to become commonplace members of the lower middle classes'.[2] Finally, we may note the extreme sensitivity of the clerk to these charges, and the care with which they are explicitly refuted; by a proud reference, for example, to the way in which clerks have distinguished themselves militarily; or, in a different vein, by the occasional revengeful gloating of some clerk who has helped to break a strike by performing arduous physical labour.

This work which already carried the stigma of being 'unmasculine' was one of the first middle-class occupations to become a feminine preserve of employment. 'Born a man, died a clerk' took on an added social significance as a result. The influx of women merely strengthened the popular stereotype of the clerk and further detracted from the prestige of the occupation. The effect of a high proportion of women in an occupation on the social status of that occupation is a function of the general status of women in society. And here the relationships of sexual inequality within the family have been duplicated in the relationships of sexual inequality in the occupational world. The kinds of work to which women were confined by physical, customary and family limitations were, for the most part, badly paid and poorly regarded. The more the work called for sheer muscular power the less was the threat of female competition; and hence the strong value placed on 'manliness' by such workers. At the other extreme, professional work was generally protected from feminization by the expense and length of training

---

[1] Quoted from the *Newcastle Weekly Chronicle* by *The Clerk*, December 1930, p. 181.

[2] *Principles of Economics*, 1920, p. 310. This attitude still persists. A recent study of secondary modern school boy leavers revealed that clerical work was their least frequent choice, and that they were disposed to regard manual work 'as the only kind of "real" work'. Mary D. Wilson, 'Vocational Preferences of Secondary Modern School Children', *British Journal of Educational Psychology*, June and November, 1953.

necessary for entry as well as by conventional barriers. As a consequence, 'women's work' came to connote work which required neither superior masculine strength nor superior masculine intellect. On both counts its prestige was low. When women began to pour into those jobs which required neither manual strength nor prolonged training—clerical work and elementary-school teaching being the supreme examples—it was wellnigh inevitable that these occupations should suffer a fall in status. This is in fact what happened. The decline in the prestige of office work associated with the influx of women during the early decades of the twentieth century exactly parallels the process observable in the elementary teaching profession at the end of the nineteenth.[1]

Finally, women have largely gone into office jobs that require little skill and carry small responsibility. Their chances of promotion are poor, and as a group they are characterized by relatively high rates of mobility from firm to firm. A large proportion are young, unmarried women and for many of them clerical work is 'just a job like any other' taken up in the interval between leaving school and getting married. It is known that girls are especially attracted to clerical work because of its social status,[2] and also, it may be surmised, because of the opportunity it affords for meeting desirable marriage partners in the blackcoated class. In short, the strictly vocational nature of office work is here very much attenuated. It is a far cry from the blackcoated male careerist of the counting house, whose aspirations and successes helped to confer the substance of prestige on the occupation, to the routine girl clerk or typist of the modern office, whose future status depends less on her own career than on that of the man she ultimately marries.

## STATUS AMBIGUITY

The twentieth century has witnessed the progressive social devaluation of clerical work. Yet it would be a mistake to assume that because the clerk is no longer clearly part of the middle classes he is now indistinguishable from the working class. Strictly speaking the clerk belongs neither to the middle class nor to the working class. In terms of social background, education, working conditions,

[1] 'The increase in the proportion of women in the elementary teaching profession (from 45% in 1862 to 74% in 1900) was both a sign of the low status of the profession and a causal factor in lowering its status further. . . . As more women entered the profession the male teacher tended to be despised for working at a "woman's job".' Asher Tropp, 'Factors Affecting the Status of the School Teacher in England and Wales', *Transactions of the Second World Congress of Sociology*, 1954.     [2] Wilson, *op. cit.*

proximity to authority and opportunity of upward mobility, clerks can still perhaps claim a higher status than most manual workers. In terms of productive contribution, income, skill, masculinity and group loyalty, they may be accorded a lower status, especially by manual workers themselves. To speak of ambiguity of status, then, is to recognize that the prestige of an occupation may be determined by many criteria which are not always entirely consistent with one another. If, as a result, clerical workers are divided among themselves on the question of their proper position in the social hierarchy, then we may speak of status ambiguity. Or if the grounds on which they generally claim a higher status than manual workers are regarded as inadmissible by the latter, so that an expectation of respect is met with contempt, then this again is a sign of status ambiguity. In both senses the social status of clerical work has become increasingly ambiguous.[1]

On the other side of the same coin there is the growing haziness of the middle- and working-class frontier itself as a consequence of the increase in skilled manual and routine non-manual occupations. To be sure, the social centres of gravity of the middle and working classes today are still located in the professional and lesser skilled manual occupations. It is here that the external manifestations of the social differences that go to make up a status order in society are most clearly marked. Differences in speech, dress, age of marriage, family size, interest in education, provision for the future, political outlook, respectability and so on. But in between these two poles the differences are quantitative rather than qualitative. Although the skilled manual worker is generally closer to the working-class pattern in these respects and the blackcoated worker closer to the middle class than either one is to the other, the differences between them are a matter of degree, and there is frequently a good deal of overlap between the 'white-collar proletariat' and the 'working-class bourgeoisie'. This field of status indeterminacy is the background against which the following remarks must be set.

Recent investigations into the phenomena of social ranking have revealed that although clerical workers are generally disposed to claim middle-class status, a substantial degree of uncertainty is displayed in their responses. In 1952 Bonham found that 72% of a sample of office workers of all grades of skill who were asked for

[1] See Michel Crozier, 'L'ambiguïté de la conscience de classe chez les employés et les petits fonctionnaires', *Cahiers Internationaux de Sociologie*, January 1955; also Torgny T. Segerstedt, 'An Investigation of Class Consciousness among Office Employees and Workers in Swedish Factories', *Transactions of the Second World Congress of Sociology*, 1954, Vol. II.

their social class membership replied that they were middle class. Twenty-four per cent claimed working-class status.[1] A similar analysis, made in 1956 by the present writer, revealed an almost identical response, 71% ranking themselves as middle class and 25% as working class.[2] These results are consistent with those of the survey made by Martin which dealt with roughly the same group of occupations, 65% claiming to be middle class and 32% working class.[3] Routine non-manual workers, mostly clerks with low skill and responsibility, showed themselves to be completely divided about their class position. In Greenwich 49% claimed to be middle class and 51% saw themselves as working class, 'poor', or 'lower class'. In Hertford the corresponding proportions were 56% and 38%.[4] From these and similar studies it appears that although the majority of office workers are predisposed to identify their position as middle class, a substantial proportion claim working-class status, and this proportion increases the lower the grade of clerk. These conclusions are strengthened by the estimation of voting behaviour made by Bonham. It is known that there is a close relationship between the self-assigned status of an individual and his propensity to vote for one of the two main political parties.[5] In 1945, 53% of the votes of clerical workers went to the Conservative Party and 47% to Labour. In 1950, the corresponding figures are 61% and 39%; and in 1951, 67% and 33%. Allowing for the general middle-class swing to the Left in 1945, it is reasonable to assume that the distribution of the blackcoated vote represents the same kind of ambiguity in social identification as that to be found in studies of self-ranking. Finally, it may be noted that the overall tendency of the blackcoated worker to visualize himself as middle class is associated with an image of the working class which maximizes the social distance between them. 'Descriptions of the working class as consisting of "dustmen", "roadsweepers", "navvies" and so on—a description which may be said to maximize social distance—are given quite often by subjects who regard themselves as middle class, particularly if they are below the professional level in occupational status.'[6] It needs only

[1] John Bonham, *The Middle Class Vote*, 1954, p. 60.

[2] From the files of the British Institute of Public Opinion.

[3] F. M. Martin, 'Some Subjective Aspects of Status', being Chapter III of *Social Mobility in Britain*, edited by D. V. Glass, 1954, p. 56.

[4] *Ibid.*, p. 54.          [5] Mark Benney *et al.*, *How People Vote*, 1956.

[6] Martin, *op. cit.*, p. 59. It might be expected that the marginal social standing of the non-manual worker would also produce an exaggeration of social distance in the other direction by those clerks who consider themselves working class. This in fact seems to be the case. Those clerks who ranked themselves as working class had high standards for admission to the middle class.

to be added that a desire to maximize social distance may be taken as a good sign of status anxiety.

The middle-class orientation of the clerk is further manifested in two other measurable indices of social status: family size and attitudes towards education. A relatively small family and a strong desire for the educational success of one's children have been the hall-marks of middle-class status since the closing decades of the nineteenth century. Taken together they represent a concern with social mobility through individual achievement, and a conscious discounting of the present against the future. It has been claimed that by the nineteen-twenties clerical workers emerged 'as the class with the lowest fertility',[1] and even if they have not maintained this record to the present day there is very little reason to doubt that a very small family size is a continuing characteristic of this occupational group.[2] There is also evidence which indicates that male clerks tend to marry later than manual workers, again a fact generally associated with small family size; not however in a causal sense but rather as another reflection of the underlying attitudes and aspirations of the individuals concerned.[3] These are the same motives whose operation can be perceived in the educational field. The connection between small family size, the high aspirations of parents for their children, and the high scholastic achievement of the children, is well known.

[1] Richard and Kathleen Titmus, *Parents Revolt*, 1942, p. 80.

[2] The latest statistics on completed family size in different social strata are those to be found in *The Trend and Pattern of Fertility* by D. V. Glass and E. Grebenik, 1954. Clerical workers do not form a separate group in this survey, but are included partly under the heading of 'salaried employees' and partly under 'non-manual wage-earners'.

[3] 'Late age at marriage is not a "cause" of low fertility in the sense of mechanical causation. It is one factor in the complex of social and economic circumstances, opportunities and aspirations which distinguish, say, the professions from unskilled labourers, reflecting rather than causing the differences between them.' Glass and Grebenik, *op. cit.*, p. 7. The preliminary results of an investigation recently conducted by the Population Investigation Committee, London School of Economics, seem to indicate that male clerks tend to marry later than male manual workers. These results are based on a sample of 5,000 marriage certificates drawn from the records of the General Register Office, England and Wales, 1951. Clerks were included with shop assistants as one status group, and this may have tended to obscure the differences between clerks and manual workers. Also, differential age distributions within the occupational groups have not been taken into account. Keeping these qualifications in mind, it was found that among both the lower non-manual and manual male workers 70% of the sample married between the ages of twenty and twenty-nine. However, among manual workers 44% married between the ages of twenty to twenty-four, and only 26% between twenty-five to twenty-nine; while among clerks and shop assistants 35% were married between twenty to twenty-four and 35% between twenty-five to twenty-nine. This information was kindly supplied by Miss G. Rowntree.

With regard to educational aspirations, the clerical worker ranks considerably higher on this index of 'middle-class' identification than the skilled manual worker. Of a sample of clerks who were asked whether they would send their child to a private school if he failed to get into a grammar school, 26% replied in the affirmative as opposed to 7% of skilled manual workers.[1] Again, 59% of clerks desired university or professional education for their children as compared with 23% of skilled manual workers. In this they were even more decided in their ambitions than professional parents, of whom only 45% expressed this desire. The scholastic achievement of the children of clerks is equally marked. According to the statistics given in a recent official report something like 45% of children from this group secure places in grammar schools as opposed to approximately 17% of children from the homes of skilled and semi-skilled manual workers.[2] Inside the grammar school, too, the continuing influence of home background makes itself felt in the differential performance of children from manual and blackcoated families. Nor, as the report points out, have these differences to do 'simply or mainly with differences of income. For example, it would not be easy to say how the incomes of parents in the clerical group compare with those of the skilled and semi-skilled workers respectively. We cannot assume that the differences revealed in the performance of the children in the several occupational groups are primarily attributable to differences in parental income. One of the main influences must be sought in the outlook and assumptions of parents and children in various walks of life.'[3]

With regard to the material concomitants of middle-class status—savings, house-ownership and suburban dwelling—differences between clerks and manual workers are again noticeable, though perhaps less pronounced.[4] This is readily understandable, since here

[1] F. M. Martin, 'An Inquiry Into Parents' Preferences in Secondary Education', being Chapter VII of *Social Mobility in Britain*, edited by D. V. Glass, 1954, pp. 171–2.

[2] Ministry of Education, *Early Leaving*, A Report of the Central Advisory Council for Education, 1954, p. 17. See also the recent study by J. E. Floud, A. H. Halsey and F. M. Martin, *Social Class and Educational Opportunity*, 1956, p. 42. 'The sons of clerks had four or more times as good a chance (of being selected for grammar schools) as the sons of unskilled manual workers, and two to three times the chance of sons of skilled workers' in South-west Hertfordshire and Middlesbrough in 1953.

[3] *Early Leaving*, op. cit., p. 35.

[4] Statistics on house-ownership and savings are given in H. F. Lydall, *British Incomes and Savings*, 1955, pp. 81, 266. Households were differentiated according to the occupation of the head. Thirty-four per cent of the households headed by clerks and sales workers were owned, as opposed to 23% where the head was a

we are dealing with factors more closely determined by income than those discussed above. The aspirations of the clerk to a middle-class style of life have always been severely curtailed by the economic realities of his position, and the changes in income distribution of the last two decades have made it increasingly hard for him to distinguish himself from the mass of skilled and semi-skilled workers in respect of housing and savings. Nevertheless, the differences that are discernible may be interpreted as further evidence of the attitudes whose operation we have already traced in connection with family size and education.

While clerks on the whole tend to identify with the middle classes, manual workers do not seem willing to recognize that the black-coated worker has a claim to a higher social status than their own.[1] Indeed, a substantial proportion of workers seem radically to devalue lower non-manual work on the ground of its low contribution to social welfare.[2] But such responses do not necessarily mean that the working man is disposed to identify with office workers in a class-conscious sense even though he will not rank them socially higher than himself. The refusal of respect is not at all the same thing as class solidarity. On the contrary, whatever sense of class division between clerks and manual workers is produced by the structure of industrial and administrative relations is certainly aggravated rather than mollified by the status ambiguity of clerical work and the discrepancy in its ranking by the two groups. Martin found that in the eyes of the working class there was a genuine decline in the prestige of lower non-manual work, 'rather subtly coloured by a slightly resentful attitude, which, in the course of the interview, found expression in occasional spontaneous exclamations such as: "They're no better than we are!" '[3] Zweig emphasizes that the working-class

skilled manual worker, and 15% where the head was an unskilled manual worker. As regards savings, the data were based on the occupations of the heads of 'income units', that is, 'single persons of eighteen and over, and married couples'. By this measure, the mean liquid assets of clerks and sales workers was £191 as opposed to £150 for skilled, and £134 for unskilled manual workers. However, while 40% of the heads of income-units in the clerical and sales group were women, women formed only 7% of the total of the skilled manual group and 24% of the unskilled manual group. It is reasonable to suppose that if males only had been compared, the differences between the non-manual and manual groups would have been greater. Finally, detailed information on the dwelling areas of clerks and manual workers in the Greater London Conurbation for the years 1921 and 1951 is to be found in Appendix B of the present volume.

[1] Martin, *op. cit.*, pp. 61, 64.

[2] Michael Young and Peter Willmott, 'Social Grading by Manual Workers', *British Journal of Sociology*, December 1956.

[3] Martin, *op. cit.*, p. 64.

man rather dislikes the middle class, 'especially its lower stratum with which he often comes into contact. People of the lower middle class often snub him, regard themselves as superior to him, take away his money in the shops, or order him about in offices.'[1] In short, when the working man says of the office worker that 'he is no better than us', he by no means implies that 'he is one of us'.

This is a rather important point, because there are many indications that the division between manual and non-manual work is still a factor of enduring significance in the determination of class consciousness, despite changes in the relative economic position of the two groups. The differences between office and factory work are not merely technical, but social, and although some of them may seem trivial by any rational accounting, they are not negligible in the social relations of industry.[2] 'Being dressed up to go to work', 'sitting down to work', 'having it cushy', 'pushing pens', 'being bosses' men', 'being one of "them" up "there" ', from whom orders come and authority emanates, are terms which working men frequently use of office workers, irrespective of their actual positions in the office hierarchy, and even of their own members once they are promoted out of the workshop. As Burns has put it, 'the line between management and the worker, the widest social barrier, is so drawn that it includes in management all but the rank-and-file workman. To succeed occupationally is to abdicate from the working class'.[3] This is not a difference that is necessarily lessened by a decline in the economic status of clerical workers. It is a result of the structure of industrial organization and especially of the relations of authority in the enterprise. In other spheres, too, in labour exchanges, in local

[1] F. Zweig, *The British Worker*, 1952, p. 206.

[2] The social significance of the distinction between 'office' and 'works' is missed for example in the note of incomprehension registered in the Report of the *Unemployment Insurance Statutory Committee on the Remuneration Limit for Insurance of Non-Manual Workers*, 1936, p. 7, where it is recorded that 'the typist who strikes the keys of a typewriter, or a comptometer who strikes the keys of a calculating machine, are held to be non-manual, while a compositor striking the keys of a linotype or monotype machine is held to be manual'.

[3] Tom Burns, 'The Cold Class War', *New Statesman and Nation*, April 7, 1956. There is also evidence that the working-class boy who succeeds academically and takes a clerical job might be rejected as much as rejecting, not only by the barrier of traditional working-class culture and the frontier of industrial organization, but also conceivably by his own family. See, for example, the letter 'Bank Clerk Lucky Jim', in the *New Statesman and Nation*, July 28, 1956, written by a clerk who protests that, 'In my case, none of my many relatives went to a grammar school, they are all working class, all earn more than I do, and they pity me in my white collar. They all tell me I am middle class now, so how can I be a Socialist . . . many of us, far from trying to become "middle-class", feel that we have been taken from our friends by our nonsensical social system.'

government, and so on, the clerk is the man on the other side of the desk who is somehow associated with authority.[1]

Thus, despite the status indistinction of the middle- and working-class frontier there exist powerful and enduring features of the work situation of clerks and manual workers which prevent full class identification from either side. The difference between the two groups is nowadays not so much a matter of clear-cut status distinction as one of sheer social distance. As Centers has put it, the fact that a person is a blackcoated worker is not so much a reason for putting him in the middle class as it is a reason for not putting him in the working class.[2] Of course, the very existence of distinctions invites evaluation, so that a sense of difference readily passes over into one of superiority or inferiority. And along the division between manual and non-manual work there has been no lack of competition for status. One of the most interesting problems of the immediate future is whether this division is one that is built on traditional social values which will slowly 'wither away', or whether it is more basically derived from the social relations of modern industry and is, therefore, not so much supported by estimations of social worth already disappearing as by the inescapable conditions of daily existence. However this may be, it is tolerably clear that at the present time invidious comparisons of status across the manual/non-manual divide continue to exacerbate whatever sense of class separation is already there.

## CONCLUSION

Changes in the values underlying the relative prestige of occupations are not susceptible of exact analysis. Established values may persist after the conditions which gave rise to them have altered, there may be more or less consensus about what is really important in drawing social distinctions, and there may be greater or lesser consistency between the various criteria involved. In the case of clerks we have tried to show how their original claim to middle-

---

[1] Merton has pointed out how the clerk, 'in part irrespective of his position within the hierarchy, acts as a representative of the power and . . . prestige of the entire structure. In his official role, he is vested with definite authority. This often leads to an actual or apparent domineering attitude, which may only be exaggerated by a discrepancy between his position within the hierarchy and his position with reference to the public.' Robert K. Merton, 'Bureaucratic Structure and Personality', *Social Forces*, Vol. XVIII, 1940.

[2] R. Centers, *The Psychology of Social Classes: A Study in Class Consciousness*, 1949, p. 101.

class status has been slowly undermined during the rise of the modern office. The growth of universal literacy, the recruitment of clerks from lower social strata, the gradual transformation of office work into predominantly 'women's work', and the increased emphasis laid on productive contribution, have all adversely affected the prestige of blackcoated work. And yet we are forced to recognize that not being middle class is not identical with being working class. In certain socially relevant respects the clerk continues to be distinguished from the manual wage-earner. There is, as a consequence, a good deal of disagreement about the relative standing of manual and clerical work at the present time, depending on which differences are stressed or ignored. This 'status ambiguity' in turn presents one of the most important obstacles to the mutual identification of clerk and manual worker.

# CHAPTER FIVE

# TRADE UNIONISM

'The idea that everybody who "looks nice and dressy" is a snob and lacking in class consciousness is neither in accord with logic nor facts. Some individuals give one the impression that to be "advanced thinkers" and class conscious, one must wear a dirty collar, shabby clothes and a general air of slovenliness.'

*The Railway Clerk,*
October 1917

# TRADE UNIONISM

## UNIONIZATION AND CLASS CONSCIOUSNESS

EARLIER chapters have been concerned with the principal changes in the social and economic position of the blackcoated worker during the period of the modern office. Deliberate emphasis has been placed on those aspects of his life situation which have a bearing on the class identification of the clerk. It is now time to look at the question of blackcoated unionism, to seek the conditions affecting its growth, and to try to determine how far such concerted action exhibits a class-conscious character.

It is important to realize from the beginning that action in concert, while obviously an expression of group consciousness, is not necessarily an expression of class consciousness. There is no inevitable connection between unionization and class consciousness. A high degree of unionization and a high degree of class consciousness may go together; but so may a high degree of unionization and a low degree of class consciousness. The conditions making for concerted action among the members of an occupational group and those making for class consciousness are not identical. Concerted action is a function of the recognition by the members of the occupational group that they have interests in common; class consciousness entails the further realization that certain of those interests are also shared by other groups of employees.

In the case of blackcoated workers, class consciousness may be said to emerge when the members of a clerical association realize, first, that their common interests are engendered by the conflict of interest between employer and employee, and secondly, that their common interests are not fundamentally dissimilar in type from those underlying the concerted actions of manual workers. The trade-union movement is a working-class movement, and to the extent that clerical workers become involved in trade unionism they have to come to terms with its wider class character. Although there can be no accurate measurement of the class consciousness of blackcoated unionism, it can be traced in a variety of indirect ways: by a change in the name and purposes of a clerical association, as when a friendly society is transformed into a genuine trade union; by the adoption and use of certain types of sanctions, such as strike action, for the attainment of its goals; by the affiliation of the association

137

to the wider trade-union movement; by its identification with the political wing of the Labour Movement; by sympathetic behaviour in critical 'class' situations, such as the General Strike; as well as by the general social and political outlook of the membership and leaders of the association. It is in terms of such indices that the character of blackcoated unionism will be discussed here. First of all, however, it is necessary to determine the factors affecting the degree of unionization in different clerical fields.

## THE DEGREE OF BLACKCOATED UNIONIZATION

Nowadays, about one out of every four clerks belongs to some kind of trade union. In 1951 the five largest clerical trade unions had a combined membership in the neighbourhood of 450,000. As can be seen from the accompanying diagram, some 34% of the total was to be found in the Civil Service Clerical Association, 29% in the National and Local Government Officers Association, 20% in the Transport Salaried Staffs Association, 9% in the Clerical and Administrative Workers' Union, and 8% in the National Union of Bank Employees.[1] More interesting than the overall degree of unionization is the variation in different fields of blackcoated employment. While 80% and upwards of local government, civil service and railway clerks were organized, the National Union of Bank Employees contained only 35% of bank clerks, and the Clerical and Administrative Workers' Union less than 5% of industrial and commercial clerks. It is with this variation in the degree of blackcoated unionization that the following discussion is primarily concerned.

## FACTORS AFFECTING THE DEGREE OF UNIONIZATION

Clerical unionization shows great variations, and it cannot be assumed that these variations are purely random. What then is their explanation? Why are clerks in one industry unionized almost to saturation point while in another only 10% of the total potential membership is organized? There is, of course, no simple answer. The actual degree of unionization in any group at a particular point of time is the result of a variety of factors, many of them peculiar

[1] These exact percentages are only crude approximations because of the difficulty of estimating the clerical membership of NALGO which includes other grades of non-manual workers. A further considerable proportion of industrial clerks, some 30,000, was organized in the Transport and General Workers' Union.

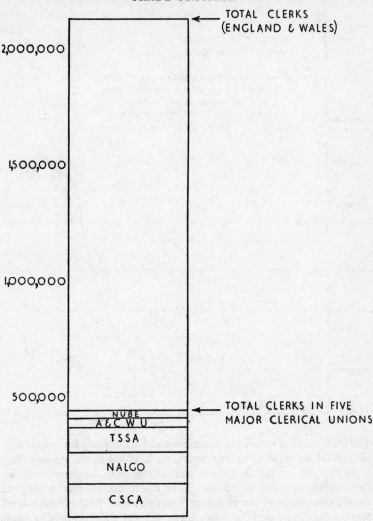

STATE OF CLERICAL UNIONIZATION
1951

to the group in question. For example, the growth curve of the Rail-way Clerks Association during the inter-war period was affected by the reduction in the numbers of railway salaried staffs, and the upswing of local government officer recruitment in the early twenties was affected by the passage of the Superannuation Act of 1922.

139

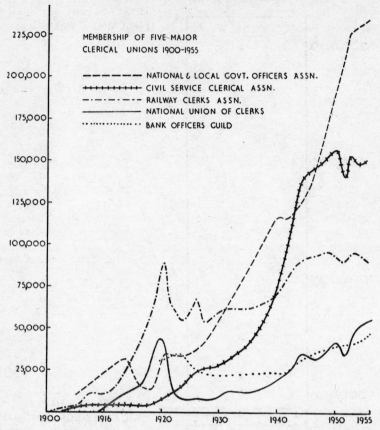

MEMBERSHIP OF FIVE MAJOR
CLERICAL UNIONS 1900-1955

— — — — — NATIONAL & LOCAL GOVT. OFFICERS ASSN.
+++++++++ CIVIL SERVICE CLERICAL ASSN.
—·—·—·— RAILWAY CLERKS ASSN.
——————— NATIONAL UNION OF CLERKS
················ BANK OFFICERS GUILD

These facts are of interest in describing and accounting for the growth of individual unions. In this sense, each union is *sui generis*. But since the present task is a comparative one, only the general conditions influencing union growth will be discussed. Insofar as the preceding discussion of the changing 'class position' of the blackcoated worker has been well founded, these general conditions have been isolated. It remains to ask how they are related to the observable variations in the degree of clerical unionism.

Is there any set of conditions generally associated with a high degree of blackcoated unionization, and does the absence of these conditions likewise explain a low degree of unionization? If such factors exist it is fairly obvious that they must be those which promote a sense of common identity among the members of a group. For concerted action ultimately depends on the awareness of the individuals concerned that they have interests in common, and therefore that they belong together. Short of this, collective action is ephemeral, sporadic, lacking in solidarity, founded on immediate and specific interests.

It would not be straining the facts excessively to argue that the unionization of blackcoated workers has been very closely associated with what may be called 'bureaucratization'. By the latter is simply meant the process by which bureaucratic rules come to predominate in administrative organization. The chief characteristics of bureaucratic organizations have already been detailed in connection with the work situation of clerks. The relevance of those characteristics to unionization is best to be understood by contrasting bureaucratic with paternalistic office administration. Paternalistic administration is usually associated with small office size, though certain of its characteristics can be produced in large-scale organizations. Basically, we may speak of paternalism in a field of clerical employment insofar as working conditions—functions, qualifications, remuneration, promotion, pensions—are determined by the personal relations of employers and clerks. One major consequence of this situation is the lack of uniformity in working conditions throughout the field of employment; that is, administrative particularism. The extreme case of paternalism is that of the counting house, where the clerks in an industry are scattered among a multitude of small, private firms. At the other pole, bureaucratic organization exists insofar as working conditions are regulated by impersonal rules which strictly exclude all forms of personal consideration between employer and clerk. To the degree that a field of employment is subject to such bureaucratic rules administrative particularism will be replaced by the standardization of working conditions. Bureaucratization is naturally greatest where an industry is brought under the central and unitary control of one employer. But between this extreme case, on the one hand, and complete paternalism on the other, there may be a whole range of mixed, intermediate stages, in which elements of both types of organization are to be found.

One further aspect of bureaucratic organization that is of consequence for unionization is the degree to which there is a blockage of upward mobility for clerical staffs. The rigid classification of functions usually leads to a clear division between 'clerical' and 'managerial' posts, and the establishment of explicit criteria for promotion from one to the other. By contrast with paternalistic administration, the process of 'fitting the job to the man', and the arbitrary distinctions which this entails, are reduced to a minimum, if not in theory dispensed with altogether. While the blockage of upward mobility

141

for clerical staffs is not necessarily associated with these conditions, such blockage may occur for the following reasons. In the first place, there may be direct recruitment to managerial positions from outside, and a consequent curtailment of internal recruitment from below. Secondly, the economies of administrative rationalization may lead to a reduction in the ratio of managerial to clerical functions. This might be expected to occur, for example, as the result of an amalgamation of several small, private concerns into a few, large-scale organizations. In varying degrees, therefore, bureaucratization is conducive to the blockage of clerical promotion and to the isolation of a separate clerical class.

Thus defined, bureaucratization represents a set of conditions extremely favourable to the growth of collective action among clerical workers. It is not too much to argue that in fostering black-coated solidarity bureaucratization has played a role analogous to that of the factory and labour market in the case of manual workers. The relationship has not been entirely one-sided. Just as bureaucratization provides fertile ground for unionization, so unionization, once established, leads to further bureaucratization by its demands for uniformity of working conditions. Bureaucratization and unionization have, to borrow a phrase from Myrdal, been 'mutually cumulative' in their effects.[1]

The civil service on the one hand, and private industry and commerce on the other, provide the two limiting cases by which the above principles can be illustrated.[2] In the civil service, especially after the reorganization of 1920, there has been a close approximation to the pure bureaucratic model of administration. A clear-cut classification

[1] Gunnar Myrdal, *An American Dilemma*, 1944, Appendix 3, 'A Methodological Note on the Principle of Cumulation'.

[2] Nationalization has provided some examples of the basic changes involved in the transition from private industrial to 'civil-service' administration, one of which—road haulage—has been described by J. H. Smith, 'The Rise of a Bureaucracy', *Transactions of the Third World Congress of Sociology*, 1956, Vol. II, pp. 64–5. He writes: 'The absence of any hierarchical system of administrative and clerical grades, with a corresponding salary scale, did not long persist in the new bureaucracy. Within two years of nationalization an elaborate grading system had been established, in which status was determined by the nature of the work and the position in the management hierarchy. Districts required more high-grade positions than groups, and so on. Personal considerations were firmly excluded. "It must be stressed," said the Executive in a statement of policy, "that *posts* are being classified and that the quality as distinct from the quantity of work arising from the duties of the post will be the determining factor . . . fitness for promotion in the absence of a suitable vacancy will not warrant regrading." Such practices were in marked contrast to most experiences of private ownership, when a clerk's salary depended wholly on his personal relations with the owner.'

of functions, qualifications, remuneration and criteria of advancement permitted a high degree of standardization of conditions throughout government departments. In particular, the resulting isolation of a clerical class, common to the service and made up of individuals whose chances of promotion were relatively small, provided the basis for the Civil Service Clerical Association, which assimilated into itself the hitherto splintered clerical associations.[1] By striking contrast with this administrative centralization and *Gleichschaltung*, industrial and commercial clerks have been scattered among a great number of private firms among which administrative particularism has been the rule. In the majority of these firms the degree of office rationalization has been low, and many of the paternalistic relationships of the counting house have persisted. In particular, the lack of a rigid division between 'clerical' and 'managerial' grades has not resulted in the explicit blockage of mobility for the clerical group which has been typical of the civil service.[2] Between the private firms there has, in addition, been little or no standardization of clerical functions or qualifications. Nor has this standardization been effected by the growth of a labour market for clerical labour. Under such conditions a sense of common identity among clerks is attenuated, and the progress of unionization is inevitably retarded.

In this context it is useful to compare the unionization of industrial and commercial clerks with that of local government clerks. At first sight the difficulties of organization appear to have been equally great. Not only were local government officers dispersed among some two thousand local authorities, but their conditions of work had little uniformity, the 'cockpit of local politics' strongly fostering local particularism. Yet in the course of the present century the National and Local Government Officers Association has emerged as the largest, and one of the most influential, unions of blackcoated workers. Side by side with the growth of NALGO, and in the main due to its efforts, there has been gradually established a bureaucratic framework for local government administration. This process culminated in the National Charter of 1946 which laid down the basic clerical and administrative grades common to local government authorities throughout the country. In the light of these facts it may

[1] B. V. Humphreys, *The Development of Clerical Trade Unions in the British Civil Service*, unpublished PhD thesis, University of London, 1954.
[2] From the point of view of unionization, the fact that upward mobility is institutionally regulated for the clerical class as a whole, as it is in the civil service, is probably just as important as the actual amount of mobility that takes place. The point is that for the commercial clerk there is no such explicit limitation of his 'chances'.

seem that the hypothesis that bureaucratization provides the basis for blackcoated unionization is falsified, and that NALGO advanced in spite of, rather than because of, the conditions of local government work.

There can be little doubt that the sense of common identity among local government employees was much less developed than that of civil-service clerks. Yet, despite local particularism, they formed a much more coherent group than industrial and commercial clerks. Despite their varying conditions of service they were all members of local government administration, and this sense of community of interest was especially strong among the senior officials and professionals who played a leading role in the formation of the association.[1] Objectively, the possibilities of uniformity were there, in the sense that local government functions were broadly comparable from one locality to another, although autonomous councils had produced a bewildering variety of actual working conditions. If there was local particularism it was much more tractable than the particularism to be found in private industrial and commercial firms. The achievement of superannuation in 1922 proved that for some purposes at least local government service could be treated as a whole. During the first flush of Whitleyism the establishment of national salary scales for local government officers was actually considered. And even after the collapse of the National Whitley Council for Local Government in 1921, work continued on making local scales comparable. In 1924 it was claimed that 'a few years ago there was not the slightest semblance of uniformity in the basic rates of remuneration of the staffs of local authorities. The position today is vastly different. A considerable number of local authorities have adopted the Association's scale of salaries, or a modified form which does not disturb the principle.'[2] Moreover, the provincial Whitley Councils survived in certain areas, notably in Lancashire, the West Riding and North Wales. Where Whitleyism prevailed, and some kind of uniformity was present, NALGO membership was high.[3] The view that standardization of working conditions was necessary and practical was voiced in an official report of 1934. 'We should like to see broadly

[1] NALGO has never been a strictly clerical union. The role played by senior local government officials gave it a 'respectable' tone from the beginning. This was different in other clerical unions where senior officials and management have usually been outside and often hostile.

[2] *Local Government Service*, 1924, p. 1.

[3] In 1935, the Lancashire and Cheshire Whitley Council scales had been applied to 24,000 officers, or 90% of the total in the Area. In 1936, this particular council, together with North Wales, represented over 20% of the total membership of NALGO. NALGO Annual Conference, *Report*, 1935, 1936.

similar staff grades in force throughout the local government service. This would knit together the service in a way calculated to increase its attractiveness to recruits, and to facilitate the movement of officers between local authorities. We recognize that there must be local variations due to the different size and functions of local authorities, but apart from this difficulty we see no reason why the grades of different authorities should not be, at any rate, comparable. This has already been achieved to some extent, especially in the Areas of the three Provincial Whitley Councils.'[1] Ten more years were to elapse, however, before this ultimate aim of uniformity would be realized.

When the national standard finally came after the Second World War, it was the end-product of a slow and steady evolution that had been in progress since the end of the first. It was during this same span of time that the membership of NALGO rapidly increased. The total membership in 1939 was four times greater than it had been fourteen years previously. More significantly, the absolute growth reflected in large measure a rapid increase in unionization of the total membership potential. By 1951 some 90% of all local government clerks belonged to the union, whereas thirty years earlier the figure had been only 34%.[2] The growth of NALGO, therefore, has gone hand in hand with the subordination of local particularism in working conditions to a set of national standards common to the service.

The experience of NALGO gains significance if it is set against that of the Clerical and Administrative Workers' Union, the major clerical union in industry and commerce. Of a total membership potential which cannot be less than a million the union has organized not more than about 5%. The condition of clerical labour in this field has presented an immensely more difficult problem to unionization than that of local government service. The CAWU has not only had to contend with the fact that clerical conditions varied firm by firm within the same industry, but also with the additional obstacle of industrial variation in working conditions. Given these circumstances, the union was faced with a huge potential membership which had next to nothing in common, except that all of them were 'clerks', and even that was a highly ambiguous common denominator. The possibility of making a general appeal to clerks as a body that would cut across this kind of particularism was extremely limited.

The actual composition of CAWU membership and the policy pursued by the union clearly reflect the abnormal difficulty of organiza-

---

[1] *Report* to the Minister of Health by the Departmental Committee on Qualifications, Recruitment, Training and Promotion of Local Government Officers, 1934, p. 35.　　[2] NALGO Annual Conference, *Report*, 1951, para. 58.

tion among a membership with little sense of corporate identity.[1] Recruitment was necessarily adventitious and opportunistic. Particular groups of clerks whose employers were favourable to unionization formed the core of the membership. Headway was also made in fields where powerful manual workers' unions were operating. But the policy of promoting standard working conditions for clerks throughout the field, the very policy adopted by NALGO, met with little success for obvious reasons. The opportunity afforded by Whitleyism was not exploited, partly because the union had insufficient membership, but also partly because the attitude of the union towards Whitleyism was, to say the least, lukewarm.[2] The mass of the membership was, for a long time, formed by clerks working in the cocoa trades, where there was a progressive Quaker management which encouraged union activity, and in the offices of trade unions, friendly and co-operative societies.[3] In addition, colliery clerks were

[1] The high rate of lapsing members is one indication of this. During the four years ending December 1947 the membership of the union increased by 1,625. But this increase involved the recruitment of 58,098 new members, because during this period the total number of lapses was no less than 56,473. Granted that this took place during the last two years of war and the first two post-war years, it still represents an incredibly high rate of turnover. One of the main reasons for lapsing is the 'penny-in-the-slot' attitude to unionism. This in turn reflects the personal and individualistic interests of the members. A sense of corporate solidarity among the membership of an association demands something more, namely, impersonal and collective interests, which again only emerge if there is a sufficient degree of uniformity in the working conditions of the group. *The Clerk*, 1949, p. 1.                                  [2] *The Clerk*, 1919, p. 76.

[3] In 1922, the Food, Drink, Tobacco and Allied Guild and the Industrial, Political and Friendly Societies Guild formed 43% of the total membership of the Union. A large proportion of these Guild members were drawn from the chocolate trades—Frys, Rowntrees and Cadburys—which were highly organized, or from Co-operative Society and Trade Union staffs. *The Clerk*, 1923, p. 104. During the collapse of the membership between 1922 and 1931 these members, in contradistinction to the rest, remained extremely stable, as the table shows:

| Guild | 1922 | 1925 | 1928 | 1931 |
|---|---|---|---|---|
| Food, Drink, Tobacco and Allied Trades | 3,550 | 3,536 | 3,295 | 3,421 |
| Industrial, Political and Friendly Societies Staffs | 1,022 | 1,254 | 1,113 | 1,078 |
| Printing and Kindred Trades | 499 | 205 | 849 | 746 |
| Building and Furnishing | 181 | 105 | 60 | |
| Engineering, Shipbuilding and Metal Trades | 2,328 | 779 | 537 | |
| Mining and Quarrying | 430 | 132 | 48 | 2,237 |
| Public Services | 1,206 | 556 | 425 | |
| General Guild | 1,484 | 1,043 | 1,077 | |
| | 10,700 | 7,610 | 7,404 | 7,532 |

Source: Annual *Reports* of the NUC for the years specified.

recruited to some extent by the union, especially in those areas where the mineworkers' union was pressing for overall coverage of workers.[1] A certain number of clerks in the engineering industry, particularly those who work in contact with manual workers, have been organized, but taken as a whole engineering still forms an undeveloped area so far as clerical unionism is concerned.[2] Since the Second World War the hold of the union has been strengthened in the mining, electricity and transport industries as a consequence of nationalization.

While the working conditions in commerce and industry have been just as unfavourable to clerical unionization as those in the civil service provided an ideal setting, the position of the bank clerk provides an interesting example of an intermediate stage. The general depersonalization of relations that followed the large-scale amalgamations in banking was a potent factor in the initial success of the Bank Officers' Guild after the First World War.[3] This point was emphasized quite clearly in the early issues of the union's journal. 'The elimination of that element of personal intercourse between bank servant and his employer, which has such fine possibilities and which was justly esteemed by both', was seen as a direct result of the reorganization typical of bureaucratization. 'In a word, the system is dehumanized.'[4] The change in the nature of the working relationship was held to be as much responsible for unionization as the question of salaries. 'Bankmen have grievances. Salaries are a burning question with them in these times of high prices, from which there is little hope of reduction at present; but unhesitatingly we affirm, from a close and extensive knowledge of the bankman and his point of view, that it is the grim factor of cold, impersonal treatment that hurts him most of all. It cuts across his manhood, and he feels that he is being ground down to a contemptible part in a soulless mechanism. It used to be the proud boast of a general manager in the old days that he knew every man in his service down to the junior clerk, and to many he was guide, philosopher and friend. This cannot be today, and we do not yearn for the impossible, for we

---

[1] In South Wales in 1943 the Union was 'fast approaching the 100% target. Our members were conscious of the fact that each of the four (largest) companies were operating an agreement between the Monmouthshire and South Wales Coal Owners Association and the South Wales Miners' Federation for 100% trade union membership amongst all grades of workers covered by the Federation'. *The Clerk*, 1943, p. 7.

[2] See 'Clerk or Labourer?', *The Clerk*, 1949, p. 8.

[3] Founded in 1918, the Bank Officers' Guild had one out of every two bank clerks in its ranks three years later. This is still roughly the proportion unionized today. [4] *The Bank Officer*, August 1919, p. 3.

recognize much merit in the economy of the big corporation; but we deplore the soullessness of much of the relations between the higher official and the rank and file.'[1]

The passing of the paternalistic work situation of the counting house and its replacement by the more highly standardized relationships of bureaucratic organization did not mean, however, that paternalism and particularism in banking were completely swept away. In the first place, there was no blockage of upward mobility for the bank clerk comparable with that institutionalized in the civil service, and this factor undoubtedly retarded unionization.[2] Secondly, between the major banking houses themselves differences in working conditions persisted. Salary scales were not identical, clerks could not move freely from one bank to another, the banks did not act in concert *vis à vis* their employees, and they encouraged particular loyalties, especially in the form of 'internal' staff associations. The resulting lack of uniformity in conditions went a long way to vitiate the efforts of the Bank Officers' Guild as a union for all bank employees. The lack of full community of interest between bank clerks may be traced directly to the endurance of this particularism in the industry. 'If for example,' one interested observer argued, 'the Big Five or the Big Six decided that on the 1st of June there should be an all-round cut of 10% then I imagine that bank officers would become conscious of community of interest as between one bank and another. That is why you have Civil Servants organized. The governmental action affected them all equally. The bank officer has not been aroused; he has not opened his eyes to the fact that there is a subtlety about the treatment meted out to him. One bank acts now, another next year, so as to keep you blind to the universality of your fate.'[3] These particular differences have continued as a characteristic

[1] *Ibid.*, October 1919, p. 4.

[2] 'There is an impediment to the close organization of the permanent male clerks. Up to about his fifteenth year of service a clerk is "on the scale"; provided he behaves with reasonable courtesy and shows average efficiency his salary will go forward by predictable annual increments. After this point, however, the male staff tends to become divided into those who will "get on" and those who will not, and here we have a real (though rarely admitted) disparity of interest. The man who thinks he is going forward by stages to a good managership looks at the world with eyes very different from those used by his former comrade who has come to realize that he stands little chance of progressing beyond a till. In the Civil Service this division is in effect made when the clerks enter the service; it is explicit, everybody knows it and organizes accordingly; in banking it creeps on a man so that at no point in his career can he be certain that he is destined for a particular fate, and this makes any organization along lines of economic category virtually impossible in the vital thirties and early forties of a clerk's life.' 'The Bank Officers' Guild and the Future of Staff Organization', *The Bankers' Magazine*, June 1943.        [3] *The Bank Officer*, July 1934, p. 9.

of banking, and have likewise continued to confound the universal appeal of the union. After pointing out that 'the foundation of any union is a common economic and social bond', one recent reviewer of the activity of the Bank Officers' Guild goes on to say that the banking industry lacks the 'necessary homogeneousness' for unified action. 'A male clerk in one of the big Clearing Banks works in an institution which receives him in youth and keeps him all his life. He cannot transfer to one of the other Clearing Banks and thus he comes to develop a group loyalty limited to the concern which employs him. Thus there does not exist that strong common interest which is required to bind him to those employed outside his own bank; at most, he will be bound to them only for such a time as the economic sun is shining.'[1]

The pertinent comparison here is with the railway clerk. During the early days of the Railway Clerks Association, the railway industry was similarly divided among a small number of large-scale bureaucratic organizations. The main difference was that the various railway companies acted in a much more concerted fashion than the banking companies with regard to working conditions of employees. Railway clerks were, as a consequence, faced with a much more unified opposition to their interests, in the form of the Railway Companies Association and later the Railway Executive Committee. In addition, railway amalgamation had resulted in diminution of promotion opportunities for clerks. All these factors were extremely favourable to collective action.[2] In 1904 the RCA contained slightly less than 7% of railway clerks. By 1918 it had a clear majority of 61%.

Variations in the degree of blackcoated unionization can, therefore, be primarily attributed to variations in the work situations of different clerical groups. This is not to say that 'economic' factors are entirely unimportant. Bureaucratization is frequently associated with a decline in the chances of upward mobility for clerks, and occupational mobility forms one aspect of their market situation. Nevertheless, 'blocked mobility' in itself would appear to be an insufficient cause of unionization; the individuals whose chances of promotion are curtailed must, in addition, be aware of their common identity as an occupational group, and this awareness is first and foremost a product of standard working conditions. Moreover, even when mobility is not blocked, as in banking for example, a consider-

<hr>

[1] *The Bankers' Magazine, op. cit.*, p. 9.

[2] The facts are set out in A. G. Walkden, *The RCA and Its Path of Progress*, 1928. See also *The Life of the Railway Clerk*, seventh edition, December 1911; *The Future of the Railway Service: Permanency or Dismissal?*, 1913.

able degree of unionization is apparently possible simply on the basis of large-scale bureaucratic organization.

There is little demonstrable connection between unionization and 'economic' position in the narrow sense of level of income, and degree of job-security. Those clerks with the least income and security of tenure are not those with the greatest degree of organization. On the contrary, it is among the more highly paid and secure clerical population that the degree of unionization is highest.

The same is true of social status. It is not generally true to say that the blackcoats with lowest prestige are the most highly organized. Conversely, it does not hold that the clerks with fairly high social standing, such as bank and civil-service clerks, are those with the lowest degree of unionization. There is in fact no general correlation between social status and trade unionism in the clerical field. This does not contradict the earlier generalization that the status ambiguity of blackcoated work is one of the major factors preventing the mutual class identification of clerk and manual worker. Trade unionism and class consciousness cannot be so easily equated, as will be seen later. The point is simply that status differences seem to have played no decisive role in the varying degree of clerical trade unionism.

In connection with social status it is useful to examine more closely the familiar attribution of the failure of clerical unionization to the 'snobbishness' of the blackcoated worker. To those who have been concerned with blackcoated unionism this explanation has appeared *simpliste*. 'There are those who would impute these barriers to trade unionism to suburban or middle-class snobbery', noted the General Secretary of the National Federation of Professional Workers. 'That in my view is altogether too easy an explanation. Certainly snobbery was not at all unknown before the war among such workers. Nor has it entirely vanished since. But was it ever their monopoly, anyway? I suggest that snobbery in one form or another was and is shared by both the social and industrial strata above and below the non-manual and professional grades. These latter may in many instances be rather more adept at it than are the workers in the factories and workshops, who have usually less urge towards pretentiousness. But nevertheless, it would be idle and erroneous to blame snobbery entirely for the lateness of the conversion of the salariat to trade union principles.'[1] What is fundamentally weak about 'snobbishness' as an explanation of the facts regarding clerical trade unionism is that it is a general factor. It cannot, therefore, throw any light on the variations in the degree of clerical unionism which are precisely of interest here. Has snobbish-

[1] *The Bank Officer*, October 1937, p. 9.

ness varied through time? If so, assuming that it has lessened, say between 1921 and 1951, why has the proportion of commercial and industrial clerks in unions hardly increased at all? If not, how is the fact to be explained that twice as many blackcoated workers are unionized nowadays as thirty years ago? Is snobbishness a factor which operates 'all along the line', something displayed by all clerks equally? If so, why are there very significant differences in the degree of clerical unionization from one field to another? Alternatively, is snobbishness connected with relative social status among blackcoats? If so, why have certain groups of clerks with high social status been highly unionized, and others with a relatively low social status poorly organized? Most perplexing of all, why have two groups of clerical workers, both with a relatively low standing in the blackcoated world—railway clerks and industrial clerks—joined their respective unions to such radically different degrees? It is unnecessary to pursue this line of argument in order to conclude that no clear connection can be established between a factor such as 'snobbishness' and the empirical variations in clerical trade unionism. Whatever influence snobbishness has on the mutual relations of clerks and manual workers it does not seem to have prevented the former from organizing themselves in trade unions.

A second factor has often been suggested as playing a significant role in clerical unionization: namely, the degree of feminization. It was Bernard Shaw who said that the two groups most resistant to trade unionism were clerks and women. Women clerks, therefore, might well be considered a most formidable obstacle to the development of blackcoated unionism. There are many impressions which, in principle, would seem to support this generalization. The young woman clerk working for 'pin-money' at the beginning of the century, the young girl machine-operator of today who regards her job as a stop-gap, the older woman secretary, loyal to her employer after years of faithful and confidential service, are all types of clerks whose enthusiasm for trade unionism could reasonably be expected to be small. Despite these considerations, the generalization is not in accordance with the facts. A high proportion of women in a clerical occupation is not universally associated with a low degree of unionization, nor does unionization necessarily proceed farthest where women are in a minority. Indeed, if a generalization is to be made, it is that the proportion of women in clerical unions is usually roughly equal to their representation in the field of employment which the unions seek to organize. Differences in the degree of unionization are therefore to be attributed to something other than differences in the sex ratio of the group.

151

To take an example. The following table contrasts the proportion of women in the membership of the National Union of Clerks with their representation in the total clerical labour force for four Census

| Year | Total Membership of N.U.C. | Women as percentage of N.U.C. Members | Women as percentage of Total Clerks |
|------|---------------------------|---------------------------------------|-------------------------------------|
| 1911 | 12,680[1] | 12[1] | 24 |
| 1921 | 14,204 | 24 | 46 |
| 1931 | 7,482 | 39 | 43 |
| 1951 | 39,203 | 46 | 60 |

years. The proportion of women in this particular union has generally been rather less than their share in the clerical labour force as a whole. But until 1941, when the two unions were amalgamated, women clerks were also represented by the Association of Women Clerks and Secretaries, the chief rival of the NUC. In 1920, for instance, a further 6,000 women belonged to this association; in 1931, a further 3,500. The sex composition of the membership of the NUC is much less significant, however, than the course of its total membership. The outstanding fact about commercial and industrial clerks is not that women have been slightly underrepresented in their union, but that there has been a comparative failure to unionize clerks. The situation was well summed up recently by the chief organizer in the following way: 'How do women appear in this picture? Are they more or less difficult to organize than men? I think the answer is that they are neither better nor worse than male clerks.'[2]

This point is brought home by considering another blackcoat union, the NALGO. The proportion of women employed in local government service has always been high, and yet, after a steady and continuous growth, the membership of the union in this field was nearing effective saturation point in 1952.[3] The same picture is true of the civil service, where again a high proportion of women is employed. In 1947 there were about 132,000 men and 158,000 women employed in the clerical and typing grades, a female percentage of 54·5. In the Civil Service Clerical Association women members formed approximately 57% of the total, or, in absolute figures, 80,000 out of 140,000.[4] In banking, too, the representation of the

[1] The NUC figures are for 1914.
[2] *The Clerk*, September 1954, p. 108.
[3] NALGO, *Annual Report*, 1952–3; also *Public Service*, March 1953.
[4] *Red Tape*, November 1947, p. 50.

woman clerk in the National Union of Bank Employees appears to be strictly proportional to her distribution in the industry. In 1954, women members formed 27·5% of the total membership of the union. In 1953 it was estimated that there were 90,000 bank employees, 25,000 of these, or roughly 28%, being women.[1] The same is generally true of railway salaried staff, who have a much smaller proportion of women clerks. Clearly the factor of sex is of relatively small importance among the conditions affecting unionization. In other words, the differences between different types of clerical employment are much more significant than differences in their sex-composition. This consideration is reinforced by the experience of a non-clerical blackcoat union—the National Union of Teachers—which has emerged as an extremely cohesive interest-group in an occupation in which women form a majority.

Degree of contact with manual workers and their unions is one condition of the work situation of the non-manual worker which has affected the distribution of membership within clerical unions, and which goes some way to explain why certain groups of clerks have been strongly organized. Railway, mining, engineering, dockside, printing clerks have all been stimulated in their organization by the support coming from the powerful manual workers' unions.[2] In the case of railway, mining, dockside and printing clerks, there has been direct recruitment by the manual unions concerned. Even within other blackcoat unions, this factor has been of some importance. Lancashire and Yorkshire have been the birthplaces of many of them, and the industrial areas have generally shown up well in the membership. 'An examination of our membership shows that very often we are strong in places where the bankman comes in direct contact with industry and weak in places where our great industrial concerns are little more than names to him. In London, for example, he may work in an office where are kept the accounts of great engineering firms, cotton companies, or chemical combines. He may even do nothing else than post their ledgers or deal in other ways with their affairs, but what do these firms mean to him? In most cases, they are the names of shares to watch on the Stock Exchange; they are the people who occupy great blocks of offices in the City and elsewhere or they are the people who expend huge sums in very well

---

[1] *The Bank Officer*, October 1954, p. 10.

[2] See, for example, *The Growth of the Trade Union Idea and Spirit Among the Staffs of the Port of London*, 1923, Transport and General Workers' Union (Administrative, Clerical and Supervisory Group); also, *Quayside and Office*, Organ of the National Union of Docks, Wharves and Shipping Staffs, October 1920 to January 1922. (Ceased publication on amalgamation with T. & G. W. U.)

got-up advertisements in the Press and on the hoardings of the underground. It may be that some bank clerks better informed than the majority say, "Ah, but I know men who work at Lever Bros., or the ICI, and I know a great deal about the conditions in these places." Yes, no doubt he does know these men—men who live in the same suburbs as himself and travel up to town every day by the 8.45 or the 9.15 wearing clean collars, neat suits and perhaps spats. They are very decent fellows and when they reach their offices do almost the same work as the bank clerk does and use the same tools, i.e. a pen and a piece of blotting paper. This, however, is not "industry" as the word here is used. It is administration, distribution, commerce, if you will, and very important work, but it is not productive industry. Turn now to the bank clerk who lives in an industrial area and ask him what he knows about the great firms. What do these names mean to him? Why, blast furnaces, at certain times belching forth flame and smoke to heaven and at other times emitting a stream of glowing, molten metal. Does he know the men who work there? Aye, of course he does, and the women too—indeed, these people form the major part of his acquaintance. They go to work some time before eight in the morning, either walking or on the tram. Their clothes, when not covered by overalls, are stained and shiny and they certainly do not wear a clean collar every day. At 12.30 a buzzer sounds and they all troop to dinner—not lunch—and an hour later they are back again until 5.30 or thereabouts when they go home to tea and recreation till bedtime. A very different picture surely from the one conjured up in the mind of the bank clerk in a non-industrial area.'[1]

Degree of contact with manual workers and their unions,[2] then, is one of those factors which affect the distribution of membership within clerical unions, but are not generally decisive in determining the differences in the degree of concerted action between one union and another. Civil servants, for example, are not a group of blackcoats who frequently come into contact with manual workers in their day-to-day routine, yet they are highly organized. On the other

[1] *The Bank Officer*, December 1928, p. 20.

[2] Another factor working in the same direction here is that the clerical workers in these areas are likely to contain a higher proportion from working-class backgrounds than is the case in non-industrial areas. This has been especially true of a group such as railway clerks. 'Many Railway Clerks Association members sympathize with the claim of the National Union of Railwaymen,' said the General Secretary in 1939, 'because they were born in the homes of railwaymen in the lowest paid grades and therefore they had first-hand and unforgettable experience of the inevitable hardships and handicaps.' *Transport Salaried Staff Journal*, May 1954, p. 174.

hand, there are approximately 300,000 clerks employed in the metal, engineering, shipbuilding, vehicle, metal goods and precision instruments trades, which is about five times greater than the *total* membership of the Clerical and Administrative Workers' Union—the union responsible for their organization.

## THE CHARACTER OF BLACKCOAT UNIONISM

So far the discussion has been concerned with the general social conditions which have determined the degree of clerical unionization in different fields. But the various clerical associations which have grown up in the last fifty years have differed considerably in character and outlook. They have developed in different environments and with different kinds of membership. Some have experienced rather rapid growth, especially in the inter- and post-war periods; others have stagnated. These factors have all been influential in deciding their policies and conduct. They are in a sense peculiar to each association. In addition to these particular factors, however, each blackcoat union has had to face certain *general* problems by virtue of its status as a defensive organization of employee interests. These have taken the form of decisions regarding the industrial status of the association, whether it is to be registered as a trade union, whether it is to be associated with the wider trade union movement made up preponderantly of manual workers, whether it is to be affiliated for political action with a party, whether it will seek parliamentary support and if so in what form, and whether, finally, it will resort in the last instance to strike action in the defence of its members' interests.

In the next section the character of five major representative blackcoat unions[1] will be traced with respect to these general questions of policy. Finally, the degree to which common developments are visible in their histories will be briefly discussed.

### TRANSPORT SALARIED STAFFS ASSOCIATION
(Previously the RAILWAY CLERKS ASSOCIATION)

Of all the blackcoated unions that have emerged in the course of the present century, the RCA deserves special notice. Not only has it achieved a high degree of unionization, but its members have

[1] The Guild of Insurance Officials has not been included because its history is very similar to that of the Bank Officers' Guild.

displayed a sense of allegiance to the Labour Movement which, going far beyond that of any other organized group of clerks, has in some respects even surpassed the class consciousness of traditional working-class unionism. Its history stands as a living refutation of the charge that blackcoated workers lack the necessary virility for a manly defence of their interests. The study of the development of trade unionism among railway clerks can only lead to a rejection of the common stereotype of the clerk, and to an awareness of the actual variations in class consciousness which that stereotype obscures.

Founded in Sheffield on May 8, 1897, the association grew slowly, after almost collapsing, and by 1904 it had 4,000 clerks and station-masters enrolled out of a possible total of 60,000. The decision in 1899 to register the association as a trade union instead of merely as a friendly society gave rise to a great deal of controversy. Many members felt that the young organization, by taking this step, would alienate clerical workers still outside who were generally regarded as Conservative and extremely unwilling to be identified with manual workers' associations. Bolder council prevailed and the step was taken. Membership, instead of stagnating, actually trebled in the next three years. The same doubts about the 'progressiveness' of the railway clerk were voiced regarding TUC affiliation which was effected in 1903. Similar arguments were repeated when the question of Labour Party affiliation was raised, and at the annual conference of 1907 the motion for affiliation was defeated by 2,440 votes to 2,006. 'There are 60,000 railway clerks in the kingdom,' noted one member the same year, 'and I think I am well inside the mark when I say that quite 50,000 of them are Conservative in politics'.[1] Affiliation was carried through in 1909, and by the end of the war the member-ship at last formed a majority of railway staffs—61,000 out of a possible total of 100,000 clerks had joined. At every stage at which working-class association had been sought for the union, then, arguments appeared which every clerical association has had to face in the course of its economic and political development. In the case of railway clerks, each of the steps was taken early in the career of the union and was in the nature of an experiment. The success which attended these moves did much to make those both inside and out-side revise their views on the feasibility and nature of blackcoated unionism. This was only the beginning.

In the pre-war years the RCA had still only a minority influence and its policy was informed by this fact. In the industrial field it was largely hampered by the companies' utter refusal to recognize the union. The only means open to it were the traditional 'memorializing'

[1] *The Railway Clerk*, 1907, p. 7.

of directors, publicity and deputation. As a result, most of its battles during this period were fought through political action. It launched a vigorous campaign against the injustice of uncompensated Sunday duty, irregularities in the superannuation funds administered by the companies, and pressed for the inclusion of railway office workers within the scope of industrial legislation. These aims were sought generally through political action, which took the form of holding up Railway Bills to secure discussion of their grievances. This was achieved through the Parliamentary Committee of the TUC and the Labour Party. Legislation was secured in 1906 on the question of compensation for accidents, bringing clerical workers within the scope of the new Workmen's Compensation Bill. Similarly, in 1907 as a result of parliamentary action, the Board of Trade agreed to set up a Departmental Committee to 'Inquire into the Constitution, Rules and Administration and Financial Position of the Superannuation and similar Funds of Railway Companies'. This later showed that serious deficiencies in the funds had resulted from the companies' failure to pay their proper share. By the same methods the RCA also secured representation on the Parliamentary Committee instituted to investigate the question of railway agreements and amalgamations. But the idea of a permanent association of clerks was still highly repugnant to the railway companies who were incensed by these interferences, and their reaction resulted in deliberate and determined attempts to crush the RCA. The North Eastern Company, from September 1907 onwards, persecuted and penalized men who dared to join the RCA and to continue their membership against the advice of the company's officers. This move was nonplussed with TUC help by a five weeks blockage' of a Bill submitted by the company in 1909 until the embargo on unionism for clerks was withdrawn. Similar efforts were made by the Midland Company to intimidate, interrogate and penalize, including the practice of 'red-ink records' of men who were trade unionists. Effective opposition by the Labour Party to the General Railway Bill of 1913 was necessary to break this opposition. Thus, action aimed at improving the status of railway clerks and defending the association itself was undertaken at this period through political representation, and this was the situation until the outbreak of the war. The experience of these early struggles confirmed the association's wisdom in its industrial and political affiliations, without which it might very well never have survived.[1]

After 1918, the association, heartened by its unionization of the

[1] On the RCA's activity in this field, see Walkden's *The R.C.A. and Its Path of Progress*, 1928, p. 71.

majority of railway clerks and by the general tone of industrial relations set by the governmental sponsorship of Whitleyism, decided to press for recognition as a bargaining unit for clerical workers throughout the railway industry. In the matter of trade unionism the companies had already acquired a reputation for reaction, and in the course of events leading up to the strike of February 1919 it became increasingly obvious that the RCA was being forced into a trial of strength with the employers. The question of policy revolved around the desirability of strike action, and the ability of the membership to make effective use of this weapon. At a hastily convened meeting in London it was decided to issue strike notices. At the eleventh hour the companies yielded and decided to accord recognition, but not before strike preparations and actual stoppages of work had taken place throughout the country and emphatically underlined the solidarity and confidence of the mass of railway clerks. The degree of concerted action was remarkable, especially since this was the first time non-manual workers had been called upon to defend their interests collectively in such an extreme manner. The past traditions of railway service had all been on the side of producing a blackleg rather than a striker. No wonder then that the Journal referred to the experience as a 'rebirth'. As the report from Leeds put it: 'The strike idea was at first something wonderful, but fearful; a monster hideous and repulsive; impossible, undesirable, awful and unthinkable. Despite all this it was a grim necessity. That was seen, that was understood, that was *felt*. It had to be.'[1] 'The manifest determination of the RCA members to strike if recognition was not conceded has been an eye-opener to the members of other trade unions,' the Journal proudly announced; 'we believe, too, that those prominent members of the RCA who were quite ready to strike themselves, but had doubts about "the other fellows" have realized that they had too little faith in the rank and file, and had underestimated the spirit and power of the association. However, even the most optimistic were somewhat surprised at the manner in which the members generally realized their responsibility and intimated their intention of "going over the top".'[2] 'The decision to strike marked a new epoch in the history of the association which once bore on its banner: "Defence not Defiance".'[3]

Further evidence of the new spirit was manifested the same year during negotiations on national scales when the association was ready to strike again if its demands were not granted. And again, during the NUR strike in the September of that year, clerks resolutely refused

[1] *The Railway Service Journal*, 1919, February, p. 18.
[2] *Ibid.*, 1919, February, p. 28.      [3] *Ibid.*, 1919, December, p. 264.

to blackleg despite the 'loyalty pay' lavishly offered by the companies.[1]
A new testing time came seven years later with the General Strike.
When the miners came out, the transport workers were in the 'front
line' of defence, and the RCA could not remain neutral. For the
second time in its short existence, the association called on its members to withdraw their labour, this time not in defence of their own
immediate interests but in sympathy with the miner's cause. It was
one of the very few blackcoat unions that actually called an official
strike. Later that year, the president, in the course of his annual
address to the conference, strongly justified the action: 'There was
only one way in which the RCA could rise to the occasion. Had we
failed to go that way we should have forfeited our self-respect; our
standing in the trade union movement would have gone, and we
should have demonstrated that the blackcoated workers were not
fit to belong to the working-class movement.'[2] Of course, the reper-
cussions followed, from within the movement in the form of resigna-
tions and protests, and from the railway companies who, several
months later, had refused to reinstate hundreds of clerks who had
gone on strike. On the whole, however, the membership was solid,
and it is perhaps eloquent of their attitude that when legislation
altered the status of their political fund, 83% of railway clerks
contracted-in to the political levy. Moreover, the RCA's high reputation in the trade union and labour movement was enhanced still
further, and unlike other clerical unions its action brought in 3,000
new recruits in the months following the General Strike.[3]

Although the threat and actual use of the strike weapon by the
RCA distinguished it from most other influential blackcoat unions,
and showed that it was prepared to take the ultimate step on sufficiently serious occasions, this aspect of its policy should not be
allowed to overshadow the quiet and undramatic nature of the
negotiating machinery, which, after its establishment in 1922,
became the chief industrial channel through which its claims and
counter-claims were expressed. In 1921 it was agreed that in future
conditions were, in the absence of agreement between the union and
the companies, to be submitted to the Central and National Wages
Boards, which essentially constituted an industrial court, composed
of equal numbers from both sides and interested outside parties.
Thus committed to arbitration,[4] there were proposals that the strike
weapon should be relinquished, but the overwhelming opinion was

---

[1] *Ibid.*, p. 262.　　　　　　　　　[2] *Ibid.*, 1926, July, p. 224.

[3] *Ibid.*, 1926, November, p. 367.

[4] *Ibid.*, 1908, p. 1. The RCA policy had always favoured arbitration as opposed
to strikes.

in favour of its retention as a last resort. In fact it was never used again, even during the thirties, when the claims of the companies for reductions in salaries were partly granted by the Board. In the negotiations before the Board, the skill of the blackcoated leadership has been amply demonstrated, particularly in the mastery of A. G. Walkden, later Lord Walkden, who was the general secretary of the association throughout the period of its critical growth.

As regards its general role in politics, it is perhaps worth noting that the RCA has, almost from its inception, financed its own candidates for Parliament, and as the Labour Party grew in strength in the Commons, RCA representatives increased *pari passu*. The first RCA member was elected in 1924; in 1929 eight of its candidates were successful; and in the General Election of 1945 no less than fifteen official and unofficial RCA candidates found seats in the House.[1] When the relatively small size of the association is taken into account, these are remarkable facts, indicative of the resources and energy devoted to political action. Outside of central government, the RCA has a record of equally intense political activity. The political statement published in its official organ shortly before the 1945 election rendered the following account: 'This issue of the *Railway Service Journal* contains a large proportion of political articles urging RCA members to work and vote for Labour Party candidates. For that we make no apology. The RCA has been affiliated to the Labour Party since 1909 and has supported it actively ever since. Nearly 90% of its 90,000 members have contracted to pay the political levy, and we doubt if any union in the country can claim a higher proportion of its members as active workers and office-bearers in the local Labour Parties and Trades Councils, and as Labour members of Local Authorities. Five of its members were in the House of Commons which was dissolved last month. It has provided two chairmen and a treasurer to the Labour Party. When the present treasurer, the Rt. Hon. Arthur Greenwood, recently appealed to the affiliated trade unions for additional grants to build up a fighting fund for the General Election, the first donation to reach Transport House was from the RCA.'[2]

Another index of the remarkable degree of class consciousness of the railway clerk can be seen in the following figures which give the proportion of members of the union who were members of the Labour Party in 1946 and 1952, that is, before and after the repeal of the 1927 Trade Union Act, the earlier figure representing a membership which had to 'contract-in' to the political levy for the Labour Party. In all other unions Labour Party membership as a proportion

[1] *Ibid.*, 1929, p. 276; 1945, p. 268.   [2] *Ibid.*, 1945, July.

of total union membership affiliated to the TUC rose considerably between 1946 and 1952, but the political affiliation of the Transport Salaried Staffs Association rose by only 2%.

### MEMBERSHIP OF THE LABOUR PARTY AS A PERCENTAGE OF TUC MEMBERSHIP

| Union | 1946 | 1952 |
|-------|------|------|
| Transport Salaried Staffs Association | 83 | 85 |
| National Union of Mineworkers | 77 | 108 |
| National Union of Railwaymen | 53 | 80 |
| Amalgamated Engineering Union | 32 | 77 |

Source: G. D. H. Cole, *An Introduction to Trade Unionism*, 1953, p. 301.

The 1946 figure was extraordinarily high at 83% even by comparison with such militant unions as the National Union of Mineworkers and the National Union of Railwaymen. In terms of its support of the Labour Movement, then, this non-manual union seems to have been even more active than the traditionally class-conscious manual unions.

The relations between the RCA and the NUR have been variously hostile and amicable. At first, the NUR was suspicious of the 'potency' of the RCA.[1] It also recruited clerks separately, though these were never a real threat to the integrity of the RCA. During the early twenties the old fears of the clerk as a weak link in the union front and memories of blacklegging led to several sharp exchanges between the two unions. The RCA debated at length the desirability of joining with the larger union, but fears of being 'submerged' and a consciousness of the differential interests of the salaried staff[2] have kept it outside, although in later years the two unions have worked in close co-operation.[3]

---

[1] *Ibid.*, 1919, p. 2.

[2] 'We have never opposed the claims of the NUR in respect of their lowest paid members,' said the General Secretary in 1954, 'but what we have done is to emphasise that our grades also deserve recognition, and that we object to being tied to a Wages Index and related to average earnings when in fact the majority of our people have no opportunity of enhanced earnings. We have also argued that there is a greater affinity between the work performed by administrative staff on the railways and comparable posts in other industries, than there is between the salaried and conciliation grades in the railway industry.' *Transport Salaried Staff Journal*, May 1954.

[3] See *Railway Service Journal* for the following years: 1920, pp. 25, 50, 99; 1921, p. 67; 1923, p. 233.

## CLERICAL AND ADMINISTRATIVE WORKERS' UNION
### (NATIONAL UNION OF CLERKS AND
### ADMINISTRATIVE WORKERS)

The National Union of Clerks is one of the oldest blackcoat unions, with a continuous history from 1897 to the present day. It is the chief craft union for the heterogeneous mass of clerks and administrative workers in commerce and industry outside the great divisions of railway, banking, insurance and government clerkdom, although it regarded these fields as falling within its jurisdiction until, and in some cases after, strong industrial unions had grown up to cater to their special needs. Throughout the whole period of its existence the NUC has exhibited a thorough-going trade-union spirit and has identified with and greatly contributed to the working-class movement in both its industrial and political wings. It made great headway immediately after the First World War and during and after the Second, and the shape of its growth has corresponded closely to the general movement of trade-union membership between 1900–50. Nevertheless, its total membership in 1951 was approximately the same as it had been in 1921 despite the fact that the number of clerks had more than doubled in the intervening years, as had the proportion of clerks in trade unions.

The union was founded in 1897 by the coming together of the spontaneous growths at Leeds (1894) and London, the latter association having been sponsored financially partly by the Amalgamated Engineering Union when it was first founded in 1890. The NUC made little progress for almost a decade. The membership in 1906 was a bare 150, kept together very largely by the personal loyalties of a few convinced trade unionists. Then, immediately before the war, clerks began to join in increasing numbers, undoubtedly stimulated by the rising price level and the general increase in trade-union activity. This growth persisted throughout the war years, and reached its peak in 1919–20 when the union had some 43,000 members.

The NUC had been founded as a trade union, and was early affiliated to the TUC; its Labour Party affiliation dates from 1907.[1] Its professed goal was to become one of the largest trade unions in the country: 'we want to see that half-million in', said the president optimistically in 1909[2]: and the means to this goal was to be political action. 'Long and painful experience has convinced all but the most conservative trade unionists that the weapon of the strike, and the

[1] Annual Conference 1907, *Report*, p. 8.
[2] Annual Conference 1909, *Report*, p. 3.

162

milder one of negotiation by delegate committees and boards, however necessary on occasion, are alike costly and unwieldy when compared with the newer and more effective methods of influencing public opinion and law.'[1] The immediate objectives of the union—the attainment of a minimum standard of remuneration, the abolition of unfair agreements between employer and clerk, the prevention of boycotting by secret character-notes, and the regulation of office hours and sanitary conditions—could all be pursued by negotiation and by withholding labour, 'but every one of these objectives can be more easily, cheaply, and (what is more to the point) effectively reached by legislative enactment and by the influence of public opinion upon administration'.

But the lack of interest in politics on the part of the membership as a whole was soon apparent and was to be a continuing theme, like that of lapsing members, haunting the successive annual conferences. At the twenty-third annual conference, in 1914, it was announced that 1,844 members were in favour of parliamentary action and only 540 against it, although the total voting membership was 10,578.[2] In 1919 only 8% voted on the choice of a candidate. 'I do not wish to enter into the merits for or against political action,' the president remonstrated, 'but it is surely the duty of the rank and file, once they have decided to finance a Parliamentary candidate, to take a real interest in the matter and vote as to who is to be the candidate. The votes cast on this occasion are so few that one wonders if the membership is really in earnest about the business.'[3]

The union was also committed to work in close harness with the rest of the Labour Movement. 'We should do all we possibly can to keep in touch with and impress ourselves upon other Trade Unions, Trades Councils and Local Labour Organizations, remembering that in the homes of many manual working trade unionists there are sons and daughters, brothers and sisters, who are clerks. We must, I say, be prominent in all local Labour Activity, and win the goodwill and respect of other organized workers. Our association with other workers will, I am confident, have its mutual advantages. The organized Labour forces of this country have much to gain from the presence in their midst of a body of men who, by reason of their very means of living, possess on the whole a large measure of that business capacity, a greater share of which would do much to benefit and consolidate the whole Labour Movement in this country.'[4] In fact,

---

[1] Annual Conference 1908, *Report*, p. 3.
[2] Annual Conference 1914, *Report*, p. 9.
[3] Annual Conference 1919, *Report*, p. 9.
[4] Annual Conference 1911, *Report*, p. 12.

local Labour Parties proved to be among the best recruiting agencies for the initial membership of new branches.[1] But some of the relations of the NUC with other trade unions were not always so happy as it might have wished. By 1919, the NUC had agreed with the Iron and Steel Trades Federation on the organization of clerks in those industries, but it was lodging complaints against what it considered to be poaching by the Amalgamated Union of Co-operative Employees, the National Warehouse and General Workers' Union, the National Amalgamated Union of Labour, the National Union of Dock Labourers, the Dock, Wharf, Riverside and General Workers' Union, and had failed to come to agreement with the Miners' Federation of Great Britain, the Nottinghamshire and Derbyshire branches of which were actively recruiting colliery clerks.[2]

Between 1910 and 1920, the union had its first experience of strike action. The year 1913 saw the first lockout of clerks who refused to blackleg in the big dock strike. The following year the union called its first strike at Rees Roturbo Company in Wolverhampton because of a refusal of recognition. Twenty-six clerks came out in March, and by May it was decided that the strikers should find positions elsewhere, which they did, being supported in the meanwhile by strike pay from the NUC.[3] In July 1915 some fifty-seven clerks struck over a case of victimization at Nobel's Explosive Factory, and they were supported in their action by the manual workers employed there. This strike was regarded as a landmark in the history of industrial relations. 'Nobel's dispute ought to make history in the Trade Union Movement. For the first time in an industrial struggle between employer and employed the worker in the office and the worker in the factory have presented a solid front to an employer.'[4] Such unity was not always forthcoming however. For instance, during a strike called by the NUC at the Butterly Colliery Company in 1920, jurisdictional rivalry with the Miners' Federation reared its head, and the clerks' strike was actually blacklegged by the Derbyshire and Nottinghamshire Miners' Association.[5] In the following years there were other strikes. It was becoming increasingly evident that 'clerks were kicking', and that they were not above acting like 'real' trade unionists if pushed far enough.

When Whitleyism appeared in 1919 the NUC was not really firmly established enough in many industries to make use of the new

---

[1] Fred Hughes, *By Hand and Brain*, 1953, p. 21.
[2] Annual Conference 1919, *Report*, pp. 17–20.
[3] Annual Conference 1915, *Report*, p. 13.
[4] *The Clerk*, July 1915, p. 77.
[5] Annual Conference 1920, *Report*, p. 28.

machinery. It was, moreover, very lukewarm about the principles underlying the proposals for joint consultation. At the conference of 1919, general endorsement of Whitleyism was not given, but it was suggested that the question of entering the scheme should be decided by the section of the membership directly concerned. An amendment was also added: 'This Conference declares that no attempted *rapprochement* between employers and employees can bridge the gulf which separates those who live on profits from those who live by labour, and is of the opinion that the only way in which industrial unrest can be allayed and the smooth and efficient working of industry and increased production be secured is by national ownership of all industries and services and democratic management by the workers engaged in each industry or service.'[1] This statement reflects the influence which the ideas of Guild Socialism were having on the NUC leadership at this time. To these ideas, and to the fact that large numbers of clerks were being organized outside the union along industrial lines, can be attributed the reorganization of the union on an Industrial Guild basis in 1920.[2] The constituent guilds were given great autonomy, and were urged to seek the closest cooperation with manual workers' unions in their respective industries. 'The experience of the last few years has shown that the "general" appeal to clerks now fails to elicit enthusiasm or to achieve effective results. The "Industrial" appeal, on the other hand, not only arouses more zeal and unity of purpose, but it conserves energy in propaganda, organization and trade movements. It also has the great moral and psychological advantages of linking the union up more definitely with the progressive and virile trends in other organizations of manual and professional workers and thence derives much encouragement and support.'[3] But the experiment was condemned almost from the start. Membership reached its peak in these years, and thereafter fell precipitously. The gains in membership in the main industries, such as engineering and shipbuilding and mining, were wiped out in the course of the next few years, and for almost a decade the industrial activity of the NUC was largely confined to the interests of clerks in the cocoa trades, in co-operative societies and in trade unions or friendly societies, who made up the mass of the membership during the years 1925 to 1935.

The social significance of this first upsurge of clerical unionism between 1910 and 1920 was summed up in the words of the president at the conference of 1921. 'The NUC, even if it has not yet achieved all that it might or should have done, stands today as a testimony

[1] *The Clerk*, July 1919, p. 76.     [2] *Ibid.*, May 1920, p. 69.
[3] *Ibid.*, July 1921, p. 105.

that clerks can be persuaded to join a Trade Union, and that they can through their Trade Union develop the purpose and courage to improve their material conditions, and finally that they can through their Trade Union express their sense of the common interests which unite all workers.'[1]

In the year of the General Strike the membership stood at 7,311, and the exceptions to the strike call by the TUC 'were sufficiently numerous and important to leave quite a substantial number of the NUC's members at work, but many were affected either directly by the call to strike or indirectly, because the interruption of business caused their offices to be closed'. A Contingencies Fund was opened in support of the strike and £3,561 was subscribed to the Miners' Fund. But in the conclusion of the official report on the strike, there was a note of disappointment. 'While expressing our appreciation of these efforts made by many of our members, it is evident from our experience in connection with the National Strike that there is much to be done in educating our general membership as to their responsibilities as Trade Unionists.'[2]

The political action of the union was largely hampered by the low degree of interest shown by the mass of the membership in things political. In 1929, the number of members who had contracted-in to pay the political levy was only about 28% of the total membership; in addition, not all those who had contracted-in had actually paid their contributions to the political fund.[3] By 1936, the contractors-in formed 15% of the total membership; in 1940, only 10%. At the annual conference of 1939, it was resolved that 'with a view to obtaining further unity among the working-class movements, this Conference strongly recommends each Branch of the Union to affiliate to as many County, Borough and Constituency Labour Parties as possible, and participate fully in all their activities'.[4] The same year a survey was made of branch affiliations to local Labour Parties. Out of a total of 163 branches, only 39 replied, and of these 30 were affiliated to the party. An additional 65 branches were known to be without contractors-in.[5] By 1944, the contracted-in membership formed only 7% of the total. The Act of 1946 completely reversed the position, for by 1951 84% of the membership were contributing to the political fund of the union, while only 16% had contracted-out.[6] Far from indicating a rise in political consciousness on the part of the general member, this fact merely seems to

[1] *Ibid.*, p. 104.　　　　[2] Annual Conference 1926, *Report*, p. 8.
[3] Annual Conference 1931, *Report*, p. 11.　　[4] *The Clerk*, June 1939, p. 109.
[5] Annual Conference 1939, *Report*, p. 17.
[6] *The Clerk*, January–February 1951, p. 170.

confirm the continuance of the previous trend of political apathy.

The low degree of political interest displayed by the mass of the membership contrasts strangely with the outlook of the leadership of the NUC which was extremely active in this sphere during the thirties. Over these years, the space given in the *Journal* to political discussion and the number of motions at conferences on political events, both domestic and foreign, appear to have been greater than in any other comparable clerical trade union. Again and again, the delegates supported the Communist Party in its claim for affiliation to the Labour Party, they were active in denouncing Fascism at home and abroad, they contributed to the International Solidarity Fund money earmarked for Spanish workers, and as late as 1943 the union was still donating funds to the International Brigade.[1] How far these activities were duplicated at branch level it is hard to estimate, but it may very well be that many clerks outside the union were deterred from joining because of its left-wing policy.[2]

The revival in industrial unionism which began in the middle and late thirties expanded the union's membership in engineering and mining again. In South Wales, organization was especially strong, and in 1944 there was an important strike by colliery clerks to force recognition of the union by several large companies, which succeeded after the intervention of the Ministry of Labour.[3] In 1945, the union could claim that 'after many years of negotiation with isolated firms in the Engineering industry we have established District agreements in eight important districts, covering junior salary scales, length of working week, and payment for overtime and night-shift work'.[4] The nationalization of the mines and of the aircraft and electricity industries also helped along the growing membership of the union, and incidentally brought to a head once more the long-standing jurisdictional dispute with the mineworkers' union. Both the NUC and the NUM claimed the right to represent the staff grades in negotiation. After considerable delay, during which the South Wales colliery clerks in the NUC struck for two days, the NUC was eventually recognized as the bargaining unit.[5]

[1] For an account of these years and the internal politics of the NUC, see Fred Hughes, *op. cit.*, Chapter VIII.

[2] See for example the letter from the secretary of a general branch in London, *The Clerk*, February 1939, p. 31: 'It is my firm opinion that one of the principal reasons for the smallness of the union, for its backwardness in recruiting and holding its membership, is this continual foisting of political opinions down people's throats, whether they like it or not,' and the ensuing correspondence on this subject.                     [3] *The Clerk*, January–February 1944, p. 103.

[4] *Ibid.*, July–August 1945, p. 149.

[5] *Ibid.*, January–February 1947, p. 5.

## CIVIL SERVICE CLERICAL ASSOCIATION

The CSCA is the largest purely clerical trade union in the world. It originated in the post-1918 reform of the civil service, one of the outstanding features of which was the creation of a homogeneous and isolated class of clerical workers, distinct in status, rewards and opportunity from the higher officials. Despite their peculiar role as government employees, the civil-service clerks have a record of militant trade unionism, and close ties with the wider Labour Movement.

The Assistant Clerks Association—the interest group of the class of civil servants established in 1895—was formed in 1904 as a protest against the low salaries then prevailing and the practice of patronage. It gave evidence before the Royal Commission of 1912, which recommended that the service grades should be thoroughly reorganized, and, after the reorganization took place in 1920, the ACA formed the core of the new Civil Service Clerical Association. Since much of the policy of the CSCA was inherited from the ACA, the history of the latter may first be briefly traced.

Throughout the war years the ACA pursued a rather vigorous and militant policy for a civil service association. At the annual meeting of 1915 it was resolved that 'in view of the existing deadlock between the Association and the Treasury on the question of conditions of service, this General Meeting of Assistant Clerks is of the opinion that the Association should be registered as a Trade Union and should affiliate with the Labour Party and the Trades Union Congress. It therefore instructs the Council to put these proposals into effect after it has been ascertained by means of a referendum that two-thirds of the membership of the Association is favourable to such a course of action being taken.'[1] Registration as a trade union took place in 1917, but it was not until 1918 that formal affiliation to the Labour Party was effected. 'The question is one that has been raised time and time again since the formation of the Association, though it was not until some three years ago that a referendum was taken and an overwhelming majority in favour obtained. The delay in giving effect to that decision has been due to a number of more or less technical causes and in no sense to considerations as to the wisdom of second thoughts.'[2] It was argued on this occasion that not only did the association now have organized support in the Commons, but that 'our linking up with the general Labour Movement of the country will serve the double purpose of broadening our own

[1] *Red Tape*, December 1915, p. 56.      [2] *Ibid.*, September 1918, p. 89.

outlook and removing the distrust with which organized Labour has tended to regard such bodies as ours in the past'.[1] On the question of strike policy, the association's objection was based on expediency not principle: 'At present the Service seems to be divided into two classes—one of which wants to strike immediately, irrespective of the strength of the Association; the other to whom the word "strike" is synonymous with "Bolshevism". Both sections are wrong. The strike used as the last resort after all other means of negotiation have failed, but not before, is a perfectly legitimate weapon. On the other hand, the strike is a boomerang weapon which often hits the users as hard as the men against whom it is directed. Particularly is this so when the users are not adequately prepared for a strike, and this is the position in the Service. There is no organization of the salaried classes which has resources sufficient to undertake a strike with any prospect of success at the present time.'[2]

The railway strike of 1919 forced the 5,000-strong association to clarify its policy on trade-union solidarity, for during the strike assistant clerks had been bribed to act as blacklegs.[3] At the annual meeting in 1919, W. J. Brown moved that 'Assistant Clerks who, in future industrial disputes, are invited to take service outside their departments which would weaken the position of the body of workers involved, should decline to do so'.[4] He asked the meeting to consider what regard a Labour Government would have for a body of civil servants who were prepared to blackleg upon other sections of the Labour Movement. He knew that the railway leaders had been called Bolsheviks and anarchists. That was to be expected. The Press which described them by these names was owned and controlled by people whose interests were diametrically opposed to the Labour Movement. He asked the meeting to say that the Labour Movement was their movement, the labour struggle their struggle, and that they would do nothing to hinder the efforts of any other section of badly paid workers to improve their position. But the meeting called for even more positive action than this, and carried the amendment that 'Assistant Clerks in future industrial disputes should give the utmost moral support to the body of workers involved by declining to undertake any service (other than ordinary duties) either inside or outside of their Departments which would weaken the position of

---

[1] *Ibid.*, September 1918, p. 94. W. J. Brown gives the date of actual affiliation to the Labour Party as 1920, *So Far*, p. 128. But the Association of Civil Service Assistant Clerks is listed as affiliated to the Labour Party in the *Report of the 19th Annual Conference of the Labour Party*, 1919, p. 67.
[2] *Ibid.*, April 1919, p. 60.    [3] *Ibid.*, November 1919, p. 28.
[4] *Ibid.*, December 1919, p. 38.

the strikers; further, it is considered that members should be given the opportunity to subscribe (by levy or other means to be determined by the Executive) to the strike funds of any body of workers which the Executive of the ACA shall consider to be worthy of such financial support.'

Further consideration of the strike weapon came in 1920, when a special meeting was held to consider the proposals of the Treasury concerning the assimilation of old grades into the new on reorganization. 'What the staff side needs,' argued Brown on this occasion, 'is the backing of a Service organized on a Trade Union basis, possessing the power and the will to strike if its just claims are not reasonably met. The superficial amenities of Whitleyism cannot hide the underlying antagonism of interest between the two sides, and it is the relative strength of the two sides which decides the fate of claims. The official criterion is not "what is just?", but "what is the least we can give without incurring too serious trouble?" And the only trouble they fear is the strike.'[1] The meeting unanimously supported their general secretary and instructed the council to take the necessary steps for the institution of a strike fund.

The last political act of the ACA was a motion at the annual meeting of 1920, 'that a grant of fifty pounds from the political fund be made to the *Daily Herald*'. It was urged that 'it was the duty of the members, as part of the working class, to support the paper of the working class', but after debate the amendment that 'voluntary contributions be invited' was passed instead.[2]

The end of the war brought the negotiating machinery of Whitleyism, the reorganization of the civil service grades in 1920, and the consequent amalgamation of most of the hitherto splintered clerical associations in the new CSCA with the ACA as its nucleus. The spirit of the small Assistant Clerks Association and that of its leader were transfused to the new organization and dominated its policy during the next stage of its growth, that is, until the Trade Disputes Act of 1927.

The CSCA decided to affiliate to the TUC in 1923.[3] The earlier affiliation to the Labour Party stood, but during the first Labour Government there was dissatisfaction with the Government's treatment of the clerical classes in the civil service, and at the 1924 conference the party was strongly censured although there was no attempt to disaffiliate. It was resolved, however, that 'this Con-

---

[1] *Ibid.*, July 1920, p. 186.  [2] *Ibid.*, 1920, p. 45.
[3] *Ibid.*, 1923, p. 126. The decision to register as a trade union was not taken until 1950, and then it was as a matter of administrative convenience. *Ibid.*, 1950, p. 394.

ference deplores the failure of the responsible Labour Ministers at the Treasury to apply the approved principles and policy of the Labour Party to Civil Service questions with which they have dealt since Labour assumed office. The Conference draws attention to the invidious position in which as a result Service Associations affiliated to the Labour Party are placed and affirms its view that the continued ignoring of Labour principles on the part of Ministers must lead to a revision of the present relations between the CSCA and the Labour Party, which the Executive would deplore.'[1] The relation of the CSCA to the party was held to be primarily an economic rather than a political affiliation, if only because of the varied political sentiments of the members of the association. Brown, examining the affiliation in 1925, wrote: 'On what, then, does our policy on these matters rest? On the political faith of our members? Not at all. Who shall say of what political faith our membership is? One thing is clear— it is not Socialist, at any rate not in the bulk. At a guess I should say that we have about 10% convinced and enthusiastic Socialists; another 30% benevolently inclined to Labour; about 20% Conservatives; a few Liberals, and the balance not interested in politics at all, but Conservative rather than Labour in their instincts. . . . We knew of course that only a minority of our people were politically Labour. But it was not a "political" proposition we were putting to them— it was an economic one. We were not catering for their private political convictions—which were their own concern—but their common needs as civil servants. Accordingly, we hoped and believed that all would contribute to the necessary political fund irrespective of their private political views. Exemption was claimed in a number of cases, but broadly speaking our members, irrespective of their personal political convictions, backed the policy very well.'[2]

But to draw the line so sharply between political and economic interests in affiliation was not easy; and the language of conference was not free from political overtones. Moreover, the policy which the CSCA was following had been largely set by the small, cohesive and radically inclined group of assistant clerks. Now it was a much larger association with a rapidly growing membership, four times what it had been in the early days, and political opinion was by no means unanimous about the closeness of the relationship with the Labour Party. At the conference of 1925, it was moved that 'a referendum be taken as to whether this Association shall be affiliated to any political party', but it was defeated by 546 votes to 237.[3] The problems arising out of the relationship between the association and the

[1] *Ibid.*, 1924, pp. 364–8.     [2] *Ibid.*, February 1925, p. 185.
[3] *Ibid.*, June 1925, p. 26.

Labour Party were overshadowed completely by the General Strike, and the policy adopted then resulted in the political and industrial isolation of the CSCA from the rest of the Labour Movement for almost twenty years.

When the strike began, the CSCA asked the Treasury for an assurance that no compulsion would be placed on civil servants to volunteer for duties outside the ordinary range of their work.[1] There was no strike of civil service clerks, but the association placed itself materially and morally on the side of the miner. As Brown said afterwards, 'No question of affiliation or disaffiliation would have altered the mental outlook of our people last year in forming their judgement of the mining dispute. We didn't back the miners because we were affiliated—we took that course because we felt that they were right— and that issue would be the same whether we were affiliated or not. Another offence which is charged against us is that we dragged the Civil Service into the field of party politics. There is a simple remedy in the hands of the Government for that difficulty. That remedy is to give their servants a square deal without making it necessary for them to apply political pressure. Major Cadogan, with whom I have the dubious pleasure of serving on the National Whitley Council, wants to know why it is that the civil servants have become politically and industrially conscious. The reason is the same reason that made the masses industrially and politically conscious—it is the realization of the fact that political power must be won by the exploited masses if they are to be successful in conducting the struggle against those who employ them.'[2] Nineteen years later, during the debate on the repeal of the 1927 Bill, Brown recalled the policy of the CSCA during the critical days of the General Strike. 'My union was involved in the 1926 dispute, although we were not called out. Our functions were limited. My own function in that dispute was to pledge every asset that the CSCA had in this world, including the office furniture and the building we worked in, in support of the strike. We did that. Why? Because we wanted to be disloyal to the State? Because we were connected with some conspiracy against its wellbeing? Not at all. We did it because of the merits of that dispute. The members of my union were heart and soul with the miners in resisting reductions of wages at that time.'[3] Shortly after the General Strike, while the repressive legislation on civil service unionism was pending, the CSCA took a ballot of its members on the desirability of TUC affiliation. Some 80% of the membership voted and decided in favour of continued affiliation to the TUC by 9,986 votes to 5,645.[4] This point

[1] *Ibid.*, 1926, p. 385.      [2] *Ibid.*, June 1927, p. 442.
[3] *Ibid.*, March 1946, p. 145.      [4] *Ibid.*, November 1926, p. 49.

marks perhaps the zenith of militancy in the career of the CSCA, a time when the association was frequently referred to as 'Red' and its general secretary known as 'Bolshevik Brown'.[1]

The Act of 1927 legislated the CSCA out of the TUC and out of politics generally. Almost immediately afterwards the 'W. J. Brown Parliamentary Candidature Fund' was instituted on the basis of voluntary contributions, and this fund was used to support Brown as CSCA candidate in subsequent elections down until 1948. Throughout the years of the depression, the association was unable to demonstrate its political complexion, although from time to time it resolved at annual conference to seek the repeal of the 1927 Act. In 1931, after salary cuts had been imposed on civil servants in line with general economic policy, there was a spontaneous demonstration of resentment by over 100,000 civil servants, mainly clerical and post-office workers, in Hyde Park, and later at the Albert Hall, where Brown put their case to the Government in his characteristic style: 'What is the social significance of these immense wage-cuts in the Civil Service and the corresponding cuts in comparable professions like municipal services, the teachers, and so on?' he asked. 'Lenin once said that you might judge when the capitalist order of society was reaching collapsing point when it found itself driven by the stress of its own internal position to drive the petty bourgeois down to the level of the proletariat. The significance of the wage cuts in this country is that that class is being steadily driven down to the level of the proletariat in Great Britain. (Hear-hear.) The biggest bulwark of the present regime in Britain is the man who has a home in the suburbs and a little car. (Hear-hear.) If that man is treated in such a way that the burden of his home, which he cannot get rid of, results in his taking his lunch to the office in a paper bag, a direct blow is aimed at one of the most vital elements in the maintenance of society as we know it today. (Hear-hear and loud applause.)'[2] But the worst was almost over, and from then on until the outbreak of war the association struggled to restore the cuts and improve its position. The feeling was strong that in this it was severely constricted within the machinery of Whitleyism and had no recourse to outside influence. At the 1936 conference it was unanimously resolved that 'this Conference reiterates its condemnation of Clause V of the Trades Disputes Act of 1927, and in view of the declared policy of H.M.

---

[1] During the debate on the famous Clause V of the 1927 Bill, Mr Hannon, the government representative on the National Whitley Council, described Brown as 'one of the most ardent advocates of whole-hog, red-blood revolution'. *Ibid.*, July 1927, p. 566.

[2] *Ibid.*, November 1931, p. 89.

Treasury to regulate the conditions and rates of pay of civil servants by reference to conditions in outside industry, instructs the new Executive Committee to take all possible steps to obtain the repeal of that Clause and the removal of restrictions preventing civil servants from taking effective action to protect and prevent the worsening of their conditions and standards of life'.[1] But the passing of such resolutions only registered the will of the association, and it was left to the changing balance of power in the war situation to enable this will to be carried into effect.

The first move came in 1943 from the Union of Post Office Workers, who, in the face of the law, applied for affiliation to the TUC. Churchill regarded this as a threat to the Government and refused to negotiate unless the UPOW withdrew its application. Meanwhile, the CSCA had supported the UPOW at its 1943 conference by passing a resolution that 'this Conference notes with deep interest and appreciation the firm stand taken by the Union of Post Office Workers in the demand for the repeal of Section V of the Trades Disputes Act. Observing the manner in which the Act is drawn, this Conference instructs the incoming Executive Committee to negotiate with other Civil Service bodies with a view to: (*a*) securing the concurrence of the Trades Union Council in accepting applications from Civil Service Unions who may wish to apply for affiliation, and (*b*) obtaining an assurance that the full support of the British Trade Union Movement will be given to individual civil servants in the event of action being taken by the Government against members of those unions which enter into such affiliation.'[2] This proved unnecessary, because the UPOW withdrew its application in the hope of securing agreement through negotiation, but no progress was made, and eventually after much procrastination Churchill suggested that the coming General Election should decide the fate of the entire 1927 Act. In 1944, the CSCA annual conference carried the resolution that it was in favour of affiliation with the TUC when it was legal to do so.[3] In 1945, the general secretary reviewed the association's position *vis-à-vis* the TUC and supported affiliation by saying, 'Congress is heavily weighted on the side of the manual workers. It is in no sense of criticism that I suggest that anything which is likely to increase the influence of the non-manual workers is to the good from the point of view of all concerned. The old-time snobbery of the blackcoated worker has tended in recent years to give place to a sort of inverted snobbery which causes the manual worker to regard with some measure of disdain the clerk and office worker. The number of unions affiliated

[1] *Ibid.*, June 1936, p. 691.    [2] *Ibid.*, July 1943, p. 219.
[3] *Ibid.*, July 1944, p. 230.

to Congress competent to express the view of the sedentary worker, and the aggregated membership of those unions, is not sufficient to provide a corrective to this tendency, and to convince the manual worker that his blackcoated colleague has in recent years become more conscious of the advantage of organization and more willing to throw his weight behind the Trade Union Movement.'[1]

The repeal of the 1927 Act left the CSCA free not only to join the TUC again but to decide on political affiliation. This raised rather more complex issues. Since 1927 the membership had grown substantially to about 140,000, and there was by no means identity of opinion about the advisability of returning to the Labour Party or to political activity at all. At first the leadership seemed to be carrying the association towards affiliation, but there was also opposition from a considerable proportion of the membership. In 1945, a motion 'that this Conference views with grave apprehension the present political tendency now exhibited by the Executive in the January circular to all members, and recommends that the members' political opinions should be expressed through the medium of the ballot box. Further, that the functions of this organization be confined to welfare conditions as between the member and the employing department in accordance with the Constitution laid down' was heavily defeated. The following year the conference endorsed the view of the national executive that reaffiliation to the Labour Party was in the best interests of the membership and agreed that a ballot should be taken to decide (1) whether a fund for promoting political objects should be re-established, and (2) whether the association should reaffiliate to the Labour Party. The general secretary argued that 'the logic is that if in the interests of our membership we decide to line ourselves up with the industrial side of the workers' movement, then logically we must in the political and social field line ourselves up with the political wing of precisely the same movement ... we must, as the largest clerical organization in the world, representing an important section of the working-class movement, identify ourselves completely in the industrial and political wings with the rest of the working-class movement'.[2]

In all this, the executive were perhaps ahead of the mass of the membership, and certainly Brown, who was now parliamentary general secretary, had changed his opinions on the subject. At the conference of 1947, the motion 'that it would be in the interests of the membership for the association to affiliate to the Labour Party and urges its members to vote for affiliation when the ballot on that

[1] *Ibid.*, September 1945, p. 274.
[2] *Ibid.*, May 1946, p. 262.

issue is held', was defeated by 2,855 votes to 2,002.[1] The ballot was not actually taken until 1949 due to certain technical details of registration, but in the meantime certain events had widened the gap between the executive and the membership on this issue. In the first place, there was disagreement about the general secretary's membership of the editorial board of the *Daily Worker*,[2] and this was expressed as a formal criticism at the 1946 conference.[3] Charges of 'Communist-domination' were made against the executive in the following years, and in 1948 in particular there were strong resolutions on the undesirability of certain political actions taken by the executive.[4] In the same year, in the House of Commons, Brown denounced Mr E. J. Hicks, who was then president of the CSCA, as a Communist. At the conference that year Hicks was removed from the presidency by failing to get support from his own branch, and Brown was asked to resign as parliamentary secretary the following year.[5] After that the dissension subsided, but when the ballot was finally taken in 1949, political action, and with it Labour Party affiliation, was ruled out by a heavy majority. Only 50% of the total membership took part, and the voting was 55,569 to 14,693.[6] What the opinions of the 70,000 non-voters were cannot be ascertained except that they were obviously not strongly committed to a return to the Labour Party. The association had clearly committed itself to a non-political career.

## NATIONAL UNION OF BANK EMPLOYEES
### (Previously the BANK OFFICERS' GUILD)

Trade unionism among bank employees, socially and economically the 'aristocracy' of clerks, has been characteristically 'respectable'. All the difficulties of establishing a trade union capable of eliciting the support of this ultra-middle-class group of workers have left their mark on the policy of the Bank Officers' Guild. The need for the 'education' of the bank clerk in the principles of trade unionism, together with the necessity of weaning him away from the internal staff associations, are the two themes that recur with striking regularity throughout the history of the guild and provide the major clue to the particular brand of trade unionism it has had to offer.

The Bank Officers' Guild was founded during 1917–18 in Sheffield. Quite soon branches were formed in all the large urban centres and

[1] *Ibid.*, July 1947, p. 276.
[2] *Ibid.*, February 1946, p. 121.
[3] *Ibid.*, July 1946, p. 262.
[4] *Ibid.*, June 1948, p. 305 *et seq.*
[5] *Ibid.*, June 1948, p. 328.
[6] *Ibid.*, December 1949, p. 77.

the headquarters was moved to London. The growth of the guild, during the post-1918 rise in the price-level, was considerable, and by 1921 it had a membership of about 28,000, or one-half of the permanent bank staffs of England and Wales.[1]

This rapid initial growth was also favoured by the conditions which had been brought about by large-scale amalgamations in the banking world, by the depersonalization of the relations between managers and their staffs which accompanied this rationalization, and by the anxieties raised by the disappearance of old grades of work and remuneration and the absence of any new scales of salaries. The almost immediate reactions of the banks to the growth of the guild were to refuse it recognition for purposes of Whitleyism, to give bonuses to their staffs, and to encourage the development of the 'internals' or house-unions, which cut across the general appeal of the BOG.

The policy of the guild, though it had been a registered trade union from the beginning, was to refrain from strike coercion and to employ moral suasion in order to gain recognition and influence the course of banking conditions. Although there were powers written in its constitution to 'proceed to drastic action in the extreme case', the guild put its faith in the 'government scheme of meetings between organized employers and employees'.[2] When the employers resolutely refused to enter into any relationship with the guild, it, recognizing its dilemma, pressed for greater and greater membership on the grounds that a recourse to strike action might alienate even its 50% membership. Even the fact that the guild was registered as a trade union was alarming enough to many bank clerks,[3] and the guild sought to emphasize quite explicitly that there were many types of trade unions and that the guild, though nominally one of their company, should not be confused with many of the more militant unions of working men. 'The Constitution and Rules of the Bank Officers' Guild has been passed by the Registrar of Friendly Societies and the guild is now a recognized trade union. There is nothing of great legal import in the action. It does confer certain financial safeguards, but it signifies the desire of the guild to have its position defined without equivocation. Registration is a formal act of definition, but in the eyes of the law any association which embodies

---

[1] July 1921, *The Bank Officer*, p. 3.    [2] *Ibid.*, August 1919, p. 4.

[3] 'How many times, when every specious argument has been disposed of, has the inveterate Guild antagonist fallen back on his last line of defence, and said, "Well, I won't belong to a trade union, anyhow; they are only for 'workmen'." Could a more ignorant or snobbish attitude be imagined? And for this reason it is so hard to combat.' *Ibid.*, February 1922, p. 8.

the desires of its members to raise their economic position is a trade union. That being the case, there is no point in not registering as such and taking advantage of any useful purpose to be obtained by recognition. In certain quarters this action of the guild has been looked upon with misgiving, but those timid ones have not really gone into the subject. Trade unions in their eyes are connected with a spirit of revolt or lawlessness. That is not the truth. Trade unions no more connote revolution or strikes or organized discontent than does the British Bankers' Association, the Bar Council or the British Medical Association. A trade union does not take its line of action from any other trade union but from the spirit and temper that animates its own members.'[1] The spirit that animated the members of the guild, when thinking of their fellows outside, was a cautious and timorous one, especially on the touchy question of strikes. Eventually, the strike clause was interpreted as an employer's safeguard against the possibility of strike action by bank clerks. 'A trade union as defined by law and common sense does not mean that the body immediately takes upon itself the worst features of the worst trade union. A trade union must be judged by the attitude of mind that animates its members. The guild was introduced to Lord Robert Cecil by a well-known public man who said, "The guild is a trade union, but a trade union with a new ideal—co-operation". The guild has a strike clause and the managements shy at it. It is the finest safeguard the directorates have. Without it there would be nothing to prevent a bare majority of the executive declaring a strike. As it is a strike can only be sanctioned when there is a five-eighths majority of all the members of the guild in favour. But why this concern? The guild has never departed from its implicit belief in the pacific aims of the Whitley Council. It is part and parcel of its objective and Whitleyism and antagonism are the very antithesis of each other.'[2]

The theme of pacific opposition and non-militant unionism dominated the conferences of those early years. 'We roundly repudiate the assumption that in having a class consciousness we have necessarily class antagonism. We have not, and our record of the hand of co-operation held out for over five years is proof enough for an unbiased person.'[3] This attitude commended itself to outsiders and received support in the Press and in parliamentary debates on the position of the non-manual worker. The guild also acted cautiously on the issue of political action. At the annual conference of 1923, it was resolved by a large majority 'that Parliamentary action be taken by putting forward our own candidates in conjunction with

[1] *Ibid.*, May 1920, p. 3.    [2] *Ibid.*, January 1921, p. 4.
[3] *Ibid.*, February 1924, p. 3.

other professional workers'.[1] But many years later, in 1933, when it was proposed that the president should seek election, it was recalled that previously 'when the time came and the election was imminent that marvellous middle-class mentality that has received attention already this morning suddenly realized that a man cannot stand for Parliament unless he belongs to a political party, and that the awful catastrophe of having a man standing as a member of any political party was such that we must shrink and step back from that particular issue'.[2] In the absence of political rules and fund, the guild acquired sponsors in both major political parties, who would support their case in the House.

In the General Strike of 1926 the guild steered a neutral course and offered its services as a mediator in the conflict. Otherwise, the bank clerk remained rather detached from the industrial struggle. 'The bank clerk tackled the difficulties of the situation with a cheerfulness and an amount of enthusiasm that should ever dispel any doubts as to his loyalty to his employers,' claimed the *Journal* shortly afterwards. And then, almost as an afterthought, 'Now that we have forgotten these little inconveniences of getting up earlier, perhaps walking a few miles extra to and from the office, may we not spare a sympathetic thought or so for the miner, his life, his ways of living, his living wage, and the risks he runs in his daily round, for he also is a man'.[3] If the Prince of Wales could express his sympathy for the miner's plight, then surely it was respectable for the bank clerk to follow suit.[4] But even the neutrality of the guild did not protect it from the bank clerk's fear of unionism. The reassurances followed. 'The Bank Officers' Guild is a trade union and in its constitution as such it reserves the right of its members to withdraw their labour in certain circumstances, but it is safe to say that not 1% of its membership would welcome this extreme measure.'[5] The president later reported that, while the guild had enrolled nearly 1,700 new members during the early part of 1926, after the General Strike hardly another member was recruited in the rest of the year. He added, 'Considering the psychology of the British public today, which is largely press-led, the wonder is that we have not felt the situation more than we have done. Trade unionism is under a ban. How extraordinarily foolish! As I said in the *Bank Officer* this month, there are two sides to trade unionism, and this is where the ignorance of the average bank clerk lets him down, and lets down the guild. He does not realize that there is a twofold function of trade unionism. *One is the legal side,*

[1] *The Bank Officer*, April 1923, p. 8.  [2] *Ibid.*, July 1933, p. 13.
[3] *Ibid.*, June 1926, p. 12.  [4] *Ibid.*, December 1926, p. 32.
[5] *Ibid.*, June 1926, p. 7.

*in which we have kept ourselves, and the other is the philosophic side, and it is the philosophic side of trade unionism which is responsible for the bitterness, the misunderstanding and the violence.*'[1]

No-politics was the straw to which the guild clung in these stormy months, but even the most non-political trade union managed to alienate some bank clerks who were expert in the detection of political sentiment. Perhaps the following letter conveys best the kind of hypersensitivity the guild was up against. It is one of many, and not the most extreme of its kind.

Dear Sir—Certain passages in recent *Bank Officers* prompt queries as follows: paragraphs on p. 7 of the April number contain these sentences: 'The only hope of bankmen in that day (of possible radical change in the banking system) will be the same as in 1918—a strong national organization—a class movement—the Bank Officers' Guild—call it what you will—it is the expression of the brotherhood of men who serve a common industry and whose economic destinies are identical. If the Council of Staff Associations is anything at all it is a tacit acknowledgment that there is a class consciousness and a class interest amongst bankmen—else why did they set it up?' I might also add that a speaker at the recent Annual General Meeting called for an increased spirit of class consciousness among bank clerks. I do not clearly understand what class consciousness is, though it is a phrase much used by persons whose proposals include the violent and bloody upheaval of our social system; while our Executive probably has no such intentions, I should like to know what the words mean in the above instances.[2]

Those outside the union did not even bother to inquire whether their association of trade unionism with 'red-blood revolution' was correct; they acted on it and avoided the guild. To the minority of convinced trade unionists the mental habits of their colleagues were anathema,[3] but the guild itself, seeking to conserve membership, was

---

[1] *Ibid.*, July 1926, p. 8.   [2] *Ibid.*, June 1926, p. 22.

[3] The following letter is typical of the minority view: 'It may gratify the vanity of many of our colleagues to think of themselves as Conservatives with identical interests with the bank's board of directors, but the facts are against them. If bank clerks are peeved at their present cuts and do nothing about it, they can have little realization of what is ultimately in store for them. The time is coming when they will have bigger problems to face than cuts, and unless they are mentally equipped, little can be accomplished. Am I for ever to witness bank clerk Fascists helping to break the General Strike or bank clerk Special Constables waiting to wipe up a few hunger marchers?' *Ibid.*, April 1934, p. 28.

on the defensive and prescribed the sedative of 'no-militancy' and 'no-politics' on every possible occasion. The year after the General Strike saw a debate at the annual conference on a motion for the deletion of the strike clause altogether from the rules of the guild. The president laboriously explained again that 'if you examine the strike clause you will see it is so hedged about with rules and regulations that it really amounts to the finest safeguard that the directors have got. If you wipe out the strike clause then immediately you give into the power of the National Executive Committee the right by a majority vote to call a strike. Of course, I am ruling out whether such a call were practical or not; I am giving the legal side of it; they will have the right on a bare majority vote to call a strike, and you are taking away certain safeguards. As a matter of fact, the strike clause as it is in our constitution makes a strike from any point of view impossible. A national strike of bank clerks in England is beyond the bounds of possibility. I do not care how Bolshevik a man may be in his ideas or how far he looks ahead. Under no known conditions today could you envisage a national strike of bank clerks.'[1] The motion was lost.

Throughout the late twenties and early thirties the guild was at a low ebb. The internal staff associations, financed by the banks, were firmly established and had as many if not more members than the union, whose membership had now sunk from the 50% achieved in the first upsurge of the immediate post-war years to a bare third of the total potential. In these years the cost of living was falling rapidly, and despite the cuts of 1931 the bank clerk was in a relatively advantageous position compared with the manual worker or even the mass of general commercial clerks. 'The fear that clutches at our bowels is that we really do get paid more for our jobs than those who do work like ours outside banks. This fear is the most paralysing of all. I have seen it in men's eyes and in their gestures. This it is which chiefly prevents them from "standing up to the brandishing of the employers' bludgeons" and makes them "continue playing at trade unionism indefinitely".'[2]

In the mid-thirties, there were signs of revival in the guild, not in the form of increased membership, which remained stable at a low level throughout the period, but in the general tenor of policy. The no-politics rule remained, though its merits and feasability were increasingly discussed.[3] The playing-down of the trade-union aspect of the guild, which had been aimed at increasing membership, be-

[1] *Ibid.*, July 1927, p. 19.
[2] *Ibid.*, March 1938, p. 11.
[3] *Ibid.*, 1934 through 1937.

came less of an obsession, and the question of affiliation with the wider trade union movement began to be raised more vigorously, though this was still obviously a minority interest. It seemed that, despite the optimism of the president, the policy of weaning the recalcitrant non-member by the avoidance of trade-union attitudes had not been particularly successful and that there was little to be gained, or lost, by its continuance. Be this as it may, the conference of 1937 appeared to be generally of the view that affiliation was ultimately desirable for the guild and that the reasons for non-affiliation were immediate and instrumental. 'It was felt that the time was not opportune for affiliation because the rank and file of our membership is not yet sufficiently trade-union minded. The cause of the great trade union movement will be better served by organizing the 45,000 bank staffs at present outside the guild than by seeking affiliation with the TUC and losing a large number of those who are now members, and delaying further the day when we have a national majority and can then, perhaps, affiliate with a convinced membership and be of real service to the movement within Congress itself.'[1] The *Bank Officer* continued to report fully the conferences of the TUC and carried numerous articles on its aims and purpose. In 1939 affiliation to that body was again rejected by the delegates on the ground that such a move would entail a loss of members, but only a few votes prevented a ballot of the membership being taken. Then, the following year, TUC affiliation was quietly secured with only two dissentients out of 123 delegates.

At the end of the war, on the occasion of the merger of the Bank Officers' Guild with the Scottish Bankers Association, the new association was renamed the National Union of Bank Employees. 'The reason why we called this union the Bank Officers' Guild was because we thought the implications of any other title would be too strong for the average bankman to swallow at that juncture. What man

---

[1] This may, as subsequent developments and general experience of other black-coat unions seem to show, have been a false estimation of the situation. It has yet to be shown that TUC affiliation by any non-manual union has led to a decrease in membership. Moreover, the fact of minority membership need not have been a real deterrent; the RCA joined as a union representing only a minority of the clerks in the railway industry, and its efficacy was certainly increased by TUC support. Indeed, if it be assumed that membership is partly a function of achievements, then precisely the opposite argument could be, and actually was, put forward—that affiliation would increase membership. This actually happened. In 1939 there were 17,646 members in the guild; by 1946 it stood at 25,352. It would be attributing too much to the undoubted class-solvency of war experience to trace it entirely to this factor. It was also the experience of the Scottish Bank Clerks Association that 'our membership has increased by more than 70% since we adopted the militant attitude'. *Ibid.*, June 1937, p. 7.

amongst you, when he is challenged for his occupation, calls himself
a bank officer?'[1] Was it true, then, that 'much of the social and
economic doctrine that commanded the interest and the support in
1918 of that middle-class society to which bank men and women
belong, is now regarded as effete',[2] and that a new era in banking
trade unionism was beginning? Between 1939 and 1942 the union
had acquired 10,000 new members, association with the general
trade union movement, and now a new name which unequivocally
announced its intention.

But the old problems remained. 'In going about the West and
South Country I find that approximately 50% of the bankmen are
TUC-minded and 50% are absolutely opposed to anything that smells
of TUC. Not all the scent of NUBE pamphlets can counteract the smell
of the TUC garlic. These gentlemen just hold their noses and say we
will have nothing to do with NUBE so long as it has anything to do
with the TUC.'[3] So far motions for disaffiliation have been resisted,
and the purely industrial character of the affiliation has been constantly reiterated. In 1951, for example, NUBE saw fit to issue the
following press statement: 'The NUBE, a non-party-political trade
union, with no political fund, makes no call for its members to vote
for any particular party or candidates in the General Election. The
NUBE is affiliated to the TUC on a purely industrial basis, as are some
other unions, and this public statement is made to demonstrate the
union's autonomous position and to make clear that its members
have an unexhorted and free choice at election times. This union is
not affiliated to any political party.'[4]

As regards recognition, the goal which has always been foremost
in the programme of the union, little has been achieved. At the outbreak of war in 1939, there was renewed pressure on the Government
to recognize the union and to force the banks to do likewise. The
Government favoured a system of negotiation, but the banks refused
to give absolute recognition to the union, reconstituted the internal
staff associations on a fee-paying basis in 1940—this despite a
majority of 959 against a subscription-paying association in Barclays
Bank—and suggested a tripartite conciliation machinery.[5] The guild
found itself unable to 'submerge' its autonomy in this way and the
machinery was never operative.[6] In 1941 the guild was recognized
as a bargaining body for its members by Barclays Bank, and by the
Trustee Savings Bank Employers' Council in 1947. The other great
banks have still refused to give recognition to the NUBE, though

[1] *Ibid.*, August 1946, p. 1.    [2] *Ibid.*, March 1946, p. 1.
[3] *Ibid.*, December 1951, p. 11.    [4] *Ibid.*, October 1951, p. 9.
[5] *Ibid.*, March 1941, p. 25.    [6] *Ibid.*, December 1942, p. 8.

undoubtedly their actions have been influenced by the existence of the guild and its propaganda.

In 1956, the NUBE could claim a membership of 48,735 out of an approximate total of 120,000 bank officials, and the total increase in NUBE membership in 1955 was almost equal to the whole of the membership rise throughout the rest of the trade unions affiliated to the TUC.[1] The goal for which the union has patiently striven for the last thirty-seven years—majority membership—is nearer than it has been for a long time.

## NATIONAL AND LOCAL GOVERNMENT OFFICERS ASSOCIATION[2] (NATIONAL ASSOCIATION OF LOCAL GOVERNMENT OFFICERS)

NALGO has experienced the most rapid growth of any blackcoat union, expanding from 5,000 members at its inception in 1905 to 230,000 in 1955. In the thirty years between 1925 and 1955 alone its membership increased by 600%. It is now the largest non-manual union in the world, and the eighth largest union in Great Britain. Catering for all grades of local government service, it includes both office boy and town clerk. The clerical grades proper form very roughly about 60% of its total membership. The growth and composition of NALGO make it perhaps unique in the history of trade unionism, and the difficulty of holding together such a vast conglomeration of disparate grades and divisions through such a period of growth has been partly responsible for the peculiar brand of trade unionism it offers. In particular, its size has made it increasingly an object of interest to the rest of the Labour Movement at the same time as its comprehensive membership has forced it to move slowly and cautiously in defining its relationship to outside associations. As in the case of other clerical associations, the questions of the status of the non-manual worker and his identity of interest with the manual worker have been raised whenever these character-defining decisions have had to be made.

In the nine years between the formation of the National Association and the outbreak of the First World War, its activities were largely those of social club and friendly society, operated through the affiliated guilds at a local level. Dances, socials, picnics, cricket matches, excursions and discount-trading were innocuous enough

[1] *Ibid.*, July/August 1956, p. 16.

[2] I am indebted to Mr Alec Spoor of NALGO who generously made available to me material collected by him and allowed me to read his unpublished history of the association.

to secure the growth of the association. The aims of NALGO in 1906 had been stated as follows: to further the interests of local government officers; to federate local and sectional societies of local government officers; to deal with questions of superannuation, security of tenure and others of national importance; to promote legislation for these and other purposes; to give legal assistance to members 'where the National Executive Council shall deem it necessary'; and to encourage the formation and working of local or district associations. None of these goals was held to involve an opposition of interest between the local government officer and his employer. The question of action on the matter of salaries generally did not arise in the members' minds, and certainly, as one writer put it, 'anything savouring of trade unionism is nausea to the local government officer'. In reality, the lot of the officer was rather better than that of the general clerk and definitely above that of the manual worker during this period. But in the few occasional instances of salary reductions that occurred before the war it was clear that, before long, NALGO would have to define its policy towards the more material interests of its members.

This decision was brought to a head by the circumstances following the end of the war. Trade unionism was in ascendancy, 'an infection going round the country like influenza', the cost-of-living was soaring, the social distance between blackcoat and fustian had somewhat diminished in the war-time community, and new, aggressive unions, such as the National Union of Clerks, were invading the local government field. In 1918 it was noted that 'the question whether they should join the Trade Union Party has been acute among civil servants and teachers in recent months, and there is a considerable element in the local government service who favour such a step'; but although 'trade unions were undoubtedly of advantage to the masses of workers and to certain classes of workers "by brain" it would be unwise not to realize that public officers are distinct from any other class of worker or professional men'.[1] The ideas of trade unionism and Labour Party affiliation seemed indissoluble to many of them, as was their association of trade unionism with strikes. At the annual conference of 1919 the council published a long report which was unfavourable to any change in the status of NALGO, and in it many of these fears were expressed.

Nevertheless, a motion for registration as a trade union was pressed at the conference. The discussion centred on the question of the best means to achieve the professed aims of NALGO. 'Constitutional' means were contrasted with the 'big-stick' policy of certain allegedly

[1] Annual Conference of 1918, *Report*, p. 28.

discontented and irresponsible elements of the membership. Others stressed the speed and efficacy with which demands forwarded by trade unions were met, as compared with the delays and postponements which were the fate of local government officers' claims. 'The very fact of having a legal standing gave a trade union a distinction, an idea of strength which was not given by an association.'[1] The other view was that NALGO was already a trade union in fact and that registration would add nothing; what was required was power, and power was spelt 'funds'. 'What were the funds of this Association? (Voices: "2s 5d" and laughter.) Talk about a lightning strike. (Renewed laughter.) "National Union of Local Government Officers. National Strike begins at 10 a.m. by the members downing pens. It ended at 10.47 a.m. owing to the exhaustion of the strike fund." (Laughter.)'[2] 'Don't bother so much about the label, so long as the stuff you have got in the pot is the right stuff.' The motion for registration was heavily defeated, as was a motion that a ballot of the members be taken, and the matter seemed to have been settled.

But only for a short while. The demobilized soldiers were avoiding NALGO and joining what they considered to be 'real' trade unions such as the NUC, the Municipal Employees Association, the Workers' Union, the National Union of Local Government Officers and the National Union of Corporation Workers. Members also began to secede from the associated guilds of NALGO, causing alarm among local organizers. A special conference had been called for January 1920 to approve an increase in subscriptions, and many of the delegates to this meeting held mandates from their branches to say that unless NALGO became a trade union the entire membership would resign.[3] At the meeting the council surprisingly announced that, despite the decision at the previous year's conference, a referendum of members on trade-union registration would be taken.

The referendum was confounded by the three alternatives given to the voters: to become a registered trade union; to become a certified trade union; or to stay unchanged. The pro-unionists, who feared that the council was still unconvinced about unionism, regarded the proposal for certification as a half-measure. When the count was taken the vote was divided: 7,916 were against unionism altogether; 5,002 wanted NALGO to become a certified trade union; and 6,992 wanted registration—20,322 members voted, out of a possible 35,000.[4] The general policy was clearly in favour of trade unionism, but the issue of registration or certification was still not settled. The

---

[1] *The Municipal Officer*, July 1919, p. 50.  [2] *Ibid.*, p. 51.
[3] Letter in possession of Mr Spoor from one of the delegates present.
[4] *Local Government Service*, May 1920, p. 52.

council declared itself in favour of certification, but others held that this was defying the opinion of the majority, and at the 1920 conference it was resolved to refer the decision again to the membership. In July of that year certification was carried by 13,707 votes to 9,180.[1]

It had been feared that the decision to make NALGO a trade union would lead to a loss of membership. This followed in isolated cases, and some of the senior officers resigned. But these losses were more than compensated for by the return of members who had left to join other trade unions before the decision, and by the influx of new members. By the end of 1920 membership had risen to 36,500—nearly 8,000 more than that of the previous year and treble the 1918 figure. This important move in the history of the association had been carried through by a majority of the membership who were in favour of more militant action and in opposition to the views of the leadership who were at that time drawn largely from the senior ranks of local government service.

Motions for affiliation to the TUC followed in 1921 and 1922 but they were heavily defeated. The opinion of conference was also sought on the desirability of establishing a political fund in 1922. Since 67 branches, representing 10,678 members, agreed to this and only 20 branches having 4,438 members were unwilling, it was moved that a fund be established at once to finance parliamentary and local government candidates. But after discussion of all the implications the difficulties of such a step were seen to be too great.[2] The following year it was announced that the best method 'would be to induce one MP from each of the three great political parties to interest himself in the affairs of the Association',[3] and this method has proved its success over the years.

Thus the association was committed to a strictly non-political existence, and the occasion of the General Strike, whilst calling for a definition of NALGO's responsibility, was regarded as a confirmation of the wisdom of this policy. 'As might be expected, the recent industrial strife was of such a nature, and so widespread, that it presented new and perplexing problems to members. It has also demonstrated the soundness of the association's policy in remaining completely non-political. The members individually hold every shade of political belief, but the association rightly holds itself entirely aloof from the world of politics, devoting its energies and force to the carrying out of its objects. The issue of the president's message undoubtedly clarified the position as regards the strike for most members, as it gave a simple statement of what may be taken as the principles

[1] *Ibid.*, August 1920, p. 94.    [2] *Ibid.*, August 1922, p. 100.
[3] Annual Conference 1923–4, *Report*, p. 42.

underlying members' positions as public officers serving all classes and all political creeds. He directed attention to the decision of the Service Conditions and Organization Committee on the question as to how members should act when requested, or instructed by councils to act as special constables, or in some similar capacity during a General Strike. This decision, which was endorsed by the executive council, was "that in the opinion of this committee this question is one which each member should decide himself or herself; but no efforts should be made to compel a member to take part in any emergency measures, which might be put into operation in connection with industrial strife". In his statement, the president also expressed the hope that "each member will, so far as his public position goes, do his very best to maintain those essential services which are necessary to the welfare of the community as a whole. Beyond this, action which may be of a party character must be left to the member's individual conscience, but I wish to say that whilst our members are left a perfectly clear hand in all action which goes beyond their official duties, it is equally expected that the local authorities will not attempt to force any member against his will to undertake duties of a partisan character, or which may be regarded as bringing him into conflict with any particular section of the community".[1] The association thus neither encouraged its members to support nor to break the strike.

After the show of enthusiasm for trade unionism immediately after the war and the defeat of motions for TUC affiliation in 1921 and 1922, the question of affiliation did not seriously arise again until the middle and late thirties. The General Strike had put trade unionism in bad odour with the middle classes generally, and the fall of the cost of living throughout the late twenties and early thirties, plus security of tenure, worked to the advantage of local government officers. Throughout this period NALGO had been working steadily, had achieved superannuation, and was striving to resuscitate the collapsed national Whitley machinery. After 1932, the general trade union movement began to revive and the affiliation issue was raised again.

The division of the membership of NALGO on TUC affiliation, which began at this time and has continued to the present day, arose out of the basic question as to whether affiliation to the TUC implied allegiance to the Labour Party. Those who thought that it did argued in the following vein: 'NALGO includes in its membership public officers who have to advise their councils on many things. These men and women have no right to let their political leanings, even

[1] *Local Government Service*, June 1926, p. 123.

if they have any, enter into their work. It does not require much imagination to see how untenable would an officer's position become if he were a member of an organization which was definitely allied to one political party. Every local government officer would be suspect. It would mean the end of impartial advice and administration, and that would probably lead ultimately to public officers coming into and going out of service with their party.'[1] The demand for 'no party politics' was supported by the president in his address to the annual conference in 1935.[2]

This kind of argument was unsatisfactory not only to other members within NALGO itself, but to certain trade unionists outside. NALGO was denounced by rival unions in the TUC in 1934, 1935 and 1936.[3] 'This annual tirade which springs from a small interested group,' NALGO complained, 'has been based upon a manufactured theory that because NALGO is not affiliated to the TUC its members are not taking their share of the burden in the struggle for the uplift of the working classes. It is a reflection upon the intelligence of anyone to assume if NALGO joined the TUC that it would take 81,000 members with it. Is it not better from a trade union point of view to leave an organization of its size, power and effectiveness to remain intact, than to cause its complete disintegration by forcing it to take a step which may have nothing more tangible than an ideal?'[4]

The outside disapproval of NALGO was carried into action in a few instances when certain Labour members of town and county councils used their positions to try to force local government officers into

---

[1] *Ibid.*, November 1934, p. 679.    [2] *Ibid.*, July 1935, p. 193.

[3] The two unions involved were those of Public Employees and Clerks. They objected to the support which NALGO had received from the Labour Movement and called for the General Council to follow the Scottish TUC in declaring NALGO not to be a *bona fide* trade union. Eventually, in 1936, Congress issued a report on the unionization of the local government service which was conciliatory and realistic in tone. Sir Walter Citrine argued thus: 'If the British TUC decided that the union was not *bona fide*, in all probability it would still remain in existence . . . the General Council have always to consider in these matters the reality of the situation. What are the realities in this case? First they are that NALGO has 80,000 members; that is the first point. The second point is that NALGO is already recognized as a *bona fide* trade union by many local authorities, some controlled by Labour majorities. Thirdly, that it has its conciliation machinery existing with practically every local authority in the country, and that it is also recognized by the London Passenger Board. Now having regard to the fact that the unions who expressed that point of view represented in point of numbers unquestionably the largest number of people affiliated to this Congress who are employed in local government and public service, the Council could not dismiss that point of view. . . .' *Report of Proceedings of the 68th Annual Trades Union Congress*, 1936, pp. 254–6.

[4] *Local Government Service*, October 1935, p. 287.

organizations that were affiliated to the TUC. Such an attempt was made in Glasgow when the secretary of the Glasgow Trades Council asked the corporation to refuse to hear representations on behalf of employees of the corporation by any persons representing bodies which were not members of the Scottish or British TUC.[1] Elsewhere, 'Branches have reported from time to time that "hints have been given" and that "threats have been used" to the effect that certain local councils hold out very little hope of favourable consideration being given to any representations made to them by NALGO unless it becomes affiliated to the TUC.'[2] These pin-pricks were regarded by NALGO as involving a serious matter of principle. 'Let it be made perfectly clear that in this question there lies a fundamental danger of supreme importance. NALGO is not out of sympathy with the policy of the TUC as regards its defence of trade unionism and its desire to protect the standards of all trade unionists, but public opinion associates the TUC with party politics, and once that same opinion associates a public service with party politics, the end of everything that the local government service stands for in this country is assured. Where the TUC stands in relation to the Labour Party was made quite clear at the Thirty-fifth Annual Conference of the Labour Party last year. Mr W. Kean, vice-president of the TUC, speaking as a fraternal delegate said: "We are not two movements, but one, with common aims, interests and activities." '[3]

The demand for affiliation came not only or mainly from outside but also from within the association. In 1936 a motion was tabled for the conference urging 'that the time has now arrived when NALGO can no longer stand aside from the overwhelming majority of organized workers by hand and brain; and that consequently we call on the NEC to approach the TUC General Council with a view to becoming affiliated to that body.'[4] In support, it was held that 'the TUC was a body distinct altogether from the Parliamentary Labour Party. The TUC was out primarily for the purpose of raising the standard of the organized trade unionists in this country.' But the amendment that 'this Conference, whilst appreciating the valuable service rendered to organized labour by the TUC, expresses the opinion that local government officers as servants of the public should be members of an independent organization, and that such organization should not be associated with party political activities' was carried instead by a large majority.

The controversy died down for five years and was then revived shortly after the outbreak of war. With the National Union of Bank

---

[1] *Ibid.*, January 1936, p. 366.　　　[2] *Ibid.*, p. 375.
[3] *Ibid.*, p. 375.　　　[4] *Ibid.*, July 1936, p. 555.

Employees inside the TUC fold, the only two blackcoated unions remaining outside were the NUT and NALGO. Moreover, the status of the TUC had been enhanced by the war-time coalition, and especially by the appointment of Mr Bevin as Minister of Labour. But the National Executive Council was adamant on the question of the political implications of affiliation. Whether the one implied the other 'technically and legally, is a question on which we hope the NEC will give all the information it can. It is, however, worthy of note that if there were any possibility of misunderstanding on the point one could have expected the TUC itself to disavow such an implication (since it must know that the question must arise in organizations such as ours which are not affiliated to it). So far as we know it has never done so. But whatever the technical position may be, the association has hitherto held the view that in practice, and in the public mind, affiliation does carry these implications'.[1] Eventually, at the annual conference of 1942, in the face of an NEC resolution that there was no reason to depart from the 1936 decision, it was decided by 48,719 votes to 32,705 to have a ballot on the problem. This was to prove very embarrassing for the NEC, because when the votes were counted they showed a majority for immediate affiliation[2]:

|            | Civilian  | Forces   | Total    |
|------------|-----------|----------|----------|
| For        | 39·53%    | 17·7%    | 33·67%   |
| Against    | 29·34%    | 8·52%    | 23·73%   |
| Not voting | 31·13%    | 73·71%   | 42·60%   |

At the next conference Mr Riley, a member of the executive, persuaded the delegates by a remarkable *tour de force* that such a momentous decision was better reconsidered and referred back to the branches for another year. He pointed out that so many voters had been absent in the forces that such a slight majority for affiliation would split the union if affiliation were actually carried out, that NALGO would lose its identity in the TUC octopus as well as many of its present functions, that NALGO was on the verge of a new Whitley Council, and that the result of affiliation would be to turn NALGO into a class union which would be mainly clerical and lose its senior officers.[3] 'It had the great advantage over other organiza-

---

[1] *Ibid.*, April 1941, p. 74.　　　　　　[2] *Ibid.*, July 1943, p. 401.

[3] In a very real sense the struggle over TUC affiliation was partly a struggle between the higher and lower grades. When it was argued against affiliation that 'many of the chief and senior officers occupied confidential and advisory posts, they not only had to carry out policy, but they had to advise their authorities on questions of policy', this obviously did not apply to the vast majority of

tions that it represented everybody from junior to chief. It was a weakness of the civil service that it was divided into clerical, executive and administrative associations, with one class set against the other. NALGO on the other hand represented local government officers as a body, and that was its source of strength, for it was better to have chief officers with the rank and file than against them. Did they want to turn NALGO into a clerical organization, with the chief officers forming a separate organization against the interests of the bulk of the service?'[1] By a narrow majority of 47,259 to 45,825 it was decided to postpone affiliation and to refer the result of the ballot to branches and districts, thus deferring the decision for another year. The answer given by this re-reference showed that 159 branches with 43,152 members were in favour of immediate affiliation, 163 branches with 39,326 members wanted the decision deferred, and 71 branches with 12,382 members were definitely opposed to affiliation.[2] It was bitterly complained by the affiliationists that the voice of the branches was not necessarily the voice of the membership as a whole, and at the next conference, which was in 1945, they asked for immediate affiliation and lost the motion by a card vote of 70,885 to 39,375. They sustained a second defeat in 1946 by 56,250 to 43,742.

The following year the NEC, sensing continuing dissatisfaction over the issue, took a new tack and moved that 'it be authorized to explore the possibility of affiliation to the TUC on a basis mutually acknowledged to be solely industrial and not implying allegiance to nor connection with any political party'. In support of this move, which seemed to bring NALGO nearer than it had ever been to a workable affiliation, the president agreed that 'it was completely untrue that affiliation automatically involved a political levy. Of the 194 unions in the TUC only 61, or one-third, were affiliated to the Labour Party.' A deputation was in fact sent to the TUC and a long report prepared by the general secretary for the 1948 conference setting out the pros and cons. But on this occasion the NEC reverted

clerical grades in the Association. The counter view ran as follows: 'It is now plain that the only reason why NALGO does not apply for affiliation is chief officer opposition. The essence of the argument about our so-called exceptional status is that, as local government officers, we occupy a position of public responsibility and must, therefore, be non-political and assert the fact unmistakably. But this cannot apply to 95% of us. The only people who might be embarrassed by association with the TUC are the principal officers. But NALGO is not composed solely of chief officers: it consists in the main of ordinary non-policy-making, anonymous meter-readers, transport inspectors, clerks, minor administrative officers and the like, whose political associations cannot possibly conflict with their official positions.' *Ibid.*, February 1948.

[1] *Ibid.*, July 1943, p. 404.  [2] *Ibid.*, February 1944, p. 29.

to its previous position and recommended the delegates not to affiliate, as a non-political affiliation was impossible. A counter-motion was heavily defeated by 101,895 to 55,254 on a card vote, but a proposal for another ballot of the membership was accepted, and it was decided that affiliation would be carried out if a majority of the membership voted in favour. Some 70% of the members voted and of these only 35·6% were for affiliation.

The last episode in this tortuous affiliation debate was acted out in 1955, when again it was resolved to take a ballot of the total membership on 'what was likely to be one of the most important decisions ever made'. The ballot revealed that 60% of the members voted, and that the affiliationists and their opponents were almost equally represented with 73,151 and 77,592 votes respectively.

Though NALGO has never engaged in strike action, in recent years the problem has been reconsidered on several occasions. In 1948, it was decided that in the event of a strike by manual workers, local government officers should continue their normal employment but should not be constrained to do other duties, and the full support of the association would be given to officers who refused orders to blackleg. But if the authority concerned made a general appeal for volunteers 'and any of the individual members decided to respond to it the Association would not place obstacles in their way'. Whatever individuals decided to do, the general policy was that the local NALGO branch should carefully refrain from taking any collective action which would give other unions the impression that the staffs were prepared to be used as strike breakers.[1]

At the 1950 conference it was reported that, during a strike of manual workers, clerical staff had been approached by the Electricity Board and asked to volunteer for essential duties in the power stations. Members of NALGO felt that they should get guidance from their trade union. The final decision of the meeting accepted this point of view and stated that 'if a section of employees withdraw or threaten to withdraw their labour, whether with or without the support of their trade union, and the authority of an electricity board desires to seek the services of administrative and clerical staffs in order to maintain supplies, the responsibility for deciding whether or not to carry out such duties should not be placed on the individuals but on their trade union'. In turn it was the duty of the local NALGO to confer with other unions involved to secure agreement upon future action.[2]

As regards NALGO's own capacity to strike, the situation was laid

[1] *Ibid.*, September 1948.
[2] NALGO Annual Conference, 1950, *Report*, p. 75.

193

bare by a special report prepared at the request of the annual conference.[1] It considered the legal, constitutional, moral and material possibilities of strike action by local government officers, and revealed that NALGO was practically incapable of striking. Some of the grounds adduced are interesting, since they are generally applicable to blackcoated workers. In the first place, superannuation rights would be endangered. Secondly, the length of notice required for certain officials would destroy all element of surprise in a cessation of work. Further, 'the policy of the manual workers' unions is no doubt conditioned by the fact that, in the main, the rates of pay of their members run roughly at the same level. The situation of NALGO members is very different. Their pay runs at very differing levels; their readiness to accept something less than their normal rates cannot be predicted, the hardships in accepting less may be greater for those on the "bread line" represented by the lower reaches of blackcoated employment than for those even on corresponding levels among the manual workers, since their career prospects are usually greater, but this very fact may have induced them to enter into commitments such as the manual worker might not venture upon.' As regards NALGO's resources, 'The situation can be chiefly illustrated by citing a recent statement reported to have been made by the joint general secretary to the London Society of Compositors: "We have got £1,250,000 in the kitty and only 15,000 members. We can stay out a long time on that." NALGO has 235,000 members with some £200,000 at present in its Special Reserve Fund. . . . The Association has obviously not enough in the "kitty" for a strike in a single large branch.' Despite these facts, the NEC did not favour any policy that would preclude strike action in all circumstances. At present strike action can only be taken if 90% of the staff in the branch contemplating such action vote in favour.

## CONCLUSION

Several generalizations may be drawn from this cursory survey of blackcoated unionism. In the first place, collective action among clerks has been moulded principally along trade-union lines. The degree to which clerks have participated in 'house unions', associations for strike-breaking, or Fascist movements is largely unknown, of course, but generally speaking the overall tendency has been for blackcoated workers to form associations fashioned after those of

[1] *Strike Action,* Special Report of the NEC to the Association's Annual Conference, 1956, p. 17.

working-class trade unions.[1] Despite the rapid increase in clerical functions between 1920 and 1950, the proportion of clerks belonging to trade unions doubled over this period of time. Although the growth of trade unionism among clerks is relatively new, it has also been relatively rapid, with the important exception of industrial and commercial clerks whose working conditions have proved a major obstacle to their unionization.

It is clear from the foregoing profiles of blackcoated unions that the foundation of trade unions for clerks, and their subsequent relations with the wider working-class movement, have been fraught with problems of class consciousness on the part of the membership and leadership alike. In some cases, the leadership has proved to be less radical in its outlook on these matters than the mass membership; in others the relationship has been the reverse. Taking the period as a whole, however, all the blackcoated unions seem to have taken a broadly similar stand on the question of their status in the Labour Movement. All have declared themselves to be *bona fide* trade unions with the express purpose of bettering the economic position of their members. All have relied heavily on negotiating and arbitration machinery for the settlement of disputes, and have tended to eschew the strike weapon as a normal instrument of collective bargaining. All have placed great emphasis upon the value of publicity and political representation. And, with the outstanding exception of NALGO, all have sought affiliation with the TUC. At the same time, all the unions have striven to maintain their identity as clerical unions, and have constantly been aware of their specific interests as non-manual workers. They have, as a result, been unwilling to submerge themselves in larger unions with predominantly manual-worker membership.

To determine the general relationship of blackcoated trade unionism to the Labour Movement as a whole, it is useful to distinguish between three types of interests, which may be called 'immediate', 'instrumental' and 'ideological', respectively. The first type of inter-

[1] Clerks have had a reputation as blacklegs. In the pre-1914 years, as in the inter-war period, clerks were certainly recruited as Special Constables, and they also figured in the Army Supplementary Reserve. *The Clerk*, 1912, p. 71; 1925, p. 51. They also formed part of the membership of the Middle Classes Union which was used as a strike-breaking organization. See Lothrop Stoddard, *Social Classes in Post-War Europe*, 1925, p. 100. C. L. Mowat, in his *Britain Between the Wars*, 1956, p. 473, also asserts that the British Union of Fascists recruited mainly from this class of the population, though he gives no evidence on this score, and I have been unable to find a single piece of evidence which would indicate the relative importance of clerks and others, such as members of the *lumpen-proletariat* and retired army personnel. In any case the numbers involved were probably quite small.

ests consists of the particular economic aims of a union with regard to such matters as salaries, hours, holidays, promotion and superannuation. The second type is derivative from the first, and includes those interests which are common to all unions of employees: matters such as the legal status of trade unionism, victimization, recognition, strike action, negotiation machinery, political representation and the like. The last type, the 'ideological', implies wider interests of a political kind, all the principles and assumptions arising out of the connection between the trade union movement and the Labour Party. Taking these three types of interests, it is possible to state more clearly the sense in which blackcoated unions have regarded themselves as sharing the same 'interests' as working-class unions.

It is the second, the 'instrumental', type of interest that has been most commonly shared by unions of blackcoated and manual workers. Immediate interests of a material nature have frequently been divergent because of the relatively privileged economic position of most clerical workers.[1] An awareness of the differences in the immediate interests of manual and blackcoated workers is the main reason why such unions as the RCA and the NUC have not become part of larger manual trade unions. For the same reason the unionization of clerks has proceeded chiefly along occupational rather than industrial lines. Interests of the second kind have been of much greater importance in creating a sense of solidarity between clerks and manual workers because they are common to all those with employee status. Even NALGO, which remains formally outside the TUC, does so on 'ideological' rather than on 'instrumental' grounds. And the explanation which Brown gave for taking the CSCA into the Labour Party was, curiously enough, one which stressed 'trade union' rather than 'political' interests. It is, indeed, with regard to the third type of interest that there has been least consistency displayed in the policies of the various blackcoated trade unions. Two out of the major five are affiliated to the Labour Party at the present time. Among the others there is more or less agreement that their trade union aims should not commit them to support a political party. They are not adverse to political activity in the form of lobbying, but they have steered clear of any formal affiliation which might be construed as 'ideological' rather than 'instrumental'. Not that this distinction can be unequivocally drawn. Whether any affiliation to the trade union movement can be purely 'instrumental' and devoid

[1] It should not be overlooked that, during periods of rising prices and wages, clerks may join trade unions not out of sympathy with the Labour Movement but in order to protect themselves from 'pressure from below'.

of political connotations has been hotly debated throughout the history of blackcoated unionism, and has given rise to radically different solutions. Brown's insistence that the attachment of the CSCA to the Labour Party was simply an extension of trade union interests may be contrasted with the conclusion of NALGO that even affiliation to the TUC inevitably carries with it, or at least is seen to imply, political sympathies. The bank clerks, after a long period of soul searching, decided that TUC affiliation would leave them politically neutral, and took the step that the RCA and NUC had taken almost as a matter of course half a decade earlier.

If it be assumed that the class-conscious feeling of the blackcoated worker is reflected in the degree to which his union identifies itself with the Labour Movement, how are the variations in the character of blackcoated unionism to be understood? Though no one set of factors suffices to explain the spirit that animates a particular corporate body, certain broad correlations may be established between the objective situation of the clerk and the character of his trade unionism.

Differences in economic position have been of prime importance. The internal economic stratification of the clerical labour force has produced differences in life-chances quite as significant as those which demarcate clerks from manual workers in the same industry. If bank clerks and railway clerks differ so considerably in their attitudes towards the Labour Movement, this is primarily due to the fact that they have formed the 'aristocracy' and 'proletariat' of the blackcoated world. During the years in which the respective policies of the BOG and the RCA took shape the railway clerk had at least as much in common with the railway worker as he had with the bank clerk. Differences in the work situation have also played their part. The railway clerk was brought into closer contact with manual workers than the bank clerk, whose employment associated him with the middle classes. The railway clerk learned his trade unionism in an industry in which manual workers were already strongly organized and militant, whereas the bank clerk had no such first-hand experience of industrial conflict and never had to meet the challenge of trade-union solidarity. Finally, the two groups of clerks differed in social origins and status. While bank clerks came mainly from the lower middle classes, a great many railway clerks were drawn from the homes of railway workers. Socially as well as economically the bank clerk had a strong claim to middle-class status, and his trade unionism, if he experimented with it at all, had to be respectable enough not to jeopardize this social standing. As for the railway clerk, his background merely confirmed him in his trade unionism, and his self-respect was in no small measure bound up with his standing in the railway community. Perhaps just because of his black coat, and the suspicions which it aroused, he felt that he had to 'prove' himself in the eyes of the railwaymen who worked by his side and to whom he was often related.

The character of blackcoated unionism, no less than its extent, is an outcome of the class situation of the clerk, and variations in the former are to be understood in terms of variations in the latter. The facts of blackcoated unionism cannot be dismissed by a facile reference to the snobbishness of the clerk. His status situation is only one aspect of his total class situation, and on the whole it has been of secondary importance in his class outlook and collective action, reinforcing rather than undermining the experiences which have their origins in his economic position and working contacts.

# CHAPTER SIX

## CONCLUSION

'Differences in the class consciousness of members of the same class are facts that simply exist; logically they can be neither true nor false.'

THEODOR GEIGER,
*Die Klassengesellschaft im Schmelztiegel*

# CONCLUSION

IT is now time to return to some of the general problems raised in the introduction. It was suggested there that the class consciousness of the blackcoated worker would best be interpreted in terms of the general concepts which had been used in the study of working-class consciousness. There was no reason to believe that the outlook and behaviour of the clerk were a function of any psychological idiosyncrasy in his make-up that could not be explained in terms of his peculiar social situation. On the basis of this assumption the intervening chapters sought to provide detailed information on the major features of the social and economic position of the clerk, and particular emphasis was given to the way in which they differed from those of the manual worker. Thus it was possible to relate differences in the attitudes and conduct of the two groups to variations in their respective social environments.

The major purpose of this study, therefore, may be seen as an attempt to relate certain general concepts to a particular set of facts. Any such attempt is fraught with difficulty. The initial breakdown of a problem into manageable categories of research does not ensure that in every instance these 'analytical boxes' will be materially filled. In fact, in many instances general theoretical considerations led the discussion into regions where information was thin or unobtainable, while in other places data were overabundant but of small relevance to the particular problem being considered. Such are the hazards of research. There remain many gaps in the information about the blackcoated worker, and the present work claims to be nothing more than a preliminary statement and exploration of the field. It is hoped, however, that the attempt to order the problem within an explicit framework of ideas has had the advantage of clearly indicating where further research is necessary and likely to be fruitful.

So far as the wider comparative aim has been realized, the study constitutes not only an analysis of the class situation and behaviour of a particular group of workers, but also relates to our understanding of the general problem of class consciousness. These general conclusions may be stated in summary form, and an attempt made to compare and contrast the salient features of the economic position, working environment, and social status of clerks and manual workers, and to relate the differences found there to variations in class identification. The first two aspects, which have been previously

201

classed under the headings of 'market-' and 'work-situation', are the basic elements of the traditional concept of 'class', while the third has usually been differentiated in sociological literature as the 'prestige' dimension of social stratification.[1]

## MARKET SITUATION

The charge of 'false' class consciousness which has been frequently levelled at the blackcoated worker is grounded in the assumption that manual workers and clerks share the same basic market situation: that is, they are both propertyless, contractual labour. The clerk, really a proletarian in a white collar, was, according to this point of view, blinded to the true facts of his class position by an obdurate snobbery, by an incurable pretentiousness. In the light of the foregoing evidence, how far is this view a valid one?

The initial difficulty of such an argument lies in the weight it attaches to the sheer fact of 'propertylessness' as a criterion of class division. In general terms, of course, there are good grounds to agree with Weber, echoing Marx, that, ' "property" and "lack of property" are the basic categories of all class situations'.[2] Indeed, the modern working-class movement owes its identity and underlying unity of interest to the fact that 'propertylessness' produced a fairly consistent pattern of life chances for the manual wage-earning class. A lack of sustained bargaining power, job insecurity, and relative social immobility, have, to a greater or lesser degree, been characteristic of those who depended for their livelihood on the sale of their labour power. Until the most recent decades, these concomitants of propertylessness constituted the reality behind the concept of a working-class 'proletariat'. At the same time there have always been marked differences within the working-class market situation itself, differ-

---

[1] In the analysis of social stratification it has long been recognized as useful to distinguish between 'class' and 'status' differences in a social system; between a hierarchy of economic positions and a hierarchy of social prestige. In recent decades, however, there has been a tendency for attention to be concentrated on the latter aspect at the expense of the former. Whatever the reasons for this emphasis, it appears as one-sided and artificial as soon as social stratification is viewed as an historical process. 'Class' and 'status' are not alternative, but complementary viewpoints of the reality of any given stratification system. See Max Weber, 'Class, Status, and Party', *From Max Weber: Essays in Sociology*, translated and edited by H. H. Gerth and C. W. Mills, 1948. Also the recent restatement of the problem by S. M. Lipset and R. Bendix, 'Social Status and Social Structure: A Re-Examination of Data and Interpretations', *British Journal of Sociology*, Vol. II, No. 2, June 1951.

[2] *From Max Weber: Essays in Sociology, op. cit.*, p. 182.

ences which belie the homogeneity of position and interest which the term 'proletariat' connotes.[1] Weber himself recognized this fact when he qualified his initial statement on class division by saying that, 'only persons who are completely unskilled, without property and dependent on employment without regular occupation, are in a strictly identical class status'.[2] The internal skill differentiation of the propertyless class with the advance of industrialization, and the increasing heterogeneity of interests associated with this development, was definitely discounted in the Marxian conception of a class-conscious proletariat. Homogeneity of position and interest were rather the order of the day. The increasing impoverishment, insecurity, and caste-like character of the propertyless class would, according to this theory, override internal differences and provide the principal dynamic of the class system of late capitalism. And into this vortex of 'proletarianization' the blackcoated workers were to be irresistibly drawn to experience their latent community of interest with the working class.[3] It is now commonplace to remark that the diversification of the occupational structure and the excursion of the State into the management of welfare have rendered obsolete the idea of a homogeneous and solidary proletarian class consciousness. It is an important truism that all those who fall into the category of propertyless and contractual labour do not necessarily share an identical market situation.

As a consequence, any empirical study of class consciousness must begin by taking into account actual differences in the market situations of propertyless groups. To define such differences out of existence at the very beginning as being irrelevant to the long-run development of class alignments and class consciousness is nothing less than an abdication from sociological understanding. Variations in class identification have to be related to actual variations in class situations and not attributed to some kind of ideological aberration or self-deception.[4]

Nowhere is this conclusion more relevant than in the case of blackcoated 'false' class consciousness. The outstanding fact which

---

[1] J. Delevsky, *Antagonismes Sociaux et Antagonismes Prolétariens*, 1924, Chapter XI.

[2] Max Weber, *The Theory of Social and Economic Organization*, translated by A. R. Henderson and Talcott Parsons, 1947, p. 390.

[3] See R. Hilferding, *Das Finanzkapital*, 1927, pp. 444–8, for a representative Marxian analysis of the position of the salariat in the stage of late capitalism. Also the interpretation of the British situation by F. D. Klingender, *The Condition of Clerical Labour in Britain*, 1935.

[4] T. Geiger, *Die Klassengesellschaft im Schmelztiegel*, 1949, Chapter VI, pp. 123–7.

all but the most biased observers of the class system must recognize is that, although he shares the propertyless status of the manual worker, the clerk has never been strictly 'proletarian' in terms of income, job security and occupational mobility. As a group, black-coated workers have enjoyed the following material advantages over the manual worker. In the first place, clerks have had a relatively high income throughout the greater part of the period with which we have been concerned. This advantage had its origins in the initial scarcity of their labour in the nineteenth century, and was perpetu-ated until the most recent decades as a traditional differential, as a 'status' reward. Their privileged economic position was also but-tressed by the small part which their remuneration plays in the total costs of the enterprise relative to wages, as well as by the interests of employers in securing the loyalty and commitment of their office staffs. As a consequence their income was regulated according to rather different principles than those governing the determination of wages. Secondly, and more important than sheer differences in income, blackcoated workers traditionally enjoyed a much greater degree of job-security than manual workers. Though this condition was never absolute and uniform throughout the clerical field, job-security was something on which the clerk could generally count. This aspect of their market situation was perhaps the most signifi-cant difference between manual and non-manual work, for, although it fell short of the full independence which comes with property, job-security did constitute a partial alternative to ownership, con-ferring on the clerk a relative immunity from those hazards of the labour market which were the lot of the working classes. Thirdly, clerks, and particularly male clerks, have had superior chances of rising to managerial and supervisory positions. Finally, in addition to the official and unofficial rights to pensions on retirement which many clerks have enjoyed, must be added the non-pecuniary advan-tages of office work—its cleanliness, comfort, tempo, hours, holidays —all of which should be included in a calculus of relative rewards.

These advantages long continued to mark off the clerk as a superior type of employee. In periods of rising wages and full employment, of course, some of these differences were submerged and there have always been considerable variations within the clerical labour force itself. The picture presented is oversimplified, and there are other reasons, shortly to be discussed, why blackcoated workers have not fully identified with the working classes, but these general differences in economic position cannot be overlooked in any sober assessment of the attitudes of the clerk. They are a first consideration in the attempt to understand his deviation into 'false' class consciousness.

## WORK SITUATION

To examine the market situation of a group is not enough to arrive at the typical sentiments and interests of its members, because interests are never purely material in character. The matrix of social relations within which material satisfactions and dissatisfactions are experienced must also be considered. Without doubt in modern industrial society the most important social conditions shaping the psychology of the individual are those arising out of the organization of production, administration and distribution. In other words, the 'work situation'. For every employee is precipitated, by virtue of a given division of labour, into unavoidable relationships with other employees, supervisors, managers or customers. The work situation involves the separation and concentration of individuals, affords possibilities of identification with and alienation from others, and conditions feelings of isolation, antagonism and solidarity.

Since the class position of the manual worker has been taken as a yardstick, it is useful to describe the typical work situation of the modern factory worker in order to illustrate the way in which the class-conscious feeling of those sharing a common market situation is reinforced by sentiments arising out of the social relations of co-operation.[1]

Both in the factory and in the labour market, the outstanding features of the work situation of modern wage-labour are, on the one hand, the physical separation and social estrangement of management and workers, and, on the other, the physical concentration and social identification of the workers themselves. Not only is the worker separated from management through the physical layout of the factory, but also socially through the impersonal and standardized relationships that result from the institution of technical and economic rationality. The work situation of the modern large-scale factory is one where instrumental action is at a premium. The calculability, rationality and discipline of machine production call

[1] It is by no means suggested that the following conditions are actually present in all factory work at all times. They are to be thought of as elements of an ideal-type, or limiting case, with which variations in concrete organization may be compared. For the source of this particular construct see, for example, the following: Karl Marx, *Capital*, I, Chapters XIII–XIV; Robert Michels, 'Psychologie der antikapitalistischen Massenbewegungen', *Grundriss der Sozialökonomik*, IX, 1926; Georg Lukacs, 'Verdinglichung und das Bewusstsein des Proletariats', *Geschichte und Klassenbewusstsein*, 1923, Chapter III; Thorstein Veblen, 'The Machine Industry', *The Instinct of Workmanship*, 1914, Chapter VII; Elton Mayo, *The Human Problems of An Industrial Civilization*, 1946.

forth relations between management and the worker that are specific and impersonal. Far from there being a probability of mutual identification between workman and employer in a personal, paternalistic working relationship, the whole atmosphere of the productive unit is conducive to impersonal antagonism. Such relationships are further reproduced outside the factory through the operation of the labour market where labour is treated as a commodity. A social situation is created in which the worker's experience of the impersonality of the factory bureaucracy is widened and generalized into a sense of class division.

The same organization of factory production throws workmen together, physically and socially, and provides the prime basis for their collective action.[1] Class identification is further promoted by the industrial emphasis upon standard conditions of work and skill which iron out individual differences within the workforce. In this process the development of machine technology has played a major role. Equally important, however, have been the social relationships created by the labour market. The common identification of masses of individual workmen is facilitated by the evolution of universal standards of work which force the workmen in one factory to realize that their conditions are bound up with those of other workmen in physically separate units of production. In general, therefore, the social relations of the work situation, which on the one hand accentuate the physical separation of worker and management, in this instance unite workers, not only by reinforcing the physical concentration of the workforce, but also by overcoming their physical separation.[2]

This type of work situation is one that clearly maximizes a sense of class separation and antagonism. Insofar as the work situation of the modern wage-earner approximated such a pattern of relationships, it took on the character of a 'proletarian' class situation. When, however, this type of 'proletarian' work situation is compared with that of the blackcoated worker, it is evident that in this respect, too, the behaviour of the clerk has been influenced by an administrative division of labour which, over great areas of clerical employment,

[1] The extreme case, favourable to class consciousness, is when there is not only factory concentration but geographical isolation of working-class communities, of which mining communities are perhaps the best example.

[2] Complementing separation at work, of course, is the social insulation of workers from management through the commensal conventions of the factory. The same holds true throughout the dual system of facilities for 'works' and 'staff'. The force of the social barrier of the work situation is amply demonstrated on those holiday occasions when such relationships are ritually relaxed and conviviality is expected.

entailed radically different relationships from those sketched above. The older, paternalistic work environment of the counting house was, as we have shown, inimical to the development of any sense of common identity among clerks. At the same time, any feeling of class identification with the manual worker was absolutely precluded by the relations of production. Physically, clerks were scattered among a large number of small offices, working in close contact with employers, and divorced from the factory workmen. Their working relationships were largely determined by personal and particular ties, which meant that there was little uniformity in standards of work and remuneration, and that individualistic aspirations to advancement were strongly encouraged.

In the period of the modern office it is necessary to distinguish between those fields of clerical employment where paternalistic influences are still operative, and those where bureaucratic forms of administration have been established. In the former, the relatively small size of the office, the internal social fragmentation of the office staff through occupational, departmental and informal status distinctions, and the absence of any institutionalized blockage of mobility, have continued to militate against the growth of collective action among clerks. In addition, the lack of any widespread, systematic criteria of job grading and remuneration—reflecting the particularism characteristic of an inchoate labour market—has, for the greater part of the period, proved a further obstacle to the development of occupational consciousness. In those bureaucracies, on the other hand, where larger office units, strict classification and grading, blocked upward mobility and unhindered horizontal mobility were the rule, there have been reproduced impersonal and standardized working relationships comparable with those created by the factory and labour market. It is here that the work situation of the clerk has been most favourable to the emergence of that feeling of collective interdependence among employees which is prerequisite to their concerted action. But even where working conditions have fostered group action by clerks, the continuing physical and social division between clerks and manual workers has generally remained a barrier to the mutual identification of the two groups. The sense of social distance between manual and non-manual worker may, in turn, be traced primarily to their relative proximity to administrative authority. Bound up as it is with the general organization of discipline and authority, the relationship between clerk and manual worker lends itself readily to hostility and resentment on both sides.

In seeking the factors underlying the tardy growth of class feeling among blackcoated workers it is principally to the structure of their work situation that we must look. It is worth reiterating that the development of class consciousness is rooted in two interrelated, yet possibly independent processes. The first is the consciousness of a division of interest between employer and employee, and the second a consciousness of a community of interest among employees. It is only when individual alienation becomes mobilized as collective solidarity that it is appropriate to speak of class consciousness as such. In the present context the decisive point seems to be that such a transformation of feeling is by no means an automatic consequence of class position conceived of in the narrow sense of 'propertylessness'. Not only does the sheer fact of 'propertylessness' admit of variations within the market situation, but it is compatible with even greater variations in the work situations of different propertyless groups. If clerk and manual worker are to be regarded as sharing the same, fundamental class situation by virtue of their relationship to the means of production, this should not obscure the fact that the varying manifestation of class consciousness among the two groups is no less fundamentally determined by the observable differences in the structure of their working relationships. Only if we adhere to the narrow definition of class situation can we continue to speak of 'false consciousness'. As soon as the term 'class situation' is understood to cover not only market situation but also work situation, it is clear that clerk and manual worker do not, in most cases, share the same class situation at all.

## STATUS SITUATION

Having dealt with the two basic elements of the 'class situation', it is now necessary to specify how the factor of 'social status' enters into the problem of class consciousness.

Class focuses on the divisions which result from the brute facts of economic organization. Status relates to the more subtle distinctions which stem from the values that men set on each other's activities. Because conflict is possible wherever power is unequally distributed, class draws attention to the sources of dissension in the society. Because prestige cannot be accorded without interpersonal judgements of worth, status emphasizes the areas of agreement. To this extent, therefore, class and status present entirely different perspectives on the phenomenon of social stratification.[1] In actual fact,

[1] For an expansion of this point see my article, 'Some Remarks On The Social System', *British Journal of Sociology*, June 1956.

however, class and status differences are closely related. There is nothing strange in this association. A dominant class has never existed which did not seek to make its position legitimate by placing highest value on those qualities and activities that came closest to its own. In modern industrial societies—to a greater or lesser degree—the dominant values underlying status distinctions have been those of the entrepreneurial and professional middle classes. The most widely influential criteria of prestige are, therefore, those which express the occupational achievement of the individual. The education required for the job, the rewards and responsibilities it offers, the fact that it is clean and non-manual, and thus 'respectable', become the key determinants of a person's social standing. We speak of 'dominant values' because, insofar as class conflict exists, there is never complete unanimity about criteria of status. 'Middle-class' values are consequently much less acceptable to the more class-conscious elements of the landed aristocracy and working class. In fact they may be completely rejected by them.[1] In this way class divisions may be seen as circumscribing the influence of dominant status values.

Contrariwise, status distinctions can aggravate or mollify class-conscious feeling. The clearest instance of the first process is to be seen in the effect which the rigid status division between manual and non-manual work has had on working-class consciousness in European countries. During German industrialization, for example, working-class antagonism was exacerbated by the social isolation of this class in prestige terms from the rest of 'middle-class' society.[2] This has been generally true of other European countries where the working class has been socially excluded from middle-class status by reason of the manual nature of its labour. It is no accident, to pursue the argument further, that even within the working class those groups which have the dirtiest and most toilsome jobs, but not necessarily the worst economic position or the least skill, are often those that exhibit most intense class feeling. In the United States, by contrast, where status distinctions were much less rigidly drawn and manual work did not carry the same social stigma, the effect was to alleviate class-conscious feeling among manual wage earners.[3] Although this was by no means the only operative cause, there can

[1] An example of *Proletarierstolz* has been provided recently by M. Young and P. Willmott in their article, 'Social Grading By Manual Workers', *British Journal of Sociology*, December 1956.

[2] E. Roberts, *Monarchical Socialism in Germany*, 1913, pp. 126–7.

[3] Werner Sombart, *Warum gibt es in den Vereinigten Staaten keinen Sozialismus?*, 1909, pp. 127 *et seq.*

be little doubt about the role played by democratic manners in the pacification of the American working class.[1]

Another instance of the way in which status consciousness can affect class consciousness is to be found in the status strivings of those working-class persons who are marginal to the middle class. Individuals who are working class in objective occupational terms may, by reason of their own middle-class origin or a desire for the upward social mobility of their children, adopt middle-class values and attitudes. Such an identification with a higher-status group is expressed in the limitation on family size, in the value set on education, in the emphasis on 'respectability', in the provision for the future, and in many other ways. This process—whereby the individualism of the middle-class culture comes to replace the collectivist ethos of working-class consciousness—has often been described as the 'bourgeoisification' of the working class. Whatever label is given to it, insofar as individuals seek their social betterment through individual rather than group action, to that extent class consciousness is weakened by status aspirations.

The purpose of these rather lengthy remarks on the effect of status divisions on class consciousness is to underline the truth that the influence of 'prestige' or 'social standing' is to be detected in all class situations and is not peculiar to that of the blackcoated worker. Class division is never a simple matter of opposition of interest but is also inextricably bound up with the notions of social superiority and inferiority current in the society. Because the distinction between manual and non-manual work provided a clearly identifiable dividing line across which many other differences—in income, security, promotion possibilities, authority, education—could also be contrasted, it was readily seized on as a line of status demarcation. The consequences of this social gulf for the mutual orientation of blackcoated and manual workers were no less significant than those stemming from economic position and working environment. Indeed, the chief result was to accentuate those other differences and invest them with a more general relevance. When differences in advantage are overlaid by differences in social worth, mutual identification is precluded; especially when superiority is asserted on the one side as vigorously as it is denied on the other. For the middle-class status of the clerk was not unequivocally recognized, particularly by the working man. It is precisely this ambiguity in the status of the clerk, deriving largely from the lack of consistency and consensus entailed

---

[1] S. M. Lipset and R. Bendix, 'Ideological Equalitarianism and Social Mobility in the United States', *Transactions of the Second World Congress of Sociology*, 1954, pp. 34–54.

by the inclusion in the middle class of all but those who work with their hands, that provides the major clue to the 'snobbishness' of the clerk. We have argued at length that the exaggerated status consciousness of the blackcoated worker was produced by his marginal social position, and by the vicious circle of clerical 'snobbishness' and working-class 'contempt' to which it gave rise. A self-perpetuating 'status' barrier between clerk and manual worker was thus brought into existence.

The lowered social status of blackcoated work at the present time is the outcome of a long and complex process of change whereby many of the former bases of the clerk's prestige have been undermined, making the line between the middle and working classes less distinct. As a group, clerical workers are now more heterogeneous and the sheer fact of 'brain work' is less and less the hallmark of middle-class status. Under these conditions the class consciousness of the blackcoated worker exhibits greater diversity. Because of his increased marginality there is perhaps a greater tendency for the class identification of the clerk to be either extreme working class or extreme middle class, though this question obviously requires much more research. What does seem tolerably clear is that the traditional superiority of non-manual work has not been entirely eradicated by the changes of the last half-century, even though it has been more frequently questioned. This is best stated by saying that the loss of middle-class status by the clerk is not tantamount to the acquisition of working-class status, either from the point of view of the clerk or the manual worker. The differences between the two groups that lend themselves most readily to status usurpation by the clerk are at the same time those which are most firmly entrenched in the hierarchy of authority of modern industry and administration. In short, differences in class situation, and especially in work situation, continue to incite status rivalry between clerk and manual worker, and status rivalry in turn weakens their consciousness of class identity.

What, then, is the role of 'status' or 'prestige' in the alleged 'false' class consciousness of the blackcoated worker? The short answer is that, while the status rivalry between manual and clerical workers has *generally* tended to weaken their sense of class identity, 'class' factors have proved more important than 'status' factors in the explanation of *variations* in the development of blackcoated unionism. Variations in the degree of blackcoated unionization can be related primarily to variations in the work situations of different clerical groups. Similarly, variations in the character of blackcoated unionization can be traced primarily to variations in the market situations of different clerical groups. Conversely, neither differences in the degree, nor differences in the character of clerical unionism are basically attributable to the relative social standing of different groups of clerks. It is true of course that status differences within the blackcoated group closely follow differences in income, job-security, responsibility and chances of promotion. But this merely seems to add weight to the conclusion that 'class' factors are of overriding importance. Lastly, the attempt to explain the attitude of the clerk to the Labour Movement in terms of 'snobbishness' is particularly inadequate because it invokes a stereotype of the blackcoated worker which diverts attention from precisely those variations in his market and work situation which provide the key to the problem.

One final word on the idea of 'false' class consciousness which has given the overall direction to the present study. Whether or not the thesis of the 'false' class consciousness of the blackcoated worker is ultimately accepted or rejected depends on the particular definition of 'class' that is adopted. In this sense, the facts presented above provide grist for either mill. If 'real' class divisions are defined solely in terms of the ownership and non-ownership of the means of production, then it is still arguable that the blackcoated worker has had a 'false' consciousness of his real class position. To argue thus is not, however, to explain the class consciousness of the clerk but simply to give it a not very appropriate label. For, after all, 'truth' and 'falsity' are logical, not sociological terms; applicable to statements about sentiments and behaviour, but not to the sentiments and behaviour themselves. In sociological terms, the 'falsity' of the class consciousness of the clerk can only mean that his attitudes and actions tend to deviate from those which are most frequently to be found among individuals of the 'propertyless' class.[1] But such a view of

---

[1] 'The differences in the class consciousness of members of the same class are facts that simply exist; logically they can be neither true nor false. This is not altered by the fact that it is possible to determine an average or normal mode of reaction. We may observe, for example, all those who live by the sale of their labour power. We attempt, on the basis of mass observation, to gain a picture of how they feel, think, react and behave on the average. From such behaviour, attitudes and reactions we can draw certain conclusions about the psychological structure behind them. Similarly, we may be able to identify closely related mentalities for a large, perhaps the greater, proportion of the class members. We may then call this or that structure of feelings, attitudes, ideas, etc., typical for the seller of his labour power; we have in other words built up a normal type. However, we are not correct if we then describe deviations from this norm as "false" ideology or false consciousness. Because the deviations themselves are also psychological facts, just as the norm, and facts cannot be false or true. They simply exist, and are, as such, conceivably subjects of true or false statements. It is, on the contrary, possible and desirable to relate the observed devia-

class position and class consciousness merely defines the problem, and does not explain it. To explain variations in class consciousness it is necessary to look for variations in class position. And if the idea of class is widened to take into account other objective differences than that of ownership—differences such as those explored in the present work—then the class awareness of the clerk is seen as a consistent and faithful reflection of his class position. To define class in this way is not to deny the importance of ownership as a criterion of class position. It is simply to argue that the latter definition of class is insufficient to explain the problem of 'false' class consciousness which it poses. 'Class', like any other sociological concept, is a device by which social facts are to be understood, and, in the last analysis, the definition of class that is adopted can be justified only by its usefulness in the explanation of particular and concrete events.

tions in behaviour to variations in the class position itself. In this way one discovers new normal types. To take an example, X is the most frequent mode of reaction for the social group of those who "sell their labour power". We also find that modes of reaction, Y and Z, are less frequent deviations. An analysis of wage earners as a whole shows that Y and Z are seldom associated with industrial workers, that Y is especially frequent among agricultural workers, and Z among blackcoated workers. On the other hand, X is relatively less frequent among agricultural and blackcoated workers. Thus it appears that a reaction of Y (or Z), which deviates from the norm for the general mass of workers, is quite typical for a certain sub-group—agricultural (blackcoated) workers—distinguishable by objective criteria.' Geiger, *op. cit.*, 1949, pp. 124–5.

# APPENDICES

# APPENDIX A

A COMPARISON BETWEEN THE PROPORTIONATE INCREASES OF CLERICAL SALARIES AND MANUAL EARNINGS BETWEEN 1905–6 and 1955. (Figures in brackets refer to the percentage increases of 1925, 1935 and 1955 on 1905–6.)

| Occupation | 1905–6 | 1925 | 1935 | 1955 |
|---|---|---|---|---|
| *Clerical* (Males aged 28)[1] | £ | £ | £ | £ |
| Bank clerk | 170[2] | 275 | 260[3] | 620 |
| | | (62) | (53) | (265) |
| Civil service clerical officer | | | | |
| (assistant clerk before 1920) | 100 | 272 | 240 | 483 |
| | | (172) | (140) | (383) |
| Local government officer | | | | |
| (general clerical grade) | 90 | 200 | 200 | 475 |
| | | (122) | (122) | (428) |
| Railway clerk | 80 | 180[4] | — | 450[5] |
| | | (125) | | (463) |
| | | | | |
| *Manual Earnings* | s | s | s | s |
| Men and boys[6] | 27·0 | 57·6[7] | 56·9 | — |
| | | (114) | (111) | |
| Men (21 and over) | 28·8[8] | — | — | 223[9] |
| | | | | (674) |
| Average hours worked (manual) | 54·4 | | | 48·9 |

[1] All the figures on local government, civil service and banking salaries, except for banking in 1905, were supplied by Mr Spoor of NALGO.
[2] *The Bank Officer*, December 1919, p. 8.
[3] This figure is for 1936.
[4] *Railway Service Journal*, January 1925, p. 15.
[5] *Transport Salaried Staff Journal*, March 1956, p. 90.
[6] A. L. Bowley, *Wages and Incomes in the U.K. Since 1860*, p. 51.
[7] This figure is for 1924.
[8] Board of Trade, *Earnings and Hours Enquiry 1906–7*, Summary Tables, p. 14.
[9] *Ministry of Labour Gazette*, October 1956.

# APPENDIX B

## A NOTE ON THE DWELLING AREAS OF CLERKS IN GREATER LONDON

The tendency for clerks to live in 'middle-class' areas can be most easily seen from the conurbation figures of the 1921 Census. Male clerks formed 11·3% of the total occupied population of Greater London, but they were much more numerous in middle-class suburban districts. Five of these districts can be identified, each centring on areas which contained more than 20% of clerks among the total occupied population. In the North-east, there was a concentration around Ilford, Wanstead and Woodford; in the North around Southgate and Hornsey; in the North-west around Harrow and Wembley; in the South-east around Lewisham and Beckenham; and in the South around Beddington and Wallington. The areas with the lowest proportions of blackcoated workers were those in which industry had developed; in particular, the Lea Valley, the Lower Thameside, the North-western area around Willesden and the Edgware Road, and the Wandle Valley around Mitcham.[1] The contrast between the high concentrations of clerks in the North and North-eastern areas on either side of the Lea Valley, and the low representation of clerks in the Valley itself, is very striking, as is that between the continuous areas of Hampstead and Willesden.

The findings of the 1931 New Survey of London revealed a similar pattern. 'Clerks tend to congregate in the predominantly "middle-class" boroughs rather than in those which are either predominantly working class or wealthy. They also tend to live more in the outer than in the inner areas.'[2]

No direct comparison is possible between 1921 and 1951 because the 1951 Census only gives details for rather large Conurbation Areas and not for the Local Government Areas on which the 1921 figures are based. As a result, contiguous areas which had high and low proportions of clerks in 1921 are frequently brought within the same Conurbation Area in 1951, and treated as a unit. The 1951 figures tend, therefore, to iron out the area differentials which existed in 1921 and which possibly also existed in 1951. Among the 1951 Conurbation Areas, the highest proportions of clerks are to be found in the Southern rural residential fringe, and in the South-western and Eastern newer residential and industrial suburban districts. These areas had more than 12% of clerks per total occupied population in 1951, as compared with 10·4% for Greater London as a whole. The lowest concentrations of clerks were to be found in the Eastern

[1] Sir Patrick Abercrombie, *Greater London Plan 1944*, 1945, Chapter IV, pp. 41–4, map p. 62.
[2] *New Survey of London Life and Labour*, 1934, Vol. VIII, p. 282.

and Southern high density, old residential, industrial and dock areas, with 5·1% and 5·8% respectively.

A broad comparison is possible between the areas in which clerks were most and least frequently to be found and those which are typically working class. The areas in which semi-skilled and unskilled workers (the Registrar-General's Social Classes IV and V) formed a high proportion of the total occupied population may be considered as predominantly working-class areas. Over the whole of Greater London, semi-skilled and unskilled workers made up 23·8% of the total male occupied and retired population. Their highest concentrations were in the high density, old residential, industrial and dock areas, and in the dense residential, mainly pre-1914 areas, that is, precisely where clerks were least well represented. On the other hand, in those areas where semi-skilled and unskilled workers formed a relatively small proportion of the occupied and retired population, clerical workers were most frequently to be found. This can be shown in a different way, by taking the proportions of total clerks, and of total semi-skilled and unskilled workers, who lived in different types of areas:

PROPORTIONS OF TOTAL CLERKS AND TOTAL CLASSES IV AND V
LIVING IN TWO DIFFERENT SETS OF AREAS IN
GREATER LONDON, 1951

| Area | Percentage of Total Clerks Living in Given Areas | Percentage of Total Classes IV and V Living in Given Areas |
|---|---|---|
| VIc, Ve, Vb, Va (newer residential and industrial suburban districts and outer-rural residential fringe) | 45 | 28 |
| IIa, IIb, IIIa, IIIb, IIIc, IIId (high density old residential, industrial and dock areas, dense residential area, mainly pre-1914) | 23 | 47 |

THREE OCCUPATIONAL GROUPS AS PERCENTAGES OF TOTAL
OCCUPIED IN CONURBATION AREAS IN
GREATER LONDON—1951 (Males)

| Area | Clerks | Semi-skilled[1] and Unskilled | Skilled[2] |
|------|--------|-------------------------------|-----------|
| | % | % | % |
| I (Metropolitan, commercial and administrative centre) | 8·1 | 28·8 | 7·7 |
| II (High density, old residential, industrial and dock area) | | | |
| A | 5·1 | 38·4 | 11·5 |
| B | 5·8 | 39·7 | 11·1 |
| III (Dense residential area, mainly pre-1914) | | | |
| A | 7·6 | 25·0 | 12·7 |
| B | 8·5 | 26·7 | 16·3 |
| C | 10·4 | 28·5 | 14·3 |
| D | 6·8 | 28·3 | 14·0 |
| IV (Hampstead type) | 8·8 | 14·5 | 7·6 |
| V (Newer residential and industrial suburban) | | | |
| A | 11·1 | 17·0 | 18·6 |
| B | 10·9 | 16·4 | 14·9 |
| C | 12·2 | 22·8 | 15·8 |
| D | 10·9 | 21·5 | 16·6 |
| E | 12·7 | 18·9 | 14·0 |
| VI (Outer rural-residential fringe) | | | |
| C | 13·4 | 16·0 | 11·9 |
| All areas | 10·4 | 23·8 | 15·4 |

Source: Census of 1951, One-Percent Sample Tables, Part II.

[1] Social Classes IV and V, occupied and retired.
[2] Order VI: Metal, engineering and allied trades.

# INDEX

Apprenticeship system, 25–6
Assistant Clerks Association,
    168–70
Association of Women Clerks and
    Secretaries, 152

Bank clerks:
    Income, 23–4, 43, 45–6, 51–2, 217
    Promotion, 64–5, 148
    Social Status, 24, 103–4, 150, 197
    Superannuation, 54
    Unemployment, 55
    Unionization, 147–9, 176–84
    Work Situation, 86–7, 147–8
Bank Officers' Guild (National
    Union of Bank Employees),
    86, 138, 140, 147–9, 153,
    176–84, 197–8; strike action,
    177–8, 179, 181; TUC affili-
    ation, 182, 183
Barclays Bank, 183
Battleaxe, B., 30
Bonham, J., 109, 126
Booth, C., 18, 20, 29, 32, 57
Bowley, A. L., 42, 46, 47
Briefs, G. A., 55
British Association for the Advance-
    ment of Science, 42
British Institute of Public Opinion,
    104, 127
Brown, W. J., 169, 171, 172, 173,
    175, 176, 196, 197
Bureaucratic administration, 85–7,
    207; and unionization, 141–9.
    See also Paternalistic adminis-
    tration
Burns, T., 131
Butterly Colliery Company, 164

Cecil, Lord Robert, 178
Centers, R., 132

Churchill, W., 174
Citrine, Sir W., 189
Civil Service Clerical Association,
    138, 140, 168–76; 'Communist
    domination', 176; Labour
    Party affiliation, 168, 170–1;
    strike action, 168, 169–70;
    TUC affiliation, 168, 170, 174
Civil Service clerks:
    Income, 23, 42, 45, 217
    Promotion, 65–7
    Social Status, 150
    Unemployment, 55
    Unionization, 142–3, 154,
        168–76
    Work Situation, 33, 85, 91, 142–3,
        148
Class consciousness, 13–16, 34–5,
    155, 180, 195–8; and unioniz-
    ation, 137–8. See also Status
    consciousness
Clerical and Administrative
    Workers' Union. See National
    Union of Clerks
Cole, G. D. H., 161
Colliery clerks, 146, 153, 164, 167
Copeman, C. H., 59
Croner, F., 113
Crozier, M., 126

Daily Worker, The, 176
Derbyshire and Nottinghamshire
    Miners' Association, 164
Dock clerks, 153, 164

Education of clerks, 20–1, 116–21
Educational aspirations of clerks,
    129
Engineering clerks, 147, 155, 165,
    167

221

Factory organization, 71, 88,
    205–6
'False' class consciousness, 14, 202,
    203, 208, 211, 212–13
Family size of clerks, 128
Fascist movement, 56, 180, 194–5
Floud, J. E., 118
Forster, E. M., 83
Friendly societies, 33–4

Geiger, T., 13, 200, 212–13
General Strike of 1926, 138, 159,
    166, 172, 179, 181, 187
Gentlemanliness, ideal of, 29–32
German clerks, 26
Glasgow Trades Council, 190
Grammar school, 117–20
Greenwood, A., 160
Guild of Insurance Officials, 155
Guild Socialism, 165

Harrison, J. S., 27
Hicks, E. J., 176
Hilferding, R., 68
Hobsbawm, E. J., 28
Holidays, 53

Incomes of clerks, 22–8, 41–53,
    217; Pre-1914, 42–4; Inter-
    War, 44–8; Post-War, 48–53
Industrial and Commercial Clerks:
    Income, 24, 43, 46, 48
    Promotion, 58–62
    Social Status, 28–32, 151
    Superannuation, 54
    Unemployment, 55–7
    Unionization, 143, 145–7, 162–7
    Work Situation, 76–81
Intermarriage between clerks and
    manual workers, 113–16
Internal Staff Associations, 148,
    177, 181, 183
Iron and Steel Trades Federation,
    164

Job grading, 85

Kean, W., 190
Kekewich, Sir George, 117
Klingender, F. D., 94, 107, 203

Labour market, 82–5
Labour Movement, 13, 14, 138,
    156, 161, 163, 168, 169, 189,
    195, 197, 212
Local Government Clerks:
    Income, 24, 42, 45, 185, 217
    Superannuation, 54, 144
    Unemployment, 55
    Unionization, 143–5, 184–94
    Work Situation, 143–5
Local Government Superannuation
    Act, 1922, 139, 144; 1938, 54
London and North Western Rail-
    way, 23
London Society of Compositors,
    194
London and Westminster Bank, 24
Lukacs, G., 87

Machine operators, 93
Management recruitment, 59–67
Marshall, A., 70, 124
Martin, F. M., 127, 130
Marx, K., 13, 15, 18, 88, 89, 202,
    205
Merton, R. K., 132
Michels, R., 71, 78
Middle class, 100, 126–30
Midland Railway Company, 157
Myrdal, G., 142

National Association of Local
    Government Officers (National
    and Local Government Of-
    ficers Association), 138, 140,
    184–94; National Charter of
    1946, 143; strike action, 186,

187–8, 193–4; TUC affiliation, 187, 188–93

National Federation of Professional Workers, 150

National Union of Bank Employees. *See* Bank Officers' Guild

National Union of Clerks (Clerical and Administrative Workers' Union), 46, 56, 106, 138, 140, 162–7, 185; Labour Party affiliation, 162, 163, 166; strike action, 164, 166; TUC affiliation, 162

National Union of Mineworkers, 101, 147, 161, 164, 167

National Union of Railwaymen, 154, 158, 161

National Union of Teachers, 153, 191

*New Survey of London Life and Labour*, 47, 53

Nobel's Explosive Factory, 164

North Eastern Railway Company, 157

Occupational Mobility. *See* Promotion

Office: organization, 72–82; mechanization, 87–95; size of, 72–6; titles, 80

Office Management Association, 41, 75, 85

Orchard, B. G., 12, 19, 21, 27, 31

Paternalistic administration, 20–2, 78–81, 86, 207; and unionization, 141–9. *See also* Bureaucratic administration

Pickard, O. G., 84

Political attitudes of clerks, 127, 156, 167, 171, 187, 196–7

Proletariat, 14, 15, 41, 55, 68, 94, 126, 173, 202–4, 206. *See also* Working class

Promotion of clerks, 24–7, 57–67

Quaker management and unionization, 146

Qualifications of clerks, 20–1, 83–4, 95, 101

Railway Clerks:
  Income, 23, 43, 49–51, 217
  Promotion, 63–4
  Social Status, 23, 151, 197
  Superannuation, 54
  Unemployment, 55
  Unionization, 33, 149, 154
  Work Situation, 92

Railway Clerks Association (Transport Salaried Staffs Association), 46, 138, 155–61, 197–8; Labour Party affiliation, 156, 160–1; strike action, 158–9; TUC affiliation, 156

Railway Companies Association, 149

Rees Roturbo Company, 164

Rowntree, B. S., 106

*Royal Commission on the Civil Service* (*1875*), 23, 24; (*1953*), 66

Scottish Bankers Association, 182

Scottish clerks, 26

Shaw, B., 151

Smith, J. H., 142

Snobbishness of clerks, 14, 31, 100, 150–1, 211, 212

Social origins of clerks, 23, 24, 25–6, 32, 106–13, 154, 197

*Social Survey of Merseyside*, 47–8, 83, 107

Spoor, A., 184

Status ambiguity, 125–32, 211

Status consciousness, 208–10. *See also* Class consciousness

Superannuation, 54–5

Tawney, R. H., 14

Thomas, G., 58, 84

*Trade Unions and Trade Disputes Act (1927)*, 173–5

Transport and General Workers Union, 138, 153

Transport Salaried Staffs Association. *See* Railway Clerks Association

Tropp, A., 125

Typing pools, 78, 80, 85, 93

Unemployment, 55–7

Unionization, blackcoated: character of, 155–98; factors affecting, 138–54; membership, growth of, 138–40

Union of Post Office Workers, 102, 174

Veblen, T., 89

Walkden, A. G. (Lord), 160

Weber, M., 16, 202

Westminster Bank, 65

Whitley Councils, 144–5, 146, 158, 164–5, 170, 173, 177

Women clerks, 36, 91–2, 110–12, 115–16, 122–5; and unionization, 151–3

Working class:
Attitudes towards clerks, 81, 101–2, 126 ,130–2
Attitudes of clerks towards, 103–5, 127
Economic position of, 28, 44, 49, 53, 67–8, 202–3
Social status of, 28–9, 99, 209–10
Work situation of, 71, 205–6. *See also* Proletariat

Zweig, F., 81, 130